GLOBAL POLITICAL PHILOSOPHY

GLOBAL POLITICAL PHILOSOPHY

LOUIS P. POJMAN
UNITED STATES MILITARY ACADEMY

Boston   Burr Ridge, IL   Dubuque, IA   Madison, WI   New York
San Francisco   St. Louis   Bangkok   Bogotá   Caracas   Kuala Lumpur
Lisbon   London   Madrid   Mexico City   Milan   Montreal   New Delhi
Santiago   Seoul   Singapore   Sydney   Taipei   Toronto

McGraw-Hill Higher Education

A Division of The **McGraw-Hill** Companies

GLOBAL POLITICAL PHILOSOPHY
Published by McGraw-Hill, a business unit of The McGraw-Hill Companies, Inc., 1221
Avenue of the Americas, New York, NY, 10020. Copyright © 2003 by The McGraw-Hill
Companies, Inc. All rights reserved. No part of this publication may be reproduced or
distributed in any form or by any means, or stored in a database or retrieval system,
without the prior written consent of The McGraw-Hill Companies, Inc., including, but
not limited to, in any network or other electronic storage or transmission, or broadcast for
distance learning.

Some ancillaries, including electronic and print components, may not be available to
customers outside the United States.

This book is printed on acid-free paper.

1 2 3 4 5 6 7 8 9 0 DOC/DOC 0 9 8 7 6 5 4 3 2

ISBN 0-07-252465-0

Publisher: *Ken King*
Sponsoring editor: *Jon-David Hague*
Marketing manager: *Greg Brueck*
Project manager: *Ruth Smith*
Production supervisor: *Carol A. Bielski*
Design coordinator: *Mary E. Kazak*
Cover design: *Andrew Byrom*
Typeface: *10/12 Baskerville*
Compositor: *GAC Indianapolis*
Printer: *R. R. Donnelley & Sons Company*

Library of Congress Cataloging-in-Publication Data

Pojman, Louis P.
    Global Political Philosophy / Louis P. Pojman.— 1st ed.
        p. cm.
    Includes bibliographical references and index.
    ISBN 0-07-252465-0 (alk. Paper)
    1. Political science—Philosophy. I. Title.
    JA71 .P598 2002
    320'.01—dc21   2002023032

www.mhhe.com

TO TRUDY

Things fall apart. The center cannot hold.

Mere anarchy is loosed upon the world.

The blood-dimmed tide is loosed, and everywhere

The ceremony of innocence is drowned.

The best lack all conviction,

While the worst are full of passionate intensity.

W. B. Yeats, "The Second Coming"

CONTENTS

PREFACE

Two shopping carts, each bearing a small child and loaded with groceries, came zooming around the corner from opposite aisles, colliding with incredible impact. Tomatoes, oranges, apples and green peppers went ballistic; milk cartons broke open as they hit the floor; cakes and pies smashed into the spilt milk; a jar of jam broke open; and everywhere chaos reigned, as the two hurried shoppers stood in apoplectic shock. Then from one of the carts a small voice spoke calmly, "Daddy, use your words!" And from the opposite cart followed another small voice, "Yes, Mommy, use your words, too!" The two shoppers, realizing the wisdom of their children's advice, began to laugh, quickly realizing how silly they had been in trying to race against time and cooperated in the cleanup, while the two four-year-olds celebrated their achievement in averting a potential catastrophe between their parents.

Human beings alone can use words to communicate, to settle disputes and resolve conflicts that might otherwise explode into violence and war. They can use words to embody reason, to communicate their fears, their problems, their aspirations, their interests. Of course, they can also use words to wreak havoc and incite violence. We can choose how we use our words. The history of the human race has taught us to embody the wisdom of the two children in the shopping carts and use our words to embody reason to prevent catastrophe and violence, to ameliorate human suffering, and to work out strategies for improving our common life together. Politics is the art or process of using words to organize people into groups, to create institutions that further our interests, to invent rules of behavior that embody our values and can guide our actions. Political philosophy is the attempt to provide a rational structure for our rules, to make sense of politics, to critically assess and justify institutions and governmental systems. Political philosophy, then, is the art of using words about politics. It is a vital process that distinguishes us from all the other animals and sets us apart as homo linguisticus. Through linguistic behavior, we enter into contracts and devise rules to govern groups, nations, and eventually all of humankind.

If we are to survive as a world community, it is vital that we use our words to develop a global political philosophy, based on the best possible reasoning. Political philosophy is a subdiscipline of moral philosophy, a subdiscipline that goes beyond individual relationships to involve nationhood, the state and its institutions, especially its laws. Thus, the Introduction contains a defense of ethical objectivism over against its ubiquitous rival, ethical relativism. I give considerable attention to the relativism–objectivism debate, because it is crucial to understanding what political philosophy is about and because it is common to see relativism confused with situationalism, the idea that moral principles apply differently in different situations. Unless we are justified in believing there is moral truth and have an idea of what that truth is, it is impossible to develop comprehensive global political philosophy. This work aims at exactly that, developing a comprehensive global political philosophy. After an introductory discussion of the background theories on the nature of political philosophy and ethical objectivism, I begin in Chapter 1, with the justification of political authority, providing answers to the question, Why not anarchism? In Chapter 2, I turn to the concept of liberty and examine Hume's arguments for the liberty principle and the harm principle, applying them to contemporary issues. In Chapter 3, I examine the nature and value of the prominent political ideal of equality, sorting out several versions of the idea and distinguishing the idea of equal citizenship or equality before the law from equal human worth. In Chapter 4, an extension of the discussion on equality, I examine the idea of equal opportunity. In Chapter 5, the concept of justice is the central focus, where the works of Rawls, and Nozick and the desert theory are scrutinized. Chapter 6 concerns the debate between state neutrality regarding conceptions of the good and moral perfectionism, the idea that the state not only is permitted, but also has a duty, to inculcate virtues in its citizens. Chapter 7 is concerned with the nature and value of rights. Chapter 8 deals with punishment, including capital punishment, as the opposite side of the coin from distributive justice, discussed in Chapter 5. Chapter 9 takes up the subject of nationalism versus cosmopolitanism. Does morality, especially with its emphasis on impartiality, require that we become world citizens and abridge our national commitments (is nationalism an infantile disease like measles, as Einstein charged?), or does nationalism have a morally significant role to play in our lives? Should we move to world government? We examine the reasons for and against doing so, including the need to pass on a healthy environment to posterity. Finally, Chapter 10 explores the threat of terrorism on the world order, taking the tragic events of September 11, 2001, as the point of departure. How should moral people respond to the growing threat of international terror, including suicide bombings, chemical and biological warfare, and the use of nuclear weapons? To stimulate sustained thinking on all the issues, I conclude each chapter with a set of questions entitled "For Further Reflection." A short bibliography for each chapter appears at the end of the book.

This book is distinguished from others of its kind in that it gives more rigorous analyses of equality, the idea of perfectionism, globalism, the debate between cosmopolitanism and nationalism, and the threat of international terrorism.

I have tried to be impartial and fair in assessing various theories in this work; nevertheless, my conclusions are often clearly stated. I invite each of you to develop your own ideas on these important subjects, and would be happy to hear from you regarding your views and comments on these matters.

The formation of my political views began with teenage experiences. When I was 16, a black family moved into my then all-white suburb of Cicero, Illinois. The day the family began to move in, many community members came out to greet them with bricks, guns, and fire bombs. The next day, I visited the site and met schoolmates, including many youth from my church, who invited me to join them in attacking the home that evening. I argued that what they were doing was evil, that it violated everything we had been taught about morality, religion, and the dignity of human beings; black and white citizens should be allowed to live wherever they liked. That night my friends rampaged, destroying the house. The National Guard was called in, and in the melee, two rioters were killed. The following Sunday I attended the youth meeting at church; we discussed the events of that June day of violence, and I listened to my friends' strained and jejune justification of their racist viewpoints. We had been taught the importance of marrying within our own faith, and I asked these devout Christians, "Would you rather marry an atheist white person or a black Christian?" They had to admit that the former would be their choice, if those were the only options. "So much for your Christianity," I said and left the group, never to return. Instead, I began to work in a mission in the black ghetto of Chicago, working with poor children, helping educate them. I carried on this ministry for four years throughout my high school and junior college years.

In the late 1950s and 1960s, I was a student radical, civil rights activist, antiwar protestor, and minister of an inner-city, predominately black church in Bedford-Stuyvesant, Brooklyn. I participated in civil rights workshops, protests, and marches, including the 1963 March on Washington, where the Reverend Martin Luther King, Jr., gave his famous "I Have a Dream" speech. In 1968 I was part of the student movement that took over buildings at Columbia University, shutting down the university for much of the spring semester. My master's degree was on black culture, and my first published articles were about the promise of the civil rights movement in the 1960s. These facts had the effect of confusing people about my identity. After getting my PhD in philosophy, I was invited to a university as a candidate for a tenure-track position. When I arrived, the hosts were in shock. I finally figured out that I had been listed as a black philosopher with a doctorate from Oxford University. When they discovered that I was just another white philosopher, I was dropped from the short list.

I have had the privilege of studying under or working with many of the philosophers discussed in this book. While at Columbia University and Union Theological Seminary, I had the privilege to study political philosophy with the late Reinhold Niebuhr, who helped disabuse me of any illusions about the prospects of Marxists' bringing about utopia. One Wednesday in April I came to his apartment, where he was holding the last seminar he ever taught on political philosophy, and reported that the Students for a Democratic Society (SDS) had just invaded the Loeb Library, taking the university president hostage. Niebuhr seemed disturbed, so I tried to reassure him, saying that students wanted only to create a movement to end the war in Vietnam and to end institutional racism at the university. Niebuhr gravely stared at me and gave me a lecture on the vulnerability of liberal institutions. Our freedoms, he argued, were not enhanced, but dangerously threatened, by anarchic revolutionaries such as the SDS. Liberal institutions such as universities could survive only when people refrained from lawless action and pursued their aims through democratic processes, most notably, open discussion and debate. Niebuhr's philosophy was that human beings are sufficiently sinful that even their ideals are likely to be corrupted by flawed character, so eternal vigilance is necessary to protect our liberties and social virtues. The self-serving intolerance and hedonism I observed in the behavior of many radical students seemed to confirm Niebuhr's diagnosis. The Left could be as peremptory and narrowminded as the Right. Finally, I concluded that only a commitment to the moral point of view, based on careful reasoning, could provide guidance in working through our social antagonisms. My faith is in rational discourse, in using words and reason to communicate, to settle disputes, and to resolve conflicts that might otherwise explode into violence and war.

This early radical background might well seem to make me an unlikely person to teach philosophy at the U.S. Military Academy at West Point. The truth is that there is as much academic freedom at West Point as anywhere else in academia, and that I have been able to discuss these ideas with cadets who run the usual gamut from conservatives to liberals. The U.S. Military Academy, "a bit of Sparta in the midst of Babylon," as Samuel Huntington has called it, is one of the best-kept secrets in academia, where highly intelligent, deeply moral, and strenuously disciplined colleagues and cadets work in an atmosphere of loyalty, integrity, and mutual respect, searching for truth. I have never worked with more congenial or honorable colleagues, and am grateful for the considerable support they have given me. I also want to thank the Philosophy Department of Princeton University for making me a Visiting Fellow for the Summer of 2001, enabling me to write the first draft of this book while at their university. The Firestone Library is the best American library I have worked in, a scholars' paradise.

I want to thank the cadets in my Political Philosophy class of 2000, Michael Rosol, Peter Boyd-Bowman, Caleb Cage, Rob Falzone, Kevin Stacy, Jeffrey Hay, Tom Grwyalski, April Smith, Meagan Dempsey, Chad Piechocki, Tom Schaughnessy, and Scott Taylor, whose questions, research, and insights helped me think through more deeply many of the issues discussed in this book. I am the happiest man in the world, earning a living by doing what I love to do most, teaching philosophy to bright young people. Wallace Matson, Robert Audi, Gary Foulk, Jonathan Harrison, Michael Levin, Jim Landesman, Richard Schoonoven, Burt Louden, and Sterling Harwood each read parts of this work and provided excellent criticisms. Stephen Kershnar read through the entire manuscript, made trenchant criticisms on early drafts, and helped me see the salient issues more clearly. I am grateful to Monica Eckman, who signed me up to do this project, and to Jon-David Hague, who graciously supported me throughout the writing of it. Ruth Smith did an excellent job of bringing this book into production. Most of all, I owe a debt of gratitude to my wife Trudy, who carefully worked through every chapter of this book with me. She has been my best friend, the joy of my life, and my keenest critic for 39 years. Without her, my life would have been poorer and this book would not have been written. To her, this book is gratefully dedicated.

Louis P. Pojman
Princeton University, Princeton, New Jersey
United States Military Academy, West Point, New York

A WORD TO THE STUDENT

EVER SINCE THE END OF THE WORLD WAR II we have lived under the threat of a nuclear explosion brought about by the conflicts of the cold war. What no one anticipated was the fall of the U.S.S.R. and the series of political implosions that have transpired in the past 10 to 15 years. A radically new situation has arisen as on the one hand, the world has shrunk, with international travel, free trade, and the Internet bringing us all closer together; and on the other hand, with rampant nationalism, including secessionist movements, ethnic cleansing, international terrorism, religious fundamentalism, and increasing antipathies [doing what—tearing us apart?]. The AIDS pandemic; the ease with which diseases affecting humans, animals, and crops are spread; the threat of global warning, air pollution, and ozone depletion in the stratosphere; and a global shortage of fresh water have all given rise to a new global constellation of problems and possibilities that calls for a fresh examination of our political structures and strategies.

A few incidents will help illustrate my point. The world was shocked on September 11, 2001. Four planes were hijacked by Arab Muslim terrorists, becoming in their hands massive, murderous missiles. Two of them crashed into New York's World Trade Center, destroying both towers; a third crashed into the Pentagon in Arlington, Virginia, and a fourth, headed perhaps for the Capitol building or the White House, in Washington, D.C., crashed into a Pennsylvania field. An estimated 3,000 unsuspecting, innocent people were killed, as well as the 19 terrorists. Thus a new era in the history of warfare has been inaugurated, one which portends a new dimension of evil and a different type of war. Politics changed on that fateful day. The history of our world will henceforth be divided into "before September 11" and "after September 11."

But we should not have been taken by surprise by the terrorist attacks of 9-11 (note the number!). Terrorist incidents had been occurring all over the world, increasingly since 1970. On July 24, 2001, for example, 13 suicide bombers of the rebel Tamil Elam broke into Sri Lanka's Bandaranaike International Airport and air force base and blew up eight military and three Sri Lankan aircraft; the rebels have been fighting a civil war against the Singhalese majority for 18 years, and thousands of people have been killed in the war. On the same day, thousands of miles to the west, a member of the Basque separatist group ETA blew herself up and injured seven bystanders in a popular tourist town in southeast Spain; the ETA has killed 800 people since 1968 (*New York Times*, July 25, 2001). On still the same day, crowds attacked the American Consulate in Macedonia, protesting NATO policies in that country. In mid-July a fire in a train tunnel in Baltimore burned some Internet cables, knocking out regional service and disrupting Internet service throughout the United States. One shudders to think of the possibilities of worldwide sabotage of the Internet system.

New strategies are called for, but world leaders seem to be stuck in old ruts, reacting to yesterday's problems with the day before yesterday's thought patterns and institutions. Missile defense systems, geared to the cold war threat of a nuclear war, won't stop suicide bombings or sabotage of the Internet.

Politics is about the use of power. When we look at the past century, one feature that leaps out is the enormous abuse of political power. Early in that century the British philosopher Lord Acton wrote, "Power tends to corrupt, absolute power corrupts absolutely," perhaps a fitting epitaph to the carnage of that era. The twentieth century was marked by mass violence and extermination of people as no other century in recorded human history. In his work *Death by Government*, R. J. Rummel has conservatively estimated that governments from 1900 until 1987 killed over 169 million people. Joseph Stalin is the all-time megamurderer, accounting for 42,672,000 deaths; Mao Tse Tung is second, with 37,828,000 deaths; Adolf Hitler is third, responsible for 20,946,000 deaths*. He is also credited with starting World War II, which resulted in some 60 million deaths.

Rummel documents that 353 wars were waged from 1816 to 1991, mostly by authoritarian regimes. Not one war was fought by a democracy against another democracy. Winston Churchill once said that democracy, with all its faults, in producing mediocrity and crude compromise, was the

---

*R. J. Rummel, *Death by Government* (City: Transaction, 1994). Long before Acton, in the eighteenth century, Edmund Burke wrote, "Power gradually extirpates for the mind every humane and gentle virtue."

worst possible political system, except for all the others. Because democracy distributes power more widely and slows the possibility of decisive autocratic action, cooler heads have time to consider the costs of war, which generally has a salutary effect.

In this work I invite you to critically examine the basic concepts and theories of political thought. I have tried to set forth a comprehensive overview of the major ideas in political philosophy with the intention of challenging you to think more clearly, critically, and comprehensively about these important issues. I have quoted W. B. Yeats's epigraph on p. vi with the intention of challenging you to be "the best" who have convictions based on solid reasoning. Your generation will face its own challenges, and how you address them will determine the course of history and the fate of the earth. Thinking clearly about the philosophical bases of politics should help shape a better understanding of the issues that lie before you. Illumination can lead to more informed decisions and policies that reflect our deepest moral principles. Such a broad vision of the world as an arena for moral action, where each of us can make a difference for good or ill, is the presumption of this work. I hope you will develop your own version of a morally informed, critical political philosophy. I would be happy to hear from you on the important matters discussed in this book.

Louis P. Pojman
United States Military Academy
West Point, New York

INTRODUCTION

Man is a political animal

—ARISTOTLE

If men were angels, no Government would be necessary.
If they were devils, no Government would be possible.

—ALEXANDER HAMILTON

Bridges are built; harbors opened; ramparts raised; canals formed; fleets equipped; and armies disciplined; everywhere, by the care of government, which though composed of men subject to all human infirmities, becomes, by one of the finest and most subtle inventions imaginable, a composition, that is, in some measure, exempted from all infirmities.

—DAVID HUME[1]

I N PART ONE of this Introduction, I introduce the subject of political philosophy, distinguishing the two features of the modern state: the nation and the state. In Part Two, I provide a context for political philosophy in moral philosophy, defending moral objectivism against moral relativism.

PART ONE: ON POLITICAL PHILOSOPHY

Political philosophy inquires into the meaning of political concepts and the justification of theories about the nature and purpose of government. It seeks to provide understanding regarding such questions as, Why should I obey the laws of the state? How should the state be constituted? What is the justification of the state? What are the principal functions of the state? Should the state be a national or an international body? Should the nation–state be sovereign, or should we create a cosmopolitan government, transcending nationalism?

In seeking to answer, or at least understand, these questions and the competing answers to them, we encounter a series of secondary concepts and theories, including the nature and value of justice, liberty, equality, political obligation, moral perfectionism, nationalism, globalism, and sovereignty. In the various chapters of this book we will examine most of these concepts and the theories surrounding them.

Political philosophy, unlike political science, is not primarily descriptive, concerned with an explanation of why government exists the way it does (though it does consider this issue), but is prescriptive or normative, dealing with how political institutions *ought* to function, concerned with setting forth arguments and justifications for the best or most morally justified ways of organizing society.

Before we can engage in considering the justification of political theories, we need to clarify some concepts and inquire what we mean by *state, nation, justice, liberty, equality, sovereignty,* and the like. This we will do in detail in the relevant parts of this book, but here we undertake an initial, condensed discussion.

Consider the fundamental concepts of the state and the nation. The *state* is an association that includes such formal ideas as a legislative body with an executive and a judicial component. The state is the ultimate authority, a sovereign body, having sole comprehensive authority over a geographical domain. A *nation*, on the other hand, is a group of people who are tied together through common sources of meaning and identity, through ethnic similarity, through language, literature, history, myth, religion, and other cultural phenomena. A state may be made up of many nations, and one nation may be divided by many states. An example of the former is Great Britain, which is made up of the nations of England, Wales, Scotland, and Northern Ireland. An example of the latter is Canada, a state made up of two nations, the French-speaking people of Quebec and the English-speaking people of the rest of Canada. Until the early 1870s, when Bismark united the German people, the German nation was divided into several separate states. After the Second World War until the fall of the German Democratic Republic in 1991, the German nation was divided into two states, East and West Germany. One could argue that Austria makes up yet another state of Germans. The ancient Greeks, a nation, were divided into several city–states, yet they joined in a military federation to defend their cities against the Persians. The distinction between state and nation is sometimes vague. Is Switzerland, with its three cultural and language groups, one state with three nations or one nation-state or several minicanton states? The goal of every nationalist is, in the words of the 18th century Italian nationalist Giuseppe Mazzini: "Every nation a state, only one state for the entire nation."[2] When we read of the conflicts in Israel between Jew and Arab, in Northern Ireland between Protestant and Catholic, or of the ethnic cleansing in Bosnia or Kosovo, we get a sense of just how penetrating and volatile nationalism can be.

In the 19th century the German sociologist Ferdinand Tönnies (1855–1936) distinguished between *Gemeinschaft* (community) and *Gesellschaft* (society), the former referring to the natural, communal ties (such as friendship, family, and clan) that cause people to commit themselves to a common cause or way of life; the latter referring to those features of social organization constituted by contract and formal rules. Tönnies says that *Gemeinschaft* is formed by natural will, whereas *Gesellshaft* is formed by rational will. *Gemeinschaft* is constituted by a covenant rather than a contract, something informal and deeply rooted in human relationships, even sacred to its members—like a religious heritage or sacred myth. In the Old Testament God does not contract, but covenants, with the people Israel. Indeed, the very term *testament* literally means "covenant." There is a relationship of personal loyalty, obedience, and trust on the part of the people of Israel, which Yahweh will honor by his guidance and protection. When Israel becomes a formal state in 1 Samuel, choosing Saul as its king, the prophet Samuel deplores the act as a betrayal of the covenantal relationship between Yahweh and Israel, but permits it as a concession to human weakness. It would be better to live in a relationship of direct trust in God, as a special community of faith, but since Israel's faith is weak, formal rules and an executive branch are permitted as a distant second best. The state, as a formal society, typically emerges from the nation or community when formal structure of rules and separation of powers are desired. Spontaneous acts of beneficence, as well as a notion of reciprocity, characterize the morality of the community, but it lacks the impartiality and consistent application of behavior. The state or society goes beyond such "natural morality" and formalizes rules of law, enforcing them impartially with sanctions. Whereas life in the community is characterized by virtue (or vice) and loyalty, society superimposes laws, rights, and contractual obligations.

When we organize a group of friends into a professional association or organization, giving it a constitution with goals and rules or laws, we superimpose society on community. A group of hikers, trekking together in the mountains, form a community, but not a society, even though they may have a common purpose (say climbing Mt. Marcy); but when they agree on a common set of rules and responsibilities, they are transformed into a primitive association, say, the Adirondack Mountain Club or the Sierra Club, which gradually may lose many of its communal characteristics, becoming more powerful, but also more impersonal, bureaucratic, and legalistic. A group of tenants may constitute a caring community, but they become an association or society when they form a tenants' association, with a constitution and set of rules, to fight more effectively for reduced rent and better maintenance. When workers in a company or organization unite in a union to advance their interests, they are changed from a community to a society. The process of transformation can have powerful effects. In a classic study of group interaction, Muzafer Sherif and associates took two sets of preteenage, average American boys, let them form into groups, and noticed that they took on all the traits of passionate patriots, turning competitive with each other until it led to violence.[3]

We can apply Tönnies's distinction to the concepts of the nation and state. When we refer to a state, we mean a large, anonymous body (the members need not know each other personally) that creates and enforces laws over a geographical area or group of people who usually reside in the geographical area. A nation, on the other hand, refers to the societal aspects, to the culture, and to the myths and history of the group. Nations, as communities, grow like trees, whereas states, as associations, are constructed like buildings. Typically, states, as artificial institutions, are invented, whereas nations are neither created by our will nor chosen, but are natural, primitive givens, based on shared history, beliefs, love, and loyalty, constituting a vital part of our self-identity. One does not choose to be of German, French, or English ancestry, with all that goes with that; rather, one is chosen by the lottery of nature. One then finds one's identity constituted by these factors. The fate of our nation is our fate, though we may not suffer physically or economically from its defeat or loss of power. In the community or nation, particular loyalties are the dominant motif. We have a special obligation to specific people, to a common identifiable tradition, whereas the society takes on a more universal aspect, characterized by a constitution, laws, and a set of requirements for membership. It constructs rational principles, which have a universal aspect, and so applies impartially, without respect for class or status. Whoever meets the abstract requirements is a citizen, a member of the society. Whoever breaches the law suffers the penalty.

Since the 17th century we find ourselves in a situation where the two types of political groups are combined, in the nation-state. *Gesellshaft* and *Gemeinshaft* become one. The universal and the particular merge into a single political reality. However, it is useful to distinguish between these two aspects of that reality.

When we think of a nation, such as England or the United States, we think of its history; its wars; its language; its literature, folk songs, and stories; its architecture, including its churches and skyscrapers; its landscapes; its cultural symbols—the flag, the eagle. When citizens travel abroad, they are soon reminded of their identity. The mores and manners are different in the foreign land and sometimes *feel* wrong. Travelers become nostalgic for the people, sights, sounds, and even smells and tastes of their native land. Americans abroad search for the *International Herald Tribune* to bring them news from home. And when they return, even if they have had a wonderful time abroad, they say, "It's good to be home." A sense of familiarity and wholeness spreads over them, even compensating for the jet lag they may experience. We tend to take nationalist sentiments for granted until they are threatened or until we are shocked by our nationalistic pride. David Miller tells of a friend who was unaware of how much importance he attached to being Dutch until a night in June 1988 when the Dutch football team defeated Germany in the European Cup, inspiring a mass celebration on the streets of Amsterdam.[4] The nation, not the state, provides our roots, our sense of belonging, our identity, our solidarity with others. So deep is this sense of communal covenant that many will risk their lives for the nation and even kill for it.

When we think of the state, on the other hand, we think of the laws, the institutions, including the constitution, that make up the state. These laws are impersonal and abstract, though they can have powerful personal effects, especially if one is caught breaking one of them. The authority of the state consists in its *sovereignty*. It alone can make laws and enforce them within its jurisdiction. External associations are forbidden from interfering in its internal affairs, and no internal association may override its statutes. The state is supreme.

Politicians differ in their appeal to the electorate, some appealing more to the societal and nationalistic sentiments, say, family values, religion, and tradition, whereas others appeal to institutional characteristics and may propose changing specific laws, such as those governing Social Security or taxation. Of course, there is much overlap, for some of the laws touch deeply on our heritage, say, a law against desecrating the flag. Still, the distinction is valid. Liberals, especially libertarians, emphasize the formal state aspects, concentrating on the government's role as a protector (from both internal and external harm), whereas conservatives and commutarians emphasize the cultural communal aspects, such as family values, patriotism, and religious and cultural heritage. A liberal may well tolerate, or even celebrate, wide differences in education, literature, and even language use (cultural diversity), whereas a conservative or commutarian will seek to promote tradition, a single language, the core curriculum in education. It is no accident that conservatives call for immigration restrictions while liberals promote open borders, or that conservatives fight for making English the official language while liberals tolerate a diversity of language use. Liberals celebrate cultural diversity, whereas conservatives identify so strongly with their own culture that they tend to be

suspicious of diversity until a case for it is made. These distinctions will surface in many parts of this work.

In sum, the state is distinguished by its sovereignty, its authority to rule
over its subjects, and its right to create laws and enforce them by coercive
means. It is formal, abstract, legalistic, and dominated by the universal,
but, because of its coercive authority, also potentially very powerful for
good or ill. A nation, on the other hand, represents the communal, voluntary aspects of social life, stressing the particular over the universal.
Whereas membership in the state is a matter of legal status, membership
in a nation is a matter of passion or emotion, of personal commitment,
which evokes the sentiment of patriotism.

PART TWO: THE RELATIONSHIP OF ETHICS TO POLITICAL PHILOSOPHY

WHO'S TO JUDGE WHAT'S RIGHT AND WRONG?

Political philosophy is a part of moral philosophy, the systematic study of
normative behavior, the concepts of right and wrong, as well as good and
evil. The idea of normativity denotes value judgments: what ought or
ought not to be the case, as opposed to descriptive statements. Contrast
these two statements D and N:

D: In April 1995 Timothy McVeigh blew up the Federal Building in
Oklahoma City, killing 168 people.
N: In April 1995 Timothy McVeigh should not have blown up the
Federal Building in Oklahoma City, killing 168 people.

Statement D simply describes a fact, without making a moral or normative
judgment, whereas statement N is a normative judgment, expressing condemnation of the same act that D describes.

The philosophical question is, How can one justify normative judgments? Since we will be deeply engaged in deliberations on how society
ought to be organized, we need to take some time to consider the nature
of morality and, especially, the question of ethical relativism versus ethical
objectivism.

ETHICAL RELATIVISM AND ETHICAL OBJECTIVISM

Ethical relativism (ER) is the doctrine that the moral rightness and wrong-
ness of actions vary from society to society, and that there are no objective

universal moral standards binding on all people at all times. Accordingly, ER holds that whether or not it is right for an individual to act in a certain way depends on, or is relative to, the society to which he or she belongs. *Ethical objectivism (EO)* is the doctrine that even though different societies hold different moral codes, an objective core morality exists, made up of universally valid moral principles. Accordingly, EO holds that whether or not it is right for an individual to act in a certain way depends on whether the act is covered by the set of universally valid moral principles.

One must first distinguish ER from *cultural relativism (CR)*. CR states that different cultures hold different moral codes, that there is cultural diversity. For instance, Eskimos traditionally allow their elderly to die by starvation, whereas we believe that this practice is morally wrong. The Spartans of ancient Greece and the Dobu of New Guinea believe that stealing is morally right; but we believe it is wrong. Many cultures, past and present, have practiced or still practice infanticide. A tribe in East Africa once threw deformed infants to the hippopotamuses, but our society condemns such acts. Sexual practices vary over time and clime. Some cultures permit homosexual behavior, whereas others condemn it. Some tribes in Africa practice genital mutilation on females, whereas we find such practices abhorrent. Some cultures permit abortion; others condemn it. Some cultures, including Moslem societies, practice polygamy, whereas Christian societies view it as immoral.

CR is a descriptive thesis, not a normative one. Just because a society believes that the Earth is flat doesn't mean that it is. Similarly, just because a society permits slavery doesn't mean that slavery is morally justified. In "A Word to the Student" I noted that Stalin had killed 42 million presumably innocent people in the former U.S.S.R. Even if the majority of Soviet citizens approved of Stalin's regime and these killings, that approval does not necessarily make his behavior morally correct.

Ethical objectivism accepts the anthropological data that different societies have different moral practices. It simply doesn't agree that believing P makes P true. Just as believing that the Earth is flat doesn't make it true (though the believer may be justified or excused in so believing), so believing that killing your children or enslaving people is morally right doesn't make it so (though the believer may not be culpable). The believers may have been conditioned to think that way or may not know any better.

Ethical objectivism must not be confused with ethnocentrism, which dogmatically supposes one's moral code is the true one. Today we condemn ethnocentrism as a variety of prejudice tantamount to racism and sexism. But one must hold some sort of ethical objectivism to condemn ethnocentrism, as well as racism and sexism. Otherwise, one can argue only that prejudice is wrong in our culture, but not in Afghanistan, or Rwanda, or Mali, or wherever things are different.

An Analysis of Ethical Relativism (conventionalism)

Ethical relativism holds that there are no universally valid moral principles, but rather that all moral principles are valid relative to cultural or individual acceptance.

The argument for ER consists of three premises:

1. *The diversity thesis.* What is considered morally right and wrong varies from society to society, so there are no moral principles that all societies accept.
2. *The dependency thesis.* All moral principles derive their validity from cultural acceptance.
3. *Ethical relativism.* Therefore, there are no universally valid moral principles, no objective standards that apply to all people everywhere and at all times.

We have already examined the diversity thesis in our discussion of cultural relativism and found it to be true. The heart of ER is the dependency thesis, to which we now turn.

The Dependency Thesis

The *dependency thesis* asserts that individual acts are right or wrong depending on the nature of the society in which they occur. Morality does not exist in a vacuum; rather, what is considered morally right or wrong must be seen within a context, depending on the goals, wants, beliefs, history, and environment of the society in question. As William Graham Sumner says:

> We learn the [morals] as unconsciously as we learn to walk and hear and breathe, and [we] never know any reason why the [morals] are what they are. The justification of them is that when we wake to consciousness of life we find them facts which already hold us in the bonds of tradition, custom, and habit.[5]

Trying to see things from an independent, noncultural point of view would be like taking out our eyes in order to examine their contours and qualities. We are simply culturally determined beings.

We could, of course, distinguish both a weak and a strong thesis of dependency. The nonrelativist can accept a certain relativity in the way moral principles are *applied* in various cultures, depending on beliefs, history, and environment. For example, many Asians show respect by covering the head and uncovering the feet, whereas Occidentals do the opposite. Though both groups adhere to a principle of respect for deserving people, they apply the principle differently. Some cultures practice polygamy, whereas others are committed to monogamy, but both are committed to strong intimate relations and the protection and nurturing of children. Both polygamy and monogamy may be workable, and so both are moral options. But the ethical relativist must maintain a stronger thesis, one that insists that the very validity of the principles is a product of the culture and that different cultures will invent different valid principles. The ethical relativist maintains that even beyond the environmental factors and differences in beliefs, there are fundamental disagreements among societies.

In a sense, we all live in radically different worlds. Each person has a unique set of beliefs and experiences, a particular perspective that colors all his or her perceptions. Do the farmer, the real estate dealer, and the artist, all looking at the same spatiotemporal field, actually see the same thing? Not likely. Their different orientations, values, and expectations govern their perceptions, so for each of them, different aspects of the field are highlighted and some features are missed. Even as our individual values arise from personal experience, so social values are grounded in the particular history of the community. Morality, then, is just the set of common rules, habits, and customs that have won social approval over time, so that they seem part of the nature of things, like facts. There is nothing mysterious or transcendent about these codes of behavior. They are the outcomes of our social history.

There is something conventional about *any* morality, so *every* morality really depends on a level of social acceptance. Not only do various societies adhere to different moral systems, but the same society could (and often does) change its moral views over time and place. For example, in the southern United States, slavery is now viewed as immoral, whereas about 140 years ago, it was not. We have greatly altered our views on abortion, divorce, and sexuality as well.

The conclusion—that there are no absolute or objective moral standards binding on all people—follows from the first two propositions. Cultural relativism (the diversity thesis) plus the dependency thesis yields ethical relativism in its classic form. If there are different moral principles from culture to culture and if all morality is rooted in culture, then it follows that there are no universal moral principles valid for all cultures and all people at all times. Morality is merely a matter of convention.

Subjective Ethical Relativism (Subjectivism)

Some relativists think that the conclusion noted above is still too tame, and they maintain that morality depends not on the society but rather, on the individual. As my students sometimes maintain, morality is in the eye of the beholder. They treat morality like taste or aesthetic judgments, which are person-relative. As Ernest Hemingway wrote:

> So far, about morals, I know only that what is moral is what you feel good after and what is immoral is what you feel bad after and judged by these moral standards, which I do not defend, the bullfight is very moral to me because I feel very fine while it is going on and have a feeling of life and death and mortality and immortality, and after it is over I feel very sad but very fine.[6]

This form of moral subjectivism has the sorry consequence of making morality a very useless concept, for, on its premises, little or no interpersonal criticism or judgment is logically possible. Hemingway may feel good about killing bulls in a bullfight, whereas Saint Francis or Mother Teresa would no doubt feel the opposite. No argument about the matter is possible. Suppose that you are repulsed by observing John torturing a child. You cannot condemn him if one of his principles is to torture little children for the fun of it. The only basis for judging him wrong might be if he was a *hypocrite* who condemned others for torturing children. However, one of his or Hemingway's principles could be that hypocrisy is morally permissible (he feels "very fine" about it), so it would be impossible for John to do wrong. For Hemingway, hypocrisy and nonhypocrisy are both morally permissible (except, perhaps, when he doesn't feel very fine about it).

On the basis of subjectivism, Adolf Hitler and the serial murderer Ted Bundy could be considered as moral as Gandhi, so long as each lived by his own standards, whatever those might be. Witness the following paraphrase of a tape-recorded conversation between Ted Bundy and one of his victims, in which Bundy justifies his planned murder:

> Then I learned that all moral judgments are "value judgments," that all value judgments are subjective, and that none can be proved to be either "right" or "wrong." I even read somewhere that the Chief Justice of the United States had written that the American Constitution expressed nothing more than collective value judgments. Believe it or not, I figured out for myself—what apparently the Chief Justice couldn't figure out for himself—that if the rationality of one value judgment was zero, multiplying it by millions would not make it one whit more rational. Nor is there any "reason" to obey the law for anyone, like myself, who has the boldness and daring—the strength of character—to throw off its shackles . . . I discovered that to become truly free, truly unfettered, I had to become truly uninhibited. And I quickly discovered that the greatest obstacle to my freedom, the greatest block and limitation to it, consists in the insupportable "value judgment" that I was bound to respect the rights of others. I asked myself, who were these "others"? Other human

beings, with human rights? Why is it more wrong to kill a human animal than any other animal, a pig or a sheep or a steer? Is your life more to you than a hog's life to a hog? Why should I be willing to sacrifice my pleasure more for the one than for the other? Surely, you would not, in this age of scientific enlightenment, declare that God or nature has marked some pleasures as "moral" or "good" and others as "immoral" or "bad"? In any case, let me assure you, my dear young lady, that there is absolutely no comparison between the pleasure I might take in eating ham and the pleasure I anticipate in raping and murdering you. That is the honest conclusion to which my education has led me—after the most conscientious examination of my spontaneous and uninhibited self.[7]

Notions of good and bad, or right and wrong, cease to have interpersonal evaluative meaning. We might be revulsed by Ted Bundy's views, but that is just a matter of taste.

Absurd consequences follow from subjectivism. If it is correct, then morality reduces to aesthetic tastes about which there can be neither argument nor interpersonal judgment. Although many students say they espouse subjectivism, there is evidence that it conflicts with some of their other moral views; for example, they typically condemn Hitler and his genocidal policies as evil. A contradiction seems to exist between subjectivism and the very concept of morality, which it is supposed to characterize, for morality has to do with *proper* resolution of interpersonal conflict and the amelioration of the human predicament (both deontological and teleological systems do this, though in different ways). Whatever else it does, morality has a minimal aim of preventing a Hobbesian state of nature, wherein life is "solitary, poor, nasty, brutish and short." But if so, then subjectivism is no help at all, for it rests neither on social agreement of principle (as the conventionalist maintains) nor on an objectively independent set of norms that bind all people for the common good. If there were only one person on earth, there would be no occasion for morality, because there wouldn't be any interpersonal conflicts to resolve or others whose suffering that person would have a duty to ameliorate. Subjectivism implicitly assumes something of this solipsism, an atomism in which isolated individuals make up separate universes.

Subjectivism treats individuals as billiard balls on a societal pool table where they meet only in radical collisions, each aimed at his or her own goal and striving to do the others in before they do him or her in. This atomistic view of personality is belied by the fact that we develop in families and mutually dependent communities in which we share a common language, common institutions, and similar rituals and habits, and that we often feel one another's joys and sorrows. As John Donne wrote, "No man is an island, entire of itself; every man is a piece of the continent."

Radical individualistic ethical relativism is incoherent. Thus, it follows that the only plausible view of ethical relativism must be one that grounds morality in the group or culture. This form is called conventionalism, which we noted earlier and to which we now return.

Conventional Ethical Relativism (Conventionalism)

Conventional ethical relativism, the view that there are no objective moral principles but that all valid moral principles are justified (or are made true) by virtue of their cultural acceptance, is based on the dependency thesis. It recognizes the social nature of morality. That is precisely its power and virtue. It does not seem subject to the same absurd consequences that plague subjectivism. Recognizing the importance of our social environment in generating customs and beliefs, many people suppose that ethical relativism is the correct ethical theory. Furthermore, they are drawn to it for its liberal philosophical stance. It seems to be an enlightened response to the sin of ethnocentricity, and it seems to entail or strongly imply an attitude of tolerance toward other cultures. As the anthropologist Ruth Benedict says, in recognizing ethical relativity, "We shall arrive at a more realistic social faith, accepting as grounds of hope and as new bases for tolerance the coexisting and equally valid patterns of life which mankind has created for itself from the raw materials of existence."[8] The most famous proponent of this position is the anthropologist Melville Herskovits, who argues even more explicitly than Benedict that ethical relativism entails intercultural tolerance:

1. If morality is relative to its culture, then there is no independent basis for criticizing the morality of any other culture but one's own.
2. If there is no independent way of criticizing any other culture, then we ought to be tolerant of the moralities of other cultures.
3. Morality is relative to its culture.
4. Therefore, we ought to be tolerant of the moralities of other cultures.[9]

Tolerance is certainly a virtue, but is this a good argument for it? I think not. If morality simply is relative to each culture, then if the culture in question has no principle of tolerance, its members have no obligation to be tolerant. Herskovits seems to be treating the principle of tolerance as the one exception to his relativism. He seems to be treating it as an absolute moral principle. But from a relativistic point of view, there is no more reason to be tolerant than to be intolerant, and neither stance is objectively morally better than the other.

Relativists not only offer no basis for criticizing those who are intolerant, but also cannot rationally criticize anyone who espouses what they
might regard as a heinous principle. If, as seems to be the case, valid criticism supposes an objective or impartial standard, then relativists cannot
morally criticize anyone outside their own culture. Adolf Hitler's genocidal actions, so long as they are culturally accepted, are as morally legitimate as Mother Teresa's works of mercy. If conventional relativism is
accepted, then racism, genocide of unpopular minorities, oppression of
the poor, slavery, and even the advocacy of war for its own sake are as
moral as their opposites. Even if a subculture decided that starting a nuclear war was somehow morally acceptable, we would have no basis for
morally criticizing those people. Any actual morality, whatever its content,
would be as valid as every other and more valid than ideal moralities—
since no culture adheres to the latter.

There are other disturbing consequences of conventional ethical relativism. It seems to entail that reformers are always (morally) wrong, since
they go against the tide of cultural standards. Consider the following examples. William Wilberforce was wrong in the 18th century to oppose slavery. Similarly, the British were immoral in opposing and forbidding *suttee*
in India (the burning of widows, which is now illegal there). If the villagers
believed that the widow should be thrown into the funeral pyre and
burned to death, who are we to oppose them? Similarly, if Nazi society believed it was right to exterminate Jews, gypsies, and homosexuals, we are
morally evil in opposing them by trying to impose our values on them. Ethical relativism has the consequence that all reformers are immoral since
they oppose the status quo, which by definition is the basis of morality. Indeed, Jesus himself was immoral in breaking the law of his day by healing
on the Sabbath and by advocating the principles of the Sermon on the
Mount, since it is clear that few in his time (or in ours) accepted them.

Yet (at least retrospectively) we normally feel just the opposite, that the
reformer is a courageous innovator who is right, who has the truth, who
stands against the mindless majority. Sometimes the individual must stand
alone with the truth, risking social censure and persecution. In Ibsen's *Enemy of the People*, after Dr. Stockman loses the battle to declare his town's
profitable, but polluted, tourist spa unsanitary, he says, "The most dangerous enemy of the truth and freedom among us—is the compact majority. Yes, the damned, compact and liberal majority. The majority has
might—unfortunately—but *right* it is not. Right—are I and a few others."
Yet if relativism is correct, the opposite is necessarily the case. Truth is with
the crowd and error with the individual.

Similarly, conventional ethical relativism entails disturbing judgments
about the law. Our normal view is that we have a prima facie duty to obey

the law, because law, in general, promotes the human good. According to most objective systems, this obligation is not absolute, but relative to the particular law's relation to a wider moral order. Civil disobedience is warranted in some cases wherein the law seems to seriously conflict with morality. However, if moral relativism is true, then neither law nor civil disobedience has a firm foundation. On the one hand, from the side of the society at large, civil disobedience will be morally wrong, so long as the majority culture agrees with the law in question. On the other hand, if you belong to the relevant subculture that doesn't recognize the particular law in question (because it is unjust from your point of view), then disobedience will be morally mandated. The Ku Klux Klan, which believes that Jews, Catholics, and blacks are evil or undeserving of high regard, is, given conventionalism, morally permitted or required to break the laws that protect these endangered groups. Why should I obey a law that my group doesn't recognize as valid?

To sum up, unless we have an independent moral basis for law, it is hard to see why we have any general duty to obey it; and unless we recognize the priority of a universal moral law, we have no firm basis for justifying our acts of civil disobedience against "unjust laws." Both the validity of law and the morally motivated disobedience of unjust laws are annulled in favor of a power struggle.

There is an even more basic problem with the notion that morality depends on cultural acceptance for its validity. The problem is that the notion of a culture or society is notoriously difficult to define, especially in a pluralistic society like our own. A person may belong to several societies (subcultures) with different value emphases and arrangements of principles. A person may belong to the nation as a single society with certain values of patriotism, honor, courage, and laws (including some that are controversial but have majority acceptance, such as the current law on abortion). But he or she may also belong to a church that opposes some of the laws of the state. He or she may also be an integral member of a socially mixed community where different principles hold sway and may belong to clubs and a family where still other rules prevail. Relativism would seem to tell us that if a person belongs to societies with conflicting moralities, then that person must be judged both wrong and not wrong whatever he or she does. For example, if Mary is a U.S. citizen and a member of the Roman Catholic Church, then she is wrong (qua Catholic) if she has an abortion and not wrong (qua citizen of the United States) if she acts against the church's teaching on abortion. As a member of a racist university fraternity, KKK, John has no obligation to treat his fellow black students as equals, but as a member of the university community (which accepts the principle of equal rights), he does have the obligation; but as a member of the surrounding community (which may reject the principle of equal rights), he again has no such obligation; but then again, as a member of the nation at large (which accepts the principle), he is obligated to treat his fellow students with respect. What is the morally right thing for John to do? The question no longer makes much sense in this moral babel. It has lost its action-guiding function.

Perhaps the relativist would adhere to a principle that says that in such cases, the individual may choose which group to belong to as his or her primary group. If Mary has an abortion, she is choosing to belong to the general society relative to that principle. And John must likewise choose among groups. The trouble with this option is that it seems to lead back to counterintuitive results. If Murder Mike of Murder Incorporated feels like killing Bank President Ortcutt and wants to feel good about it, he identifies with the Murder Incorporated society rather than the general public morality. Does this justify the killing? In fact, couldn't one justify anything simply by forming a small subculture that approved of it? Ted Bundy would be morally pure in raping and killing innocents simply by virtue of forming a little coterie. How large must the group be in order to be a legitimate subculture or society? Does it need 10 or 15 people? How about just 3? Come to think of it, why can't my burglary partner and I found our own society with a morality of its own? Of course, if my partner dies, I could still claim that I was acting from an originally social set of norms. But why can't I dispense with the interpersonal agreements altogether and invent my own morality—since morality, in this view, is only an invention anyway? Conventionalist relativism seems to reduce to subjectivism. And subjectivism leads, as we have seen, to moral solipsism, to the demise of morality altogether.

If one objects that this is an instance of the *slippery slope fallacy*,[10] then let that person give an alternative analysis of what constitutes a viable social basis for generating valid (or true) moral principles. Perhaps we might agree (for the sake of argument, at least) that the very nature of morality entails two people who are making an agreement. This move saves the conventionalist from moral solipsism, but it still permits almost any principle at all to count as moral. And what's more, one can throw out those principles and substitute contraries for them as the need arises. If two or three people decide to make cheating on exams morally acceptable for themselves, via forming a fraternity, Cheaters Anonymous, at their university, then cheating becomes moral. Why not? Why not rape, as well?

I don't think you can stop the move from conventionalism to subjectivism. The essential force of the validity of the chosen moral principle is that it depends on *choice*. The conventionalist holds that it is the group's choice, but why should I accept the group's "silly choice," when my own is better (for me)? If this is all that morality comes to, then why not reject it altogether—even though, to escape sanctions, one might want to adhere to its directives when others are watching? Why should anyone give such august authority to a culture or society? I see no reason to recognize a culture's authority, unless that culture recognizes the authority of something that *legitimizes* the culture. It seems that we need something higher than culture by which to assess a culture.

We have shown that ethical relativism has a lot of problems, but showing this doesn't make its opposite, ethical objectivism, true. What can be said for EO? Just this: If morality has to do with promoting human flourishing, ameliorating suffering, and resolving conflicts of interest justly, then it would seem that certain rules of behavior would be more conducive than others to these goals. What is the evidence for universal principles? Some scientists reject the diversity thesis (what we call cultural relativism). One can see great similarities among the moral codes of various cultures. E. O. Wilson has identified over a score of common features, and before him, Clyde Kluckhohn noted some significant common ground:

> Every culture has a concept of murder, distinguishing this from execution, killing in war, and other "justifiable homicides." The notions of incest and other regulations upon sexual behavior, the prohibitions upon untruth under defined circumstances, of restitution and reciprocity, of mutual obligations between parents and children—these and many other moral concepts are altogether universal.[11]

Colin Turnbull's description of the sadistic, semidisplaced, disintegrating Ik culture in northern Uganda supports the view that a people without principles of kindness, loyalty, and cooperation will degenerate into a Hobbesian state of nature. But he has also produced evidence that underneath the surface of this dying society, there is a deeper moral code from a time when the tribe flourished, which occasionally surfaces and shows its nobler face.[12]

On the other hand, there is enormous cultural diversity, and many societies have radically different moral codes. Cultural relativism seems to be a fact, but, even if it is, it does not by itself establish the truth of ethical relativism. Cultural diversity in itself is neutral with respect to theories. The objectivist could concede complete cultural relativism but still defend a form of universalism; for he or she could argue that some cultures simply lack correct moral principles.

Earlier in this chapter we distinguished between a weak and a strong thesis of dependency. The weak thesis says that the application of principles depends on the particular cultural predicament, whereas the strong thesis affirms that the principles themselves depend on that predicament.

The nonrelativist can accept a certain degree of relativity in the way moral principles are *applied* in various cultures, depending on beliefs, history, and environment. For example, a raw environment with scarce natural resources may justify the traditional Eskimos' brand of euthanasia to the objectivist, who would consistently reject that practice if it occurred in another environment. The East African tribe throws its deformed infants into the river because the tribe believes that such infants *belong* to the hippopotamus, the god of the river. We believe that these groups' beliefs in euthanasia and infanticide are false, but the point is that the principles of respect for property and respect for human life operate in such contrary practices. The tribe differs with us only in belief, not in substantive moral principle. This is an illustration of how nonmoral beliefs (e.g., deformed infants belong to the hippopotamus), when applied to common moral principles (e.g., give to each his or her due), generate different actions in different cultures. In our own culture, the difference in the nonmoral belief about the status of a fetus generates opposite moral prescriptions. The major difference between pro-choicers and pro-lifers in the abortion debate is not whether we should kill persons but whether fetuses are really persons. It is a debate about the facts of the matter, not the principle of killing innocent persons.

Moderate Objectivism

If we give up the notion that a moral system must contain only absolute principles, duties that proceed out of a definite algorithm, what can we put in its place?

The *moderate objectivist's* account of moral principles is what William Ross refers to as prima facie principles,[13] valid rules of action that one should generally adhere to but that in cases of moral conflict may be overridable by another moral principle. For example, even though a principle of justice may generally outweigh a principle of benevolence, there are times when one could do enormous good by sacrificing a small amount of justice; thus an objectivist would be inclined to act according to the principle of benevolence. There may be some absolute or nonoverridable principles, but there need not be any (or many) for objectivism to be true. Renford Bambrough states this point nicely:

> To suggest that there is a *right* answer to a moral problem is at once to be accused of or credited with a belief in moral absolutes. But it is no more necessary to believe in moral absolutes in order to believe in moral objectivity than it is to believe in the existence of absolute space or absolute time in order to believe in the objectivity of temporal and spatial relations and of judgments about them.[14]

If we can establish or show that it is reasonable to believe that there is, in some ideal sense, at least one objective moral principle that is binding on all people everywhere, then we shall have shown that relativism probably is false and that a limited objectivism is true. Actually, I believe that many qualified general ethical principles are binding on all rational beings, but one principle will suffice to refute relativism:

A: It is morally wrong to torture people for the fun of it.

I claim that this principle is binding on all rational agents, so that if some agent, S, rejects A, we should not let that affect our intuition that A is a true principle; rather, we should try to explain S's behavior as perverse, ignorant, or irrational instead. For example, suppose Adolf Hitler doesn't accept A. Should that affect our confidence in the truth of A? Is it not more reasonable to infer that Hitler is morally deficient, morally blind, ignorant, or irrational than to suppose that his noncompliance is evidence against the truth of A?

Suppose further that there is a tribe of "Hitlerites" somewhere that enjoys torturing people. Their whole culture accepts torturing others for the fun of it. Suppose that Mother Teresa or Mahatma Gandhi try unsuccessfully to persuade these sadists to stop torturing people altogether, and the sadists respond by torturing her or him. Should this affect our confidence in A? Would it not be more reasonable to look for some explanation of Hitlerite behavior? For example, we might hypothesize that this tribe lacks the developed sense of sympathetic imagination that is necessary for the moral life. Or we might theorize that this tribe is on a lower evolutionary level than most Homo sapiens. Or we might simply conclude that the tribe is closer to a Hobbesian state of nature than most other societies, and as such probably would not survive very long—or if it did, the lives of its people would be largely "solitary, poor, nasty, brutish and short," as in the Ik culture in northern Uganda, where the core morality has partly broken down.

But we need not know the correct answer as to why the tribe is in such bad shape to maintain our confidence in A as a moral principle. If A is a basic or core belief for us, then we will be more likely to doubt the Hitlerites' sanity or ability to think morally than to doubt the validity of A.

We can perhaps produce other candidates for membership in our minimally basic objective moral set:

1. Do not kill innocent people.
2. Do not cause unnecessary pain or suffering.
3. Do not steal or cheat.
4. Keep your promises and honor your contracts.

5. Do not deprive another person of his or her freedom.
6. Tell the truth, or at least, don't lie.
7. Do justice, giving people what they deserve.
8. Reciprocate; show gratitude for services rendered.
9. Help other people, especially when the cost to oneself is minimal.
10. Obey just laws.

These 10 principles are examples of the *core morality,* principles necessary for the good life within a flourishing human community. They are not arbitrary, for we can give reasons to explain why they are constitutive elements of a successful society, necessary to social cohesion and personal well-being. Principles such as the Golden Rule and those listed above are central to the fluid progression of social interaction and the resolution of conflicts of interest that ethics bears on. For example, language itself depends on a general and implicit commitment to the principle of truth telling. Accuracy of expression is a primitive form of truthfulness. Hence, every time we use words correctly (e.g., "That is a book" or "My name is Sam"), we are telling the truth. Without a high degree of reliable matching between words and objects, language itself would be impossible. Likewise, without the practice of promise keeping, we would not be able to rely on one another's words when others inform us about future acts and could have no reliable expectations about each other's behavior. But we are social beings and our lives are dependent on cooperation, so it is vital that when we make an agreement (e.g., I'll help you with your philosophy paper if you'll help me install a new computer program) we have confidence that the other party will reciprocate when we have done our part. Even chimpanzees follow the rule of reciprocity, returning good for good (returning evil for evil may not be as necessary for morality). Without a prohibition against stealing and cheating, we could not claim property— not even ownership of our very limbs, let alone external goods. And without the protection of innocent life and liberty, we could hardly attain our goals. Sometimes people question whether rule 7, "Do justice, giving people what they deserve" is valid. Each person should be judged on the basis of his or her abilities, moral character and effort, not on the basis of race, gender, or economic status. We should reward people according to their contributions and accomplishments. Conversely, they should be punished for their evil deeds. Of course, these principles are prima facie, not absolutes. They can be overridden when they come into conflict, but, in general, they should be adhered to in order to give maximal guarantee for the good life.

There may be other moral rules necessary or highly relevant to an objective core morality. A moral code would be adequate if it contained a requisite set of these objective principles, but there could be more than one adequate moral code that contained different rankings or different combinations of rules. Different specific rules may be required in different situations. For example, in a desert community, there may be a strict rule prohibiting the wasting of water, and in a community with a preponderance of females over males, there may be a rule permitting polygamy. Such moral plasticity does not entail moral relativism, but simply a recognition of the fact that social situations can determine which rules are relevant to the flourishing of a community. In matters of sexual conduct, a society where birth control devices are available may have rules that differ from those in a society that lacks such technology. Nevertheless, an essential core morality, such as that described above, will be universally necessary.[15]

TWO TYPES OF ETHICAL THEORIES

Finally, we must note that there are two types of ethical theories: deontological and consequentialist, or utilitarian. *Deontological ethical theories* place the emphasis on right action versus wrong action. It is simply wrong to torture or kill innocent people no matter what the consequences. *Consequentialist ethical theories,* on the other hand, place the emphasis on the good consequences that are likely to result from the act. If you can save a large number of people by torturing or killing one innocent person, that act may be justified. Consequentialists are likely to approve of the United States dropping an atomic bomb on Hiroshima to end the War in the Pacific, saving thousands of soldiers, but most deontologists condemn the act as unjust. Or suppose a terrorist has planted an atomic bomb somewhere in our city. We have his daughter in custody. If we think we can get the terrorist to tell us where the bomb is by torturing his daughter, are we justified in doing so? The deontologist is likely to say no, the end does not justify the means. The consequentialist is likely to say yes, the end often does justify the means. Typical deontological theories are intuitionism (roughly, Trust your deepest reflective intuitions in ethics) and Kantianism (roughly, Universalize the principles you want to act on—act in a way consistent with everyone's doing that kind of act). Consequentialists hold that morality consists in maximizing certain values. The pluralist thinks that there are a number of such values, such as happiness, friendship, knowledge, and desert. The utilitarian, or monist consequentialist, holds that happiness (or pleasure) is the only value that we should aim at maximizing.

There are two classical types of utilitarianism: *act-* and *rule-utilitarianism.* In applying the principle of utility, act-utilitarians, such as Jeremy Bentham, say that ideally we ought to apply the principle to all the alternatives open to us at any given moment. We may define act-utilitarianism this way:

Act-utilitarianism: An act is right if and only if it results in as much good as any available alternative.

Of course, we cannot do the necessary calculations to determine which act is the correct one in each case, for often we must act spontaneously and quickly. So rules of thumb (e.g., In general, don't lie, and Generally, keep your promises) are of practical importance. However, the right act is still that alternative that results in the most utility.

The obvious criticism of act-utility is that it seems to fly in the face of fundamental intuitions about minimally correct behavior. Consider Richard Brandt's criticism of act-utilitarianism:

> It implies that if you have employed a boy to mow your lawn and he has finished the job and asks for his pay, you should pay him what you promised only if you cannot find a better use for your money. It implies that when you bring home your monthly paycheck you should use it to support your family and yourself only if it cannot be used more effectively to supply the needs of others. It implies that if your father is ill and has no prospect of good in his life, and maintaining him is a drain on the energy and enjoyments of others, then, if you can end his life without provoking any public scandal or setting a bad example, it is your positive duty to take matters into your own hands and bring his life to a close.[16]

Rule-utilitarians like Brandt attempt to offer a more credible version of the theory. They state that an act is right if it conforms to a valid rule within a system of rules that, if followed, will result in the best possible state of affairs (or the least bad state of affairs, if it is a question of all the alternatives' being bad). We may define rule-utilitarianism this way:

Rule-utilitarianism: An act is right if and only if it is required by a rule that is itself a member of a set of rules whose acceptance would lead to greater utility for society than any available alternative.

Human beings are rule-following creatures. We learn by adhering to the rules of a given subject, whether it be speaking a language, driving a car, dancing, writing an essay, rock climbing or cooking. We want to have a set of action-guiding rules by which to live. The act-utilitarian rule, to do the act that maximizes utility, is too general for most purposes. Often we don't have time to deliberate whether lying will produce more utility than truth telling, so we need a more specific rule prescribing truthfulness, a rule that passes the test of rational scrutiny. Rule-utilitarianism asserts that the best chance of maximizing utility is by following the set of rules most likely to give us our desired results. Since morality is a social and public institution, we need to coordinate our actions with those of others, so that we can have reliable expectations about other people's behavior.

An oft-debated question in ethics is whether rule-utilitarianism is a consistent version of utilitarianism. Briefly, the argument that rule-utilitarianism is an inconsistent version that must either become a deontological system or transform itself into act-utilitarianism goes like this: Imagine that following the set of general rules of a rule-utilitarian system yields 100 hedons (positive utility units). We could always find a case where breaking the general rule would result in additional hedons without decreasing the sum of the whole. So, for example, we could imagine a situation in which breaking the general rule to never lie to spare someone's feelings would create more utility (e.g., 102 hedons) than keeping the rule would. It would seem that we could always improve on any version of rule-utilitarianism by breaking the set of rules whenever we judge that by so doing we could produce even more utility than by following the set.

One way of resolving the difference between act- and rule-utilitarians is to appeal to the notion of *levels of rules*. For the sophisticated utilitarian there will be three levels of rules to guide actions. On the lowest level is a set of utility-maximizing rules of thumb that should always be followed unless there is a conflict between them, in which case a second-order set of conflict-resolving rules should be consulted. At the top of the hierarchy is the *remainder rule* of act utilitarianism: When no other rule applies, simply do what your best judgment deems to be the act that will maximize utility.

An illustration of this hierarchy of rules might be the following: Two of the lower-order rules might be to keep your promises and to help those in need when you are not seriously inconvenienced in doing so. Suppose you promised to meet your teacher at 3 P.M. in his office. On your way there you come upon an accident victim stranded by the wayside who desperately needs help. It doesn't take you long to decide to break the appointment with your teacher, for it seems obvious in this case that the rule to help others overrides the rule to keep promises. We might say that there is a second-order rule prescribing that the first-order rule of helping people in need when you are not seriously inconvenienced in doing so overrides the rule to keep promises. However, there might be some situation where no obvious rule of thumb applies. Say you have $50 you don't really need now. How should you use this money? Put it into your savings account? Give it to your favorite charity? Use it to throw a party? Here and only here, on the third level, the general act-utility principle applies without any other primary rule; that is, do what in your best judgment will do the most good.

The rule-utilitarian argues that in the long run, a rule that protects legally innocent, but morally culpable, people will produce more utility than following an act-utilitarian principle.

If we accept the second intuitionist version of the remainder principle, we may be accused of being intuitionists and not utilitarians at all. But I think it is more accurate to admit that moral philosophy is complex and multidimensional; both the striving for the goal of utility and the method of consulting our intuitions are part of moral deliberation and action.

I must leave it to you to decide which type of ethical theory is best. Both deontological and consequentialist theories are objectivist, and deontologists and rule-utilitarians or rule-consequentialists often agree on issues. These concepts will be used in the succeeding chapters of this book.

Conclusion

Ethical objectivism, the thesis that a core of universally valid moral principles exists is more justified than its opposite, ethical relativism, but there is some truth in the latter position. Some aspects of morality do depend on cultural approval ("When in Rome, do as the Romans do" does have limited application). Moral principles are also situational, being applied differently in different situations. Normally, lying is immoral, but it is not immoral to lie to an assassin who asks you for vital information on the whereabouts of a diplomat. Similarly, although killing another human being is generally wrong, killing in self-defense is not wrong.

We have spent a great deal of time on ethical relativism and its opposite, ethical objectivism, as well as on ethical theories, because on these issues hangs a great deal of political philosophy. This will become increasingly clear as we proceed through the topics in this book, especially, justification of government, (Chapter 1), justice (Chapter 5), state neutrality and moral perfectionism (Chapter 6), and nationalism versus internationalism (Chapter 9), where we want to determine whether we have global moral duties, not simply intersocietal duties. The discussion of terrorism and the just war theory in Chapter 10 will also use the distinctions discussed in this Introduction.

For Further Reflection

1. Explain the difference between the nation and the state.
2. Explain the difference between community (*Gemeinshaft*) and society (*Gesellshaft*). In the light of that distinction, do you agree with this statement: The nation, not the state, provides our roots, our sense of belonging, our identity, our solidarity with others?
3. Examine the notion of subjective ethical relativism, which bases morality on radical individualism. On that basis, each person is the inventor of morality (morality is in the eye of the beholder). Consider that

assumption of individualism. Can there be a morality for only one person? Imagine that only one person exists in the world (leave God out of the account). Suppose you are that person. Do you have any moral duties? Certainly there are prudential duties—some ways of living will help you attain your goals—but are there moral duties?

4.   Now imagine a second person comes into your world—a fully developed, mature person with wants, needs, hopes, and fears. How does that change the nature of the situation of the solitary individual?

5.   Here is a puzzle for subjectivist relativists: Consider a baby who gets hold of a knife and stabs its four-year-old sister. The baby doesn't know any better. We would suppose it is innocent. Tragic though this situation is, we would not hold the baby responsible for its deed. Now consider a father who stabs that same four-year-old girl. Suppose the father explains his act by saying, "I felt good exercising my power, and what feels good must be morally good." Does the fact that he thought his act was morally permissible really make it morally permissible? Discuss your answer.

6.   Can you separate the anthropological claim (the diversity thesis—called cultural relativism) that different cultures have different moral principles from the judgment that *therefore* they are all equally good (ethical relativism)? Are there independent criteria by which we can say that some cultures are better than others?

7.   Ruth Benedict has written that our culture is "but one entry in a long series of possible adjustments" and that "the very eyes with which we see the problem are conditioned by the long traditional habits of our own society." What are the implications of those statements? Is she correct? How would an objectivist respond to the claims?

Endnotes

1. David Hume, *Treatise of Human Nature* (Oxford University Press, 1978) p. 539.
2. Quoted in Eric Hobsbawn, *Nations and Nationalism since 1780* (Cambridge, 1990), p. 101.
3. Muzafer Sherif et al., *The Robber Cave Experiment: Intergroup Conflict and Cooperation* (Weslyan University Press, 1988).
4. David Miller, *On Nationality* (Oxford University Press, 1995), p. 14.
5. W. G. Sumner, *Folkways* (Ginn, 1905), sect. 80, p. 76. Also, Ruth Benedict indicates the depth of our cultural conditioning this way: "The very eyes with which we see the problem are conditioned by the long traditional habits of our own society" ("Anthropology and the Abnormal," *Journal of General Psychology* [1934]: pp. 59–82).

6. Ernest Hemingway, *Death in the Afternoon* (Scribner's, 1932), p. 4.

7. This is a statement by Ted Bundy, paraphrased and rewritten by Harry V. Jaffa, *Homosexuality and the Natural Law* (Claremont Institute of the Study of Statesmanship and Political Philosophy, 1990), pp. 3–4.

8. Ruth Benedict, *Patterns of Culture* (New American Library, 1934), p. 257.

9. Melville Herskovits, *Cultural Relativism* (Random House, 1972).

10. The fallacy of objecting to a proposition on the erroneous grounds that, if accepted, it will lead to a chain of states of affairs that are absurd or unacceptable.

11. Clyde Kluckhohn, "Ethical Relativity: Sic et Non," *Journal of Philosophy* 52 (1955).

12. Colin Turnbull, *The Mountain People* (Simon & Schuster, 1972).

13. W. D. Ross, *The Right and the Good* (Oxford University Press, 1930).

14. Renford Bambrough, *Moral Skepticism and Moral Knowledge* (Routledge & Kegan Paul, 1979).

15. For a fuller discussion of ethical relativism and ethical objectivism, as well as the ethical theories discussed here, I refer you to my book *Ethics: Discovering Right and Wrong*, 4th ed. (Wadsworth, 2002).

16. Richard Brandt, *Morality Utilitarianism and Rights* (NY: Cambridge Univerity Press, 1992).

1

THE JUSTIFICATION
OF GOVERNMENT

Why Should I Obey the State?

The defining mark of the state is authority, the right to rule. The primary obligation of man is autonomy, the refusal to be ruled. It would seem, then, that there can be no resolution to the conflict between autonomy and the putative authority of the state.

—ROBERT PAUL WOLFF, IN DEFENSE OF ANARCHISM, 1976

Covenants without the sword, are but words, and of no strength to secure a man at all . . . If there be no [political] power, every man will rely on his own strength and art against all other men.

—THOMAS HOBBES, LEVIATHAN, 1651

INTRODUCTION: POLITICAL AUTHORITY

You are filling out your yearly federal income tax forms and become irritated at the large sum of money that you are going to have to pay—$5,000. If that isn't bad enough, you don't believe in the programs for which most of the money will be spent. You ask yourself, What right does the government have to demand payment of me? But you don't like the probable consequences of not paying—a prison sentence—so you reluctantly write out a check for $5,000, realizing that you will not be able to afford needed house repairs nor a vacation this year.

You put your tax forms and the check inside an envelope and go out to mail it at the nearest mailbox. On your way home, a man accosts you with a gun. "Your money or your life," he roughly demands. You open your wallet and hand him the $100 therein. You continue home, beaten in spirit, feeling twice robbed, and wonder which is the greater robber, the gunman or the government. After all, the government used coercion to extract 50 times the amount of money that the gunman stole.

You ask yourself if that feeling is justified. Is the government with its laws only a gunman who observes reliable rituals and procedures and, unlike the robber, warns you in advance that a percentage of your money will be taken at a certain time every year? You've always been a law-abiding citizen, but now you wonder what right the government has to demand your obedience. Why should you obey the state? The state claims sovereignty, the sole right to make and enforce laws over a people within a given territory. What is the justification of the state?

In this chapter, we examine six answers to the questions posed above:

1. *The anarchist answer.* The state is not justified in imposing its wishes on you, for your autonomy is a fundamental moral absolute, which the state has no right to violate. The state is without moral authority. This is the view of the French philosopher Pierre-Joseph Proudon (1809–65), who was the first person to call himself an anarchist; the nineteenth-century Russian prince Peter Kropotkin (1842–1921); and the American philosophers Henry David Thoreau (1817–62) and Robert Paul Wolff.

2. *The religious answer.* Governments are instituted by God for the protection of the people and the public good, so we have an obligation to God to obey the laws of our country.

3. *The social contract or consent answer.* Government is based on the consent of the governed. Thomas Hobbes (1588–1679), John Locke (1632–1704), and Jean-Jacques Rousseau (1712–78) all held that to escape the inconvenience of the state of nature and to procure security and the benefits of civilization, we form a social contract by consenting explicitly or implicitly to be governed by a higher authority. Social contract theorists agree that we give up some freedom for security, though they disagree as to the extent of the surrender. According to Locke, in consenting to obey the state, we do not give up our natural rights to life, property, representation, and other goods—better to endure a state of nature than to give up those things. Hobbes and Rousseau also held that position, though they differ on the details. Hobbes focuses on the dark side of human nature, which leads to a war of "every man against every man." The notion of a social contract has been the classic answer to the question of political obligation.

4. *The fair play answer.* The function of the state is to promote justice as fairness, an arrangement of institutions whereby maximal liberty consistent with equal opportunity and a principle to

benefit the worst-off prevails. Our obligation to the state is based on the principle of fairness. If within a social scheme, which depends on social cooperation, you are accepting the benefits of that scheme, you have an obligation to do your part to cooperate with others in maintaining that scheme. H. L. A. Hart (1907–92) and John Rawls (1921–) hold this position.

5. *The gratitude answer.* So long as we are receiving benefits from the state, we have an obligation to express our gratitude by obedience to the laws. W. D. Ross (1877–1971) is a representative of this position.

6. *The utilitarian or consequentialist answer.* Government is a tool for enabling us to coordinate our activities and live a more harmonious social life, things that are necessary for maximizing human happiness. Any government that is carrying out this function is legitimate and should be obeyed. At least we have a prima facie duty to obey its edicts, while working to improve its nature. David Hume (1711–76) and John Stuart Mill (1806–73) held this position.

PART ONE: WHY NOT ANARCHISM?

AN EXAMINATION OF POLITICAL ANARCHISM

Political anarchism is the philosophy that the state is unjustified because it improperly infringes on human autonomy. *Autonomy* is self-directed freedom, the ability to use reason to choose one's principles and to live by them. Autonomy as human freedom is, for the anarchist, the paramount moral value that no amount of efficiency, utility, or stability may justly override. We can distinguish two forms of anarchism, positive and negative. *Positive political anarchism* holds that all forms of government are bad in that they restrict the free exercise of human reason that is necessary for the attainment of perfection. Proponents typically believe that human nature is inherently good, but that oppressive society corrupts us. They echo Rousseau's words, "Man is born free but is everywhere in chains." Proudhon, regarded as the father of anarchism, rejected all forms of authority from society in favor of complete individualism. According to Proudhon, government means being "fined, vilified, harassed, hunted down, abused, clubbed, disarmed, bound, choked, imprisoned, judged, condemned, shot, deported, sacrificed, sold, betrayed; and to crown all, mocked, ridiculed, derided, outraged, dishonored."[1] It primarily preserves inequality and property, but property is theft and should be abolished, so that love and peace can reign in blissful utopia. Kropotkin, as well as the English poet Percy Bysshe Shelley (1792–1822), held similar views, advocating a future communist society without government.[2] Kropotkin thought that because animals, including human beings, were inherently cooperative, an anarcho-communist society would replace capitalist, oppressive society as humankind developed and gradually realized the injustice of inequalities of wealth and the benefits of peace and justice.[3] A sense of justice, which resides deep within the human soul, needs only to be nourished to become a self-actualizing reality. Moral perfection is possible. Utopia, the goal of anarchism, can occur only with the withering away of the state.

Negative anarchists, on the other hand, are not utopians, but confine themselves to the thesis that autonomy and political authority are diametrically opposed, so the state is unjustified. Wolff argues (see the first epigraph at the beginning of this chapter) that morality is centered in autonomy, in each person's determining what is right and wrong through his or her reason.[4] The state, however, is grounded in authority, requiring its members to obey its laws simply because it has so determined. It creates obligations even when individuals disagree with these obligations. So autonomy and authority are diametrically opposed to each other. Since moral obligations override all other obligations, its authority overrides that of the state. As responsible agents, we must decide for ourselves what is right and wrong. People may adhere to the principles the state enacts into law (e.g., keeping promises and refraining from murder, adultery, and lying), not because the state commands these laws, but because moral reason does. Since moral autonomy is sovereign, it follows that the state can have no moral authority over the individual. People may not forfeit or transfer their authority to the state. Hence, all authority is equally illegitimate. Although some states are more immoral than others, no state has moral force. All states are unjustified. To quote Wolff:

> Now, of course, an anarchist may grant the necessity of *complying* with the law under certain circumstances or for the time being. He may even doubt that there is any real prospect of eliminating the state as a human institution. But he will never view the commands of the state as *legitimate,* as having a binding moral force. In a sense, we might characterize the anarchist as a man without a country, for despite the ties which bind him to the land of his childhood, he stands in precisely the same moral relationship to "his" government as he does to the government of any other country in which he might happen to be staying for a time. When I take a vacation to Great Britain, I obey its laws, both because of prudential self-interest and because of the obvious moral considerations concerning the value of order, the general good consequences of preserving a system of property, and so forth. On my return

to the United States, I have a sense of reentering *my* country, and if I think about the matter at all, I imagine myself to stand in a different and more intimate relation to American laws. They have been promulgated by *my* government, and I therefore have a special obligation to obey them. But the anarchist tells me that my feeling is purely sentimental and has no objective moral basis.[5]

If the anarchist is correct, we have no more reason to accept the authority of the government of our own country than that of some foreign country, since no government is legitimate. Can we answer the anarchist? Can we show that an obligation exists to obey the state? To that task we now turn.

In the remainder of Part One, we will discuss four classic responses to the questions, Why not anarchism? Why do we have an obligation to obey the state? In Part Two, we will use a thought experiment to consider this issue.

RESPONSES TO ANARCHISM

Can the anarchist be answered? Can autonomy be reconciled with political authority? Can the state be justified? We turn to various attempts to do so.

The Religious Answer

The first attempt to answer the anarchist is based on religious authority. Government is given by God for the defense of law and order and for the protection of individuals from greed and injustice. St. Paul wrote that government is instituted by God and derives its authority directly from God:

> Let every person be subject to the government. For there is no authority
> except from God, and those that exist have been instituted by God.
> Therefore he who resists the authorities resists what God has appointed, and
> those who resist will incur judgment. For rulers are not a terror to good
> conduct, but to evil. Would you have no fear of him who is in authority?
> Then do what is good, and you will win his approval, for he is God's servant
> for your good. But if you do wrong, be afraid, for he does not bear the sword
> in vain. He is the servant of God to execute his wrath on the wrongdoer.
> Therefore one must be subject, not only to avoid wrath, but for the sake of
> conscience. For the same reason you also pay taxes, for the authorities are
> ministers of God, appointed to promote the public good. (Rom: 13)

Many religious people ground their political obligations in this doctrine, which for centuries was used to justify the divine right of kings. But one may read a proviso into this passage. The government is serving God only as long as it is carrying out justice and promoting the human good. When it fails in that task, it relinquishes its legitimacy. There is no doubt that religion has influenced in the past and still does influence many people's political commitments (for good and ill). While I was writing this chapter, news reports indicated that the Islamic authorities had done what virtually no other government had succeeded in doing: eliminating the growing of opium in Afghanistan, once the center of such production. At considerable financial loss, farmers ceased growing the crop because they accepted the Mullah Omar's injunction as the will of God. Of course, the Taliban, who ruled the country at that time, used the same authority to oppress women, but the point is simply that religion provides a strong incentive for political obedience.[6] Depending on how it is used, that power can be exercised for good or evil. However, there is a deep problem with religious justification. It assumes that there is a God who is providentially presiding over the world. But such a view is controversial, and many reflective people doubt the existence of a God, let alone one who presides over human affairs. Even if there is a God, how do we know that our institutions are in line with God's will, except by tailoring them to fit with our best moral theory? So whether or not God exists, we need to use philosophical analysis to provide a justification of the state's authority, assuming one can be found.

The Answer from the Social Contract and the Principle of Consent

Thomas Hobbes, John Locke, and Jean-Jacques Rousseau are the classic social contract theorists. They hold that the state's authority is grounded in the consent of the governed.[7] Each member commits himself or herself to obey the laws of the government and thereby establishes the legitimacy of the state. Without freely given consent, the government is illegitimate and subjects have no moral obligation to obey its laws. People voluntarily give up to the state their natural freedom in order to have their interests served: the interests, or natural rights, of life, liberty, property, and the pursuit of happiness. Government is a cooperative enterprise that enables us to live better than we could live in an uncoordinated social situation. These philosophers actually thought that there was an original contract whereby people agreed to live under a governing authority. Locke held that although the present generation may not have expressly contracted to live under the government, so long as people decide to continue residing in a country, they implicitly consent to the laws of the land. The only stipulation is that the government represent the interests of the people, namely, protecting their natural rights. When it ceases to do that, the citizens are morally obliged to overthrow it and establish a representative government. This was the justification of the American colonists in overthrowing the British Crown in the late 18th century. England was taxing the colonists without allowing them due representation.

The consent theory is especially appealing because it is grounded in perhaps the most fundamental positive moral principle: Keep your promises. Consenting to a government is agreeing or promising to obey its edicts. When we join a club or get married, we promise to obey the relevant rules in exchange for the benefits. As such, the consent is a deliberate, voluntary act for which we can be held fully responsible. Naturalized citizens and members of the military expressly promise to obey the laws of their country. But many of us do not ever explicitly consent to be governed. Locke held that we implicitly agree to be governed.

The idea of *implicit,* or *tacit, consent* has some force. When I join in a baseball game, I imply that I will abide by the rules of the game, including the umpire's judgment. When I enter your house, I imply that I will not violate you or your property, but abide by the rules of the house. When I visit a foreign land, I imply that I will obey its rules. Socrates gave expression to the idea of tacit consent to a government through residence in his famous speech in the *Crito,* where the Laws are imagined to address him:

> We openly proclaim this principle, that any Athenian, on attaining to manhood and seeing for himself the political organization of the state and its laws, is permitted, if he is not satisfied with us, to take his property and go away wherever he likes. If any of you chooses to go to one of our colonies, supposing that he should not be satisfied with us and the state, or to emigrate to any other country, not one of the laws hinders or prevents him from going away where he likes, without any loss of property. On the other hand, if any one of you stands his ground when he can see how we administer justice and the rest of our public organization, we hold that by doing so he has in fact undertaken to do anything that we tell him.

You have the option of leaving the country if you don't like it, so, the argument goes, you haven't relinquished your autonomy. You are bound by the state's laws. It has been objected that anarchists, spies, revolutionaries, terrorists, and gangsters can reside in a country without implying that they are committed to obeying the country's laws. But this seems wrong. These antiestablishment types do imply by their residency that they will adhere to the laws governing the country. In fact, the very success of their projects in most cases depends on their successfully deceiving the authorities on just this point, pretending to comply, but doing great mischief.

The social contract argument with its consent stipulation, for all its attractiveness, is fraught with serious problems. Only a small set of citizens has ever explicitly promised to obey the government, and the argument of *consent to obey through residence* is problematic. Hume uttered the most serious objection to it:

> Can we seriously say, that a poor peasant or artisan has a free choice to leave his country, when he knows no foreign language or manners, and lives from day to day by the small wages which he acquires? We may as well assert that a man, by remaining in a vessel, freely consents to the dominion of the master, though he was carried on board while asleep, and must leap into the ocean, and perish, the moment he leaves her.[8]

Hume's objection seems weighty. We can be so limited in our resources as to be unable to take advantage of formal opportunities, such as emigration. Jeffrey Murphy has objected to Hume's argument, maintaining that coercion does not invalidate consent. If I'm drowning and a private boater offers to save me for a fair price and I consent, I am obligated to pay that price.[9] This argument is true for explicit consent, less obvious for tacit consent. A lot depends on the operative word *fair.* If I tell you I'll save you only if you agree to become my slave or murder my rival, you would be in your rights to make a lying promise in order to save yourself. But the poor peasant or artisan has not made any explicit promise. He is like the sailor who is impressed onto the ship and simply doesn't take steps to jump overboard. It may be in his interest to seem to obey the regulations and even to do so when to disobey would have deleterious consequences, but he has no strong obligation to adhere to the rules. Surely the captain of the ship has a right to make a safe way off the ship available to him, offering him the option of adhering to the rules or getting onto a longboat bound for land, but the captain doesn't have the right to keep him on board indefinitely against his will. While the boater is not a criminal like the gunman who offered me a choice between my money or my life, and my obligation to pay the boater, after I am saved, persists, I am morally permitted to leave the boat (to board a larger vessel) as soon as I have discharged my debt. But the poor peasant who "knows no foreign language or manners, and lives from day to day by the small wages which he acquires" doesn't have the ability or liberty-making conditions to enable him to leave his country. His autonomy is greatly diminished. He has not made an explicit agreement to commit himself to the laws of the land, and any tacit consent is diminished to the point of vanishing. So the tacit consent principle doesn't seem to apply universally. Perhaps it should, though. Perhaps the social contract doctrine should be instituted by governments. There could be a neutral territory to which dissenters could emigrate. We could also institute a Citizenship Day—when each youth, say, at age 13 or 18, takes a pledge of citizenship or emigrates with government support to another country or to the neutral territory set aside for anarchists. Of course, the youths would have to apply for admission to the country they emigrated to, and go through a readmission process, but this would not be unfair. Perhaps the institutionalizing of the social contract would be inconvenient, but it would be a way of ensuring that the social contract really was observed. As it is, the consent theory seems fraught with serious objections: Few citizens explicitly consent to government, and, as Hume notes, many are not in a position to be able to give meaningful tacit consent. So the consent argument and its master theory of the social contract seem unsound and unable to justify political obligation or the legitimacy of the state.

The Answer from the Principle of Fair Play

The Oxford legal philosopher H. L. A. Hart formulates the principle of fair play this way:

> When a number of persons conduct any joint enterprise according to rules and thus restrict their liberty, those who have submitted to these restrictions when required have a right to a similar submission from those who have benefited by their submission. The rules may provide that officials should have authority to enforce obedience . . . but the moral obligation to obey the rules in such circumstances is due to the cooperating members of the society, and they have the correlative moral right to obedience.[10]

Suppose we are pushing our car up a steep hill. It is in all our interests that we move the car to the top of the hill where we can safely start it up by rolling it downhill. It would be wrong of me (without an overriding reason) to stop pushing or only pretend that I am pushing the car, leaving you and the others to do the work unaided by my strong arms. Or if we hire a car to take us to our destination, but I lie about not having money to contribute to the endeavor, I am a loathsome free rider, someone who fails to do his share in a cooperative venture, where you and others must take up the slack, but where I equally benefit. So Hart argues that if we are benefiting from a group activity, we have an obligation to bear the correlative burdens necessary to procure the success of the activity. It is morally despicable to be a freeloader. I am undeserving of the benefits I obtain.

The principle of fair play seems correct for many activities, but Robert Nozick has offered counterexamples, suggesting that benefiting within a scheme may not obligate one to cooperate with the scheme:

> Suppose some of the people in your neighborhood (there are 364 other adults) have found a public address system and decide to institute a system of public entertainment. They post a list of names, one for each day of the year, yours among them. On his assigned day . . . a person is to run the public

address system, play records over it, give news bulletins, tell amusing stories he has heard, and so on. After 138 days on which each person has done his part, your day arrives. Are you obligated to take your turn? You have benefited from it, occasionally opening your window to listen, enjoying the music or chuckling at someone's funny story. The other people have put themselves out. But must you answer the call when it is your turn to do so? As it stands, surely not. Though you benefit from the arrangement supplied by others, you may know all along that 364 days of entertainment supplied by others will not be worth your giving up one day. You would rather not have any of it and not give up a day than have it all and spend one of your days at it. Given these preferences, how can it be that you are required to participate when your scheduled time comes?[11]

Nozick concludes that the unqualified principle of fair play simply doesn't work. So long as my personal preferential scheme fails to adopt the cooperative project, I cannot be obliged to bear my share of the burdens. I would prefer that the scheme hadn't been instituted in the first place, so how can I be held responsible for keeping it going, even if I do derive some benefit from it? I must have voluntarily accepted the benefits before I can have an obligation to bear the burden of my share in the scheme. In conjunction with this point, A. John Simmons distinguishes between open benefits and benefits that are readily available. An *open benefit* is one that is available to me whether I want it or not.[12] A benefit is *readily available* if it is available but I must actively accept it. He asks us to imagine a community with two kinds of police protection: the first consisting of police walking their beats, patrolling your neighborhood; the second being special detectives who for a fee will provide additional protection, say, when you fear a paid assassin is out to harm or kill you. You do have to accept the latter, but not the former, type of protection for it to be available. So long as we cannot avoid the benefit of an open benefit, we are under no obligation to pay for it, but we are obligated to pay for (in some form or other) a readily available benefit. If you fail to do your share for a readily available benefit that you accept, you are culpable and probably should be punished. Many people who watch public television, which is dependent on listener support, without supporting it are remiss in their duty. Similarly, people who use our national parks should make a comparable contribution in terms of contributions or labor for such benefits. But national defense, the rule of law, vaccinations against diseases, parks and highways, and public schools seem open benefits, which are simply there for us regardless of whether we consciously want them or not. So Nozick's point stands: Unless we deliberately accept the benefits of a social scheme, we have no obligation to help maintain it.

We conclude that the principle of fair play must be qualified to the point where it loses the broad general applicability it was meant to have. Most benefits are open benefits, not ones we have an option to reject.

The Answer from the Principle of Gratitude

It is sometimes argued that receipt of the benefits of government creates a duty of gratitude, which translates into obedience to the state. W. D. Ross held this position.[13] Socrates first set forth this argument in the *Crito*, as he prepared to die. The Laws are addressing him:

> Are you not grateful to those of us laws which were instituted for this end, for requiring your father to give you a cultural and physical education? Then since you have been born and brought up and educated; can you deny . . . that you were our child and servant, both you and your ancestors? We have brought you into the world and reared you and educated you and given you and all your fellow citizens a share in all the good things at our disposal.

It would seem that at least most of us do have a debt of gratitude to our society, and failure to perform it constitutes moral dereliction. Perhaps oppressed people have no such duty or a lesser one, but many of us have flourished within our country and should do what we can to pay back our debt through some kind of action. The problem is that gratitude is generally a personal and indefinite relationship. Consider the notion of *indefiniteness:* I am grateful to you for saving my life, but this doesn't tell me how exactly to express my debt. Is it enough to have a disposition to help you if you need help? To simply say "thank you"? In personal relations we generally do feel positive toward our benefactors but may express these feelings in diverse ways. There is no algorithm to tell us how much we owe our parents for nurturing us or our friends for their loyalty. No one is keeping score on these matters. The best we can do is be disposed to feel gratitude to them and be ready to express it in our actions. We now come to the notion of *personalness.* The state is not a person, so the analogy seems to break down. Can I be grateful to an impersonal entity such as laws or the state? I once heard a philosopher argue that we could be grateful for good weather because we enjoyed it. I suspect she meant she was grateful to God for providing good weather, but if one does not believe in God, that argument won't work. If gratitude can be stretched so broadly, why not say we are grateful to the laws of logic for preventing contradictions from being true, to the English language for enabling us to communicate, and to atoms and subatomic particles for giving rise to macrophysical reality? But that seems absurd. The concept of gratitude seems too amorphous to

serve as the basis for political obligation. I am delighted that I live in a relatively just society, and I sense a duty to promote this society, but that does
not necessarily translate into an obligation to obey the laws of the state.
Furthermore, just as our gratitude to our friends is not absolute, but only
a presumptive duty that can be overridden by more compelling obligations, so our loyalty to the state may be overridden by any number of
moral duties. Then why not just be a moral person and dispense with a
special obligation to obey the laws? I will generally obey laws, such as traffic regulations, because they yield good consequences, but not because
the state has any special authority. It is not that we don't feel gratitude—
or at least appreciation—for the institutions and opportunities that our
country affords. It is just that such gratitude doesn't seem sufficient to
ground any special obligation; it doesn't seem adequate to ground political authority.

We have examined four arguments for grounding political authority: the religious answer, the contract or consent theory, the principle of fair play, and
the principle of gratitude. Although all of them had merit, none of them
seemed sufficient to ground a general political obligation. So let us continue our search for an answer to the question, Why should I obey the state?

PART TWO: A THOUGHT EXPERIMENT— A BOTTOM-UP PROJECT OF JUSTIFYING GOVERNMENT

Let us begin this part of our study with a thought experiment: imagining
what a utopian society might look like.

UTOPIA: THE FIRST GENERATION

Several idealistic students, saddened by the injustice, violence, and general immorality of their society, come together to start a new morally ideal
society on a lush, uninhabited island. Concerned to devise a cooperative
community with peace, justice, maximal freedom, and prosperity, they begin to set forth the rules for their community in terms of rights and obligations. The rules include (1) no killing of one another (except possibly
a criminal who is found to be guilty after due process); (2) no stealing (for
property is deemed essential to one's well-being); (3) respect for another's
autonomy (as rational beings, we should be allowed to choose how we are

to live and then be held responsible for those choices); (4) truthfulness (no one may lie or cheat); (5) cooperation in promoting the social good (each person must commit him- or herself to working for the good of the group); (6) defense (each member is to help in policing the island, both from internal crime and external threat); and (7) obedience to the law (each member commits him- or herself to obey the rules as they are instituted by their representatives). A general election is held, which chooses a small group of students to lead the community for the next year, at which time a new election will be held. Those students who have shown themselves most talented in organizing the new community, not surprisingly, are elected to this council.

The community sets to work building houses and boats, creating farms, and dividing responsibilities. Some will be hunters; others, fishers; others, gatherers of the fruit that grows on the island; still others, cooks and dieticians. Some members have an excellent knowledge of medicine and guide the community in maintaining well-being, primarily through exercise, diet, and good habits. A dining hall is built, where communal meals are eaten. A sanitary system is constructed to dispose of waste. The money brought with them from the mainland is placed in a common trust to be used for buying supplies from the mainland. Shells, which fill the sandy beaches, are collected to be used for currency and are distributed equally to the members of the community so that they can buy and sell as they have need. People are given positions of leadership based on their merit, and everyone receives roughly in proportion to his or her contribution to the common good. The gap between the best-off and the worst-off has been greatly reduced, the result of a progressive income tax, devised to aid the poor and elderly.

For a long time the scheme works well, and it is clear that every member consented to the social order. Members adhere to the rules. They also play games, write essays and poetry, paint, play music, teach each other skills, and discuss philosophical questions, such as What is the meaning of life? and What is the nature of the universe? Many of the members marry, and children are born, who are nurtured and educated by the community. Schools are constructed to meet these new needs.

Of course there are conflicts of interest, but they are resolved reasonably well, if not by the disputing parties then by the leaders, who prove to be impartial judges. Rules are complied with even though members occasionally disagree with some particulars. Members know that the system of rules is basically fair and serves the community well. And, of course, unhappy members can always leave the island, which a few do—sometimes to return, realizing that Utopia is superior to anything on the mainland.

UTOPIA: THE SECOND GENERATION AND BEYOND

Children are born and educated on the island, and some immigration occurs, among the immigrants, political and economic refugees. The population grows, wealth increases, and a growing discrepancy between the better-off and the worse-off arises, causing envy and differences in political power. The leadership of the community becomes less personal and citizenship more anonymous. Although the people have more opportunities for education and travel, they also have more time for griping, crime, and destructive behavior. Laziness, a trait almost unknown by the founders, springs up among the new generation. Similarly, envy, greed, and disregard of the social good arise.

While the life of the individuals on the island is still far superior by their accounts to that of the mainlanders, their problems begin to resemble, more and more, those of the mainland. As crime increases, so must the size of a special professional police force. Disease sweeps over parts of the island and another institution must be created, a special medical profession with hospitals constructed and medicine brought from the mainland.

The first generation gradually dies off, and succeeding generations carry on the society with less overall commitment to the original vision of the founders. Social degradation, pollution, waste of resources, and exploitation occur on parts of the island, and the average quality of life diminishes until gradually, it approximates that of the mainland, which the student founders left. And they rolled over in their graves and wept.

AN APPLICATION OF THE THEORIES OF JUSTIFICATION

As we examine the progression of life on the island utopia we must consider the relevant justifications of government discussed earlier in this chapter:

1. The Social Contract or Expressed Consent answer: Government is based on the expressed consent of the governed.
2. The Tacit consent answer.
3. The Utilitarian answer.
4. The Fair-Play or Justice answer.

In the beginning, expressed consent was clearly the basis for compliance with the authority of the government, but that consent, in turn, was based on utility, fair play, and justice. The society worked well, produced the possibility of happiness, was fair to all, and maintained justice, rewarding people on the bases of merit and desert. As the community grew in numbers, explicit consent was replaced by tacit consent. Anyone could emigrate, so by remaining on the island, people in effect agreed to abide by the rules of the society. Eventually, an offer to fund emigration was withdrawn, but nearly everyone agreed that the social scheme brought significant benefits, or utility, and gave justice. So even though (1) expressed consent and (2) tacit consent, receded, factors (3) utility and (4) justice were sufficiently viable to justify the government and compliance with its rules.

The thought experiment described above roughly approximates the history of the United States, except that the Pilgrims and other early, idealistic settlers didn't arrive at an uninhabited island, but a vast continent that was already inhabited. Although an accommodation between the settlers and natives was sometimes worked out, relationships could have been more successful than they actually were. Our history is also blighted with the evil of slavery and with a civil war, neither of which occurred on the island. What difference does all this make to questions of the justification of government?

I will let you fill in the details and debate the nuances, but it does seem that insofar as the state promotes justice and the public good, it merits our commitment. Since morality involves promoting the human good, including justice, and the state is instituted to help us carry out those tasks, we have a general obligation to cooperate with its edicts. We need to work together through the coordinated activity of parliamentary processes and representational government to form rules that are reasonable and promote utility and justice. This is largely the conclusion set forth by David Hume in the eighteenth century: "The general obligation which binds us to government, is the interest and necessity of society . . . A small degree of experience and observation suffices to teach us, that society cannot possibly be maintained without the authority of magistrates, and that this authority must soon fall into contempt where exact obedience is not paid to it."[14] Perhaps Hume overstates the case. The state will survive without universal compliance ("exact obedience"), but we can amend his point appropriately to mean general compliance. The government can survive some noncompliance, but if too many people become free riders, the state is doomed. We have a general obligation to obey the laws of our land because it is vital to our protection and the overall public good, including the efficient carrying out of justice.[15] An objection is sometimes made that the utilitarian reason obligates us to promote all states, not just our own. But rule-utilitarians would argue that just as we have special obligations to our own family over and above other families, we have special obligations to our country over and above any general duty to promote good government.

Conclusion

So we return to our original question at the beginning of this chapter: What justifies government? The answer is its function in carrying out the moral purposes of promoting justice and the public good.

It seems that there are many grounds of political obligation, which at least constitute a prima facie duty to obey the government, including adhering to traffic rules, paying taxes (even when you don't agree with all the ways your money is spent), voting (even when you would rather be doing something else) for the best candidates, supporting the police and military (especially defending one's country), and other particular laws. I will generally obey laws with which I disagree. Say I believe we should have a right to choose physician-assisted suicide or to smoke marijuana, but these acts are illegal. I will comply with the law and will attempt to persuade my representatives to change the law. Of course, these are prima facie duties, not absolute duties. They may be overridden for more stringent moral reasons. Civil disobedience is warranted when the state is unjust and all reasonable means of reforming the situation have been exhausted, as occurred during the civil rights movement in the 1960s. But civil disobedience should be used sparingly, lest it leads us into a chaotic state of anarchy, where life becomes, in Hobbes's memorable words, "solitary, poor, nasty, brutish and short." And, of course, some laws will coincide with general moral rules (e.g., don't murder, don't steal, keep your promises and contracts) so even the anarchist will obey many of the state's laws—only not because they are laws.

I have included justice as one of the consequentialist goals of the legitimate state. Many philosophers would make it the primary goal of government. Every citizen has an equal right to have his or her interests considered on their merits. We will examine the contested concept of justice in Chapter 5. Suffice it to say that my discussion of political authority and obligation can accommodate either the broadly *consequentialist* view (which incorporates justice as a means to social well-being) or the more *deontological* view (which treats justice as an inherent political value detached from utilitarian considerations). Justice is important, but so is the general social well-being, where liberty and happiness abound. We will examine the value of political liberty in Chapter 2. Political philosophy ought to recognize a plurality of values and appropriately prioritize them.

I suspect that many, if not most, people obey the law out of less than sound, well-developed philosophical reasons. They obey out of habit or inertia, out of fear of the consequences, out of patriotic love of country, for religious reasons, or even out of superstition. But in a diverse, pluralistic, secular society, we need to develop philosophical justifications for our commitments. This chapter begins the process of challenging you to work out your own political philosophy.

For Further Reflection

1.   Examine the thesis of positive anarchism—that moral perfection is possible and that we should aim at utopia. Do you think this thesis is true? What arguments can you think of for and against the thesis?

2.   The negative anarchist's argument may be set forth in this manner:

> 1.   If the state has authority over the citizens, the state has the right to command the citizens.
> 2.   If the state has the right to command the citizens, the citizens have an obligation to obey the state.
> 3.   If the citizens have a duty to be autonomous, then they are obligated to act only for reasons they themselves regard as good.
> 4.   If the citizens are obligated to act only for reasons they themselves regard as good, they cannot be obligated to obey the state qua state.
> 5.   Therefore, it cannot be the case that the citizens are both autonomous and under the authority of the state.
> 6.   But our highest obligation is to be autonomous.
> 7.   Therefore, we have no moral obligation to obey the state.
> 8.   In other words, the state has no moral authority; it is not justified.
> 9.   But if the state is not justified, all people must do what they decide to do as autonomous agents. *This is a situation of anarchy.*
> 10.   Thus, anarchy is the correct political theory.

Do you agree with negative anarchy? Are all governments unjustified? Is our obedience irrational? Analyze this argument. Is it sound? Which premises, if any, in the argument are questionable?

3.   Examine the consent or contract argument. Do you think it is a sound argument for political obligation? Could instituting a Recognition of Citizenship Day enable this principle to work? What do you think of the idea of the government's helping dissidents emigrate or have a neutral territory in which to live?

4.   Review the various other proposed answers to the question, Why obey government? Can you find problems with the reasons given in this

chapter? Can any of the theories be improved? How would you go about arguing for (or against) a general duty to obey the laws of the state?

5.   Consider the claim that in a diverse, pluralistic, secular society, we need to develop philosophical justifications for our commitments. How would you go about doing this?

6.   Consider the religious justification for political authority discussed in this chapter. How strong is it? Explain.

7.   In elementary school many of us daily recited the Pledge of Allegiance to the Flag of the United States before classes began:

> I pledge allegiance to the flag of the United States of America and to the republic for which it stands: one nation under God, indivisible, with liberty and justice for all.

Do you think reciting that pledge entailed consenting to the authority of the state? Should the pledge be recited in all schools today? Should the phrase "under God" be kept in or deleted?

8.   Discuss the concept of civil disobedience with regard to a general duty to obey the laws of the state. Give an illustration of when it might be justified and what it would entail.

Endnotes

1. P. J. Proudhon wrote:

> *To be* governed *is to be watched, inspected, spied upon, directed, law-driven, numbered, regulated, enrolled, indoctrinated, preached at, controlled, checked, estimated, valued, censored, commanded, by creatures who have neither the right nor the wisdom to do so. To be* governed *is to be at every operation, at every transaction, noted, registered, counted, taxed, stamped, measured, numbered, assessed, licensed, authorized, admonished, prevented, forbidden, reformed, corrected, punished. It is, under pretext of public utility, and in the name of the general interest, to be placed under authority, drilled, fleeced, exploited, monopolized, extorted from, squeezed, hoaxed, robbed; then, at the slightest resistance, the first word of complaint, to be repressed, . . . That is government; that is its justice; that is its morality.* (General Idea of the Revolution in the Nineteenth Century, *London: Freedom Press, 1923*)

Note: Ellipses indicate the portion of the quotation that appears in the chapter text.

2. Percy Bysshe Shelley wrote:

> And if then the tyrants dare
> Let them ride among you there,
> Slash, and stab, and maim, and hew,

What they like, that let them do.
With golded arms and steady eyes,
And little fear, and less surprise,
Look upon them as they slay
Till their rage has died away.
Then they will return with shame
To the place from which they came,
And the blood thus shed will speak
In hot blushes on their cheek.

The American writer Henry David Thoreau expressed similar anarchist views in "Civil Disobedience" (1849): "Laws never made men a whit more just: and by means of their respect for it, even the well disposed are daily made instruments of injustice. A common and natural result of an undue respect for law is, that you might see a file of soldiers . . . marching in admirable order over hill and dale to the wars, against their wills, ay, against their common sense."

3. See Peter Kropotkin, *Mutual Aid,* in which he argues that humans as well as other animals have a tendency to cooperate for individual and social development.
4. Robert Paul Wolff, *In Defence of Anarchism* (New York: Harper & Row, 1976).
5. Ibid.
6. "At Heroin's Source, Taliban Do What 'Just Say No' Could Not," *New York Times,* May 24, 2001.
7. See Hobbes, *Leviathan,* (1651), chap. 14 and his "Review & Conclusion"; Locke, *Second Treatise of Government,* (1690), sects. 23, 119, 135, and 137; Rousseau, *Social Contract* (1762), Iv.ii. An excellent discussion of the consent theory is found in A. John Simmons, *Moral Principles and Political Obligation* (Princeton, NJ: Princeton University Press,1979). I have leaned much from this fine work and am in Simmons's debt here and elsewhere.
   Here is a classic quotation from Locke on the original contract:

   Men being, as has been said, by nature, all free, equal, and independent, no one can be put out of this estate, and subjected to the political power of another, without his own consent. The only way, whereby any one divests himself of his natural liberty, and puts on the bonds of civil society, is by agreeing with other men to join and unite into a community, for their comfortable, safe, and peaceable living one amongst another, in a secure enjoyment of their properties, and a greater security against any, that are not of it. This any number of men may do, because it injures not the freedom of the rest; they are left as they were in the liberty of the state of nature. When any number of men have so consented to make one community or government, they are thereby presently incorporated, and make one body politic, wherein the majority have a right to act and conclude the rest.

8. David Hume, "Of the Original Contract" reprinted in L. Pojman, ed., *Political Philosophy: Modern and Contemporary Readings* (New York: McGraw-Hill, 2002).

Hume also argues convincingly that there is no evidence that an original contract was ever made.

9. Jeffrey Murphy, "Coercion" *Virginia Law Review*. One's response to Murphy's thesis that coerced consent still obligates will depend on one's views about positive liberty, to be discussed in Chapter 2. To the degree you think having "reasonable" options is necessary for responsibility, to that extent you will value your obligations to keep promises made under coerced consent.

10. H. L. A. Hart, "Are There Any Natural Rights," reprinted in L. Pojman, ed., op. cit. John Rawls offers a slightly more sophisticated version of the principle of fair play in "Legal Obligation and the Duty of Fair Play," in Sidney Hook, ed., *Law and Philosophy* (New York: New York University Press, 1964).

11. Robert Nozick, *Anarchy, State, and Utopia* (Basic Books, 1974), pp. 90–95.

12. A. John Simmons, op. cit., pp. 128–32.

13. W. D. Ross, *The Right and the Good* (Oxford University Press, 1930), p. 21.

14. David Hume, op. cit. The argument centers on the thesis that morality involves promoting human flourishing and survival. We need institutions to enable us to promote flourishing and survival. Government is instituted to those ends. Therefore, we need government and have prima facie obligations to obey its laws.

15. John Stuart Mill put it this way:

Though society is not founded on a contract, and though no good purpose is answered by inventing a contract in order to deduce social obligations from it, every one who receives the protection of society owes a return for the benefit, and the fact of living in society renders it indispensable that each should be bound to observe a certain line of conduct towards the rest. This conduct consists, first, in not injuring the interests of one another; or rather certain interests, which, either by express legal provision or by tacit understanding, ought to be considered as rights; and secondly, in each person's bearing his share (to be fixed on some equitable principle) of the labors and sacrifices incurred for defending the society or its members from injury and molestation. These conditions society is justified in enforcing, at all costs to those who endeavor to withhold fulfillment. ("On Liberty" [1859])

2

LIBERTY, THE LIMITS OF THE STATE, AND STATE PATERNALISM

I know not what course others may take; but as for me, give me liberty or give me death.
———Patrick Henry, at the Second Virginia Convention, 1775

Man is born free, but is everywhere in chains.
———Jean-Jacques Rousseau, 1792

The only purpose for which power can be rightfully exercised over any member of a civilized community, against his will, is to prevent harm to others.
———John Stuart Mill, 1859

INTRODUCTION

If we accept the thesis of the last chapter, that government is necessary to prevent chaos, protect citizens from crime and external threats, resolve conflicts of interest fairly, and coordinate behavior, then the question becomes, What is the extent of the state's authority over the individual? If not anarchy, nor complete liberty, what is the proper balance between individual liberty and governmental authority? Should the state be permitted to protect us from ourselves, from taking great risks? Or should we have maximal liberty—to use drugs, to drive without using seat belts, to commit suicide, to do whatever we want—so long as we take responsibility for our actions? That is, should drugs, public nudity, attempted suicide, gambling, dueling, swimming in unsupervised beaches, and pornography be legal? In his classic essay "On Liberty" (1859), John Stuart Mill attempts to set forth a defense for maximal but not complete liberty. We begin with his grand statement of purpose:

The object of this Essay is to assert one very simple principle, as entitled to govern absolutely the dealings of society with the individual in the way of compulsion and control, whether the means used be physical force in the form of legal penalties, or the moral coercion of public opinion. That principle is, that the sole end for which mankind are warranted, individually or collectively in interfering with the liberty of action of any of their number, is self-protection. That the only purpose for which power can be rightfully exercised over any member of a civilized community, against his will, is to prevent harm to others. His own good, either physical or moral, is not a sufficient warrant. He cannot rightfully be compelled to do or forbear because it will be better for him to do so, because it will make him happier, because, in the opinions of others, to do so would be wise, or even right . . . In the part which merely concerns himself, his independence is, of right, absolute. Over himself, over his own body and mind, the individual is sovereign.[1]

MILL'S THEORY OF LIBERTY

The main points of Mill's liberty principle are:

1. *The nonanarchy principle or self-protection principle.* The state ruling in a civilized society is necessary to protect people from harm. It may interfere with individual liberty when harm is likely to result to others from our actions.
2. *The harm principle.* While the state may intervene against harm likely to occur to others, it may not interfere with self-regarding action. It may not interfere with individuals for their own good, because it will make them happier, or because they are imprudent or wrong.
3. *The liberty principle.* Individuals may do whatever they desire to do, so long as they are not harming others. Over themselves, over their own bodies and minds, individuals are sovereign. This principle states the harm principle from the individual perspective. Neither the government nor other individuals should intervene to prevent an individual's doing what he or she wants to do.

Mill goes on to qualify his principle. He is speaking of mature adults living in a civilized society. He does not mean his principle to apply to children or young people below an age of maturity. Nor does it apply to those "backward states . . . in which the race may be considered as in its nonage . . . Despotism is a legitimate mode of government in dealing with barbarians" (p. 10). People must first become sufficiently rational as to deserve to be treated as autonomous agents. Mill would permit paternalism for retarded people, the temporarily insane, and people living in backward countries, where educational opportunities have not permitted the full development of the rational faculties. Secondly, his defense of liberty is not based on the idea of natural or abstract rights or deontological notions of dignity, but solely on utilitarian principles:

> I regard utility as the ultimate appeal on all ethical questions; but it must be utility in the largest sense, grounded on the permanent interests of man as a progressive being. Those interests, I contend, authorize the subjection of individual spontaneity to external control, only in respect to those actions of each, which concern the interest of other people. (p. 10)

In this vein, the state may hold individuals responsible for contributing to the common good. They can be punished for failing to do their social duty, as well as for positive wrong actions. But there is a sphere where individuals are sovereign over themselves, including the realms of conscience and of freedom of thought and speech. However, it is controversial whether Mill's utilitarian defense of liberty works. If utilitarianism has to do with maximizing of welfare or happiness, one would suppose some abridgement of the liberty principle when it actually leads to such maximization. We will examine this point below. For now, let us continue with the basic analysis.

On the value of freedom of thought and speech, no more eloquent defense has ever been penned:

> If all mankind minus one, were of one opinion, and only one person were of the contrary opinion, mankind would be no more justified in silencing that one person, than he, if he had the power, would be justified in silencing mankind. Were an opinion a personal possession of no value except to the owner; if to be obstructed in the enjoyment of it were simply a private injury, it would make some difference whether the injury was inflicted only on a few persons or on many. But the peculiar evil of silencing the expression of an opinion is, that it is robbing the human race; posterity as well as the existing generation; those who dissent from the opinion, still more than those who hold it. If the opinion is right, they are deprived of the opportunity of exchanging error for truth: if wrong, they lose, what is almost as great a benefit, the clearer perception and livelier impression of truth, produced by its collision with error. (p. 16)

The maximal opportunity for freedom of speech aids in undermining false, orthodox, and widely held dogmas, and even when received opinion turns out to be true, we are challenged to give a closer justification of such truths, growing in understanding.

To assume that we are competent judges as to which opinions to allow and which to prohibit in the public discourse is to presume infallibility.

Many opinions, like the flat earth hypothesis, were once viewed as self-evident but are now dismissed as patently false. We can never be sure that our most certain beliefs will not turn out to be undermined by new evidence. Mill reminds his readers that upright citizens and social leaders condemned the paragon of virtue, Socrates, to death for impiety and corrupting the youth, or not believing in the Athenian gods and for encouraging the young to think for themselves. Similarly, the pious, not the wicked, condemned Jesus to death for his beliefs. Even the great Marcus Aurelius, the most noble of the Roman emperors, failed to see the potential good in Christianity, persecuting its adherents.

Essentially, Mill gives four reasons for the utility of permitting unpopular, politically incorrect, speech:

1. The prohibited idea may be true, thus leading to the discovery of the truth.
2. The prohibited idea may be partially true, leading to a fuller understanding of the truth.
3. The prohibited idea may be false, but responding to it will help us better understand the orthodox position.
4. Only through deep and vigorous intellectual debate can justified beliefs become fully appreciated by us. We need devil's advocates to awake us from our dogmatic slumber.

To those who object that some unjustified beliefs have practical benefits, maintaining moral stability and order, Mill argues that intolerance ironically promotes the very opposite, dissimulation, encouraging atheists to lie and pretend to be believers. Mill would encourage debate on virtually every controversial subject, including political anarchy, legalization of drugs, average racial differences, and the value of liberty itself.

With regard to the need for devil's advocates, Mill's tolerance toward dissent is qualified by his strong ethics of belief. "No one can be a great thinker who does not recognize that as a thinker it is his first duty to follow his intellect to whatever conclusion it may lead" (p. 32). In the quest for truth, we must examine both sides of the argument. "He who knows only his own side of the case knows little of that. His reasons may be good, and no one may be able to refute them. But if he is equally unable to refute the reasons on the opposite side, if he does not know what they are, he has no grounds for preferring either opinion. The rational position for him would be suspension of judgment . . . Both teachers and learners go to sleep at their posts as soon as there is no enemy in the field" (pp. 33, 41).

IS LIBERTY AN INTRINSIC GOOD?

One of the earliest, cogent criticisms of Mill's view of liberty was set forth by James Fitzjames Stephens, who accused Mill of unwarrantedly joining liberty with utility and argued that liberty was not an intrinsic good. "The question whether liberty is a good or a bad thing appears as irrational as the question whether fire is a good or bad thing. Liberty is only good when it enables us to do good things. It is bad when it leads to bad things."[2]

But Mill's liberty principle recognizes this ambivalence. That is why he is not an anarchist, but advocates government interference when liberty is misused. His view of human nature causes him to regard liberty not as a sufficient property for happiness, but as a necessary one. Liberty doesn't guarantee social or individual happiness, but rather, social and individual happiness require liberty, without which happiness cannot endure. Although Mill's rhetoric sometimes gives the impression that he is an absolutist on liberty ("In the part which merely concerns himself, his independence is, of right, absolute"), a charitable revisionist reading suggests that he is really a rational optimist who recognizes that other values, such as social welfare, social stability, justice, and decency, also are part of our moral repertoire. He holds that there is a strong presumption in favor of liberty, so that the burden of proof is always on the side of those who would interfere or curtail liberty for social or paternalistic purposes. But then, is paternalism sometimes warranted? We will examine that question below.

Liberty is a value grounded in the nature of humans as progressive beings. It can be put to bad use, but it is also a necessary condition for the personal self-development requisite for human happiness:

> The human faculties of perception, judgment, discriminative feeling, mental activity, and even moral preference, are exercised only in making a choice. He who does anything because it is the custom, makes no choice. He gains no practice either in discerning or in desiring what is best. The mental and moral, like the muscular powers, are improved only by being used. Human nature is not a machine to be built after a model, and set to do exactly the work prescribed for it, but a tree, which requires to grow and develop itself on all sides, according to the tendency of the inward forces which make it a living thing. (p. 56)

Each person has a moral duty to reach his or her highest potential, for as the individual becomes better, society does too, and a generous portion of liberty is necessary for such development. "Many persons, no doubt, sincerely think that human beings thus cramped and dwarfed are as their

Maker destined them to be, just as many have thought that trees are much finer when clipped into pollards or cut out into figures of animals, than as nature made them." But this seems a poor understanding of religion (p. 59). It is more reasonable to believe that God made each of us unique, so that we are to develop our personalities in individualistic ways, giving rise to geniuses and eccentric paragons of virtue.[3]

NO MAN IS AN ISLAND

John Donne wrote: "No man is an island, entire of itself; every man is a piece of the continent." A second criticism often lodged against Mill's liberty principle is that almost everything we do has effects on others. My converting to a new religion from the one I was raised in may offend my devout parents; my marrying the woman of my choice may plunge 20 female admirers into the depths of despair; my suicide may harm the whole community, robbing it of a functioning member and filling it with sadness. Even wearing my favorite purple tie or earrings may shock members of my community. Or suppose you and I both want to be president of company C, which includes lucrative benefits, but you beat me out for the position in fair competition. This sends me into a deep depression and ruins my self-esteem, which in turn destroys my marriage, which in turn creates such a dysfunctional family that my children become criminals, wreaking havoc on society. From an act-utilitarian perspective, it would have been better if I had gotten the job, for the negative consequences would not have been half so bad. How would Mill deal with such objections?

First of all, Mill seems to be a rule- or indirect-utilitarian, not an act-utilitarian. He doesn't think we should determine what to do in every case by doing a utility calculus. Rather, we should accept the set of rules that has been confirmed throughout human history as having the best prospects for bringing about maximal utility. In this way, Mill derives moral duties with their corresponding moral rights, as well as sound social policy, such as merit. Thus, even though you are harmed by my marrying the woman of my choice (whom you would like to marry), you have not been unjustly harmed. Likewise, your winning the job, because you are better qualified, adheres to a proven principle of meritocracy, which in the long run will prove beneficial to the society at large. We ought to adhere to a system of utilitarian deserts, merit, and rights, including the right to be given the position we are best qualified for, even if in the short run, hiring a mediocre candidate might have better consequences.

However, the principle of noninterference is dominant. If a man chooses to be drunk, the state should not punish him, but if he gets drunk while on police duty or military watch, he should be severely punished, not because he got drunk, but because he is unable to fulfill his duty.

Mill does not go as far as the anarchists in abolishing government. Human beings need an overarching political authority to assist them in making the conditions of life better, but severe limits must be imposed on the authority of the state. A strong burden of proof always rests on the state or society at large to justify intervention into the lives of individuals.

Although Mill holds that we ought not paternalistically to interfere in people's private lives, he does not hold to state neutrality regarding the morally good (chap. 4):

> It would be a great misunderstanding of this doctrine, to suppose that it is one of selfish indifference, which pretends that human beings have no business with each other's conduct in life, and that they should not concern themselves about the well-doing or well-being of one another, unless their own interest is involved. Instead of any diminution, there is need of a great increase of disinterested exertion to promote the good of others. But disinterested benevolence can find other instruments to persuade people to their good, than whips and scourges, either of the literal or the metaphorical sort. I am the last person to undervalue the self-regarding virtues; they are only second in importance, if even second, to the social. It is equally the business of education to cultivate both. But even education works by conviction and persuasion as well as by compulsion, and it is by the former only that, when the period of education is past, the self-regarding virtues should be inculcated. Human beings owe to each other help to distinguish the better from the worse, and encouragement to choose the former and avoid the latter. They should be forever stimulating each other to increased exercise of their higher faculties, and increased direction of their feelings and aims towards wise instead of foolish, elevating instead of degrading, objects and contemplations. (p. 74)

Mill roots his idea of human freedom in his theory of human nature, stating that human beings are progressive beings, who need to be free in order to develop their highest potential. This potential is best developed within a moral community, one that is deeply virtuous. The place to inculcate good character is in childhood. We can remonstrate and argue with each other about moral improvement, but after childhood, the state should not intervene in protecting people from themselves; rather it should tolerate offensive behavior, as well as personally destructive behavior.

Mill believes that liberty requires us to tolerate offensive behavior. Virtually everyone is offended by some type of behavior, whether homosexual conduct, public defecation or copulation, public nudity, or the expression of religious difference—your practicing of religion R may involve eccentricities that are meaningful to the bearers but offensive to others—so if we want others to tolerate our eccentricities, we ought to do likewise with theirs.

Can offensive behavior ever be serious enough to warrant state intervention? Only if it infringes on our autonomy and zone of privacy do we have grounds for attaching punitive measures to it. Such a situation was the Skokie case, where American Nazis marched into Skokie, Illinois, in 1977 to insult and offend the sensibilities of the large Jewish community of that town. The Supreme Court ruled that, under the First Amendment, the Nazis were permitted to march through Skokie, arguing that the citizens of Skokie could avoid viewing the parade.

In his essay "On the Offense Principle," Joel Feinberg distinguishes between easily avoidable and unavoidable offenses. If I defecate in public, you may not be able to avoid offense, so I have infringed on your liberty, but my wearing my favorite purple tie or earrings, though they may shock you, are easily avoidable. You can turn your eyes away from me or keep away from me altogether. Feinberg approves of the Supreme Court decision in the Skokie case on the grounds that those who were offended by it could avoid it. Similarly, some people are offended by knowing that men engage in homosexual acts, but so long as homosexuals are not having sex in public, third parties can avoid witnessing such acts. Would Mill say the same thing about beastiality and pornography?[4] I think so. There may be limits to indecency, but if we prize our own liberty, we ought to extend it as far as possible, tolerating even "indecent behavior."

NEGATIVE AND POSITIVE LIBERTY

Isaiah Berlin distinguishes between two kinds of liberty: negative and positive. *Negative liberty* is simply the absence of using coercion to influence a person. Coercion "implies the deliberate interference of other human beings."[5] Negative liberty is the freedom to do whatever we want, without being interfered with by others. This is the liberty that Mill was talking about. *Positive liberty,* on the other hand, is the genuine freedom to become your real or rational self. "The 'positive' sense of the word 'liberty' derives from the wish on the part of the individual to be his own master. I wish my life and decisions to depend on myself, not on external forces." At a minimum, this is what we call *autonomy.* But it is what Rousseau meant by one's *true self,* the ideal self that is our proper goal. Rousseau went so far as to endorse society's right to "force people to become free." "Whoever refuses to obey the general will will be forced to do so by the entire body. This means that he will be forced to be free".[6] Berlin argues that it is a contradiction in terms to say one can be "coerced to be free." We ought not call positive liberty "liberty" at all, but something else. "Liberty is liberty, not equality or fairness or justice or culture or human happiness or a quiet conscience." We ought not conflate or confuse these two types of liberty. Political liberty should concentrate on *negative* liberty, but *positive* liberty does convey a useful concept and should be kept. Both negative and positive liberty have internal and external dimensions. Internal obstacles are psychological, internal to the agent. External obstacles to liberty are obstacles in the world. Negative internal liberty includes being free from such psychological obstacles as lack of talent or ability, and lack of information or understanding, which would hinder us in doing what we want to do. Negative external liberty consists in not being hindered by physical coercion (e.g., you are twisting my arm or holding me down or raping me) or threats of others or coercive incentives (you blackmail or bribe me). Positive internal liberty includes being free from such positive psychological obstacles as weakness of will, compulsive habits, neuroses, or obsessions, such as fear of the dark, which prevents us from going out at night. Positive external hindrance to liberty includes insufficient resources, such as wealth or tools. The table below presents the schema of the various relationships of liberty.

TYPES OF LIBERTY		
	Negative—freedom from	*Positive—freedom from*
Internal	Lack of information	Weakness of will
	Lack of ability	Compulsive habits
	Ignorance	Neuroses, obsessions
	Lack of understanding	
External	Physical compulsion	Deficient resources
	Coercive incentives	

Mill's defense of liberty, as purely negative and external, seems quite plausible when we read it. Certainly we want to be free and not enslaved (we identify with Patrick Henry's dictum quoted above), autonomous and not coerced by the government or anyone else. We want to assert our right to be free from external constraints. Some would say that internal negative liberty is an incoherent notion. Liberty refers only to the absence of external obstacles. Others would say that positive liberty is simply ability to do certain things, not really liberty. But consider the criticism of the notion of standard negative liberty by Clement Atlee, leader of the Labour Party during the British general election campaign of 1945:

The prime Minister [Winston Churchill] made much play last night with the rights of the individual and the dangers of people being ordered about by officials. I entirely agree that people should have the greatest freedom compatible with the freedom of others. There was a time when employers were free to work little children for sixteen hours a day. I remember when employers were free to employ sweated women workers on finishing trousers at a penny halfpenny a pair. There was a time when people were free to neglect sanitation so that thousands died of preventable diseases. For years every attempt to remedy these crying evils was blocked by the same plea of freedom for the individual. It was in fact freedom for the rich and slavery for the poor. Make no mistake, it has only been through the power of the State, given to it by Parliament, that the general public has been protected against the greed of ruthless profit-makers and property owners.[7]

Atlee is arguing that state intervention is sometimes justified to prevent exploitation of the poor and powerless. What we call liberty for some is sometimes unjustified exploitation of the poor or weak. Anatole France made a similar point as he sardonically quipped about "the majestic equality of the law that forbids the rich as well as the poor to sleep under bridges, to beg in the streets and to steal bread."[8] Social conditions can limit the resources of the poor to the extent that they cannot exercise their abilities and live a good life, being deprived of appropriate opportunities because of their poverty.

Berlin makes a significant revision of Mill's liberty principle with his addition of positive liberty and the notion of *agonistic liberalism,* a value pluralism. The term *agonistic* comes from the Greek word for rivalry, or competition. Negative liberty, which liberals tend to concentrate on, is one value among others, including positive liberty, justice, welfare, peace, and social order.[9] All these are universal and objectively valid values, but they are incommensurable and conflicting. Though objective in themselves, there is relativity in how we arrange our values. The difficult task of political philosophy is to do justice to these conflicting values. We play one value against the others, trying to bring about a harmonious combination. Whether this can be done successfully is a difficult question, a task fraught with pitfalls. Berlin, in the Millian tradition, continues to give priority to negative liberty as the primary value, but his philosophy leaves the door open for other combinations. In the end he seems to rely on intuition or a consensus of the democratic public to determine the correct balance. But this seems a heraclitian, volatile process. What restricts the possibilities is the process of rational discourse: We can reason with each other, arguing that at different times and places, different political values are needed to fulfill democratic ideals. If it is to make sense, this value pluralism must be seen in the wider context of a full theory of political justice, which we will examine in Chapter 5.

PATERNALISM

This discussion leads us to take up the issue of *paternalism*, the intervention into the lives of others for their own good, exactly what Mill's harm principle seeks to prohibit. But is it right to be so absolutistic about non-interference in another's freedom?

Consider a list of paternalistic actions:

1. Mandating that drivers wear seat belts.
2. Mandating that motorcyclists wear protective helmets.
3. Prohibiting dueling.
4. Prohibiting gambling.
5. Prohibiting suicide.
6. Prohibiting the use of certain drugs.
7. Prohibiting purchasing drugs for therapeutic purposes without a physician's prescription.
8. Giving patients placebos when doctors believe their symptoms are psychosomatic.
9. Prohibiting women and children from working at certain jobs or working long hours, say 16 hours per day.
10. Requiring immunizations against disease to protect the public health.
11. Requiring that people put part of their wages into retirement funds, such as Social Security.
12. Prohibiting swimming in lakes and seaside beaches without the supervision of a lifeguard.
13. Prohibiting people from selling themselves into slavery.
14. Prohibiting people from becoming prostitutes.
15. Requiring that life-saving blood transfusions be given to children even when it is against their parents' religious beliefs.
16. Regulating the maximum interest rates for loans.
17. Putting fluoride in the public water supply.
18. Prohibiting people from killing others even if consent is given (such as in euthanasia).
19. Prohibiting selling of pornography (or child pornography).
20. Prohibiting self-mutilation.

Review this list and consider whether any of these paternalistic actions are justified. Does the state sometimes have the right to act paternalistically? When and to what extent? And is it ever permissible or even a duty for individuals to act paternalistically?

Mill answers these questions in the negative. It is never permissible to intervene against an adult's own judgment. Mill would justify item 13 on the grounds that it is contradictory to use freedom to abolish all future freedom. Regarding item 15, he would allow the government to override the parents' wishes and give blood transfusions to their children, but respect the decisions of the parents with regard to their own lives. We may remonstrate and try to persuade, but in the end, the agent's decision is final. The paternalist argues against Mill, that none of us is completely rational, that sometimes we don't know what is good for us, that sometimes our friends and family actually have a better grasp on what is in our best interest than we do. We all have weak spots in the guise of weakness of will. Jack may occasionally be unable to resist that one drink too many. Jill may be unable to resist that piece of chocolate cake, which will ruin her diet. I tend to neglect to buckle up when driving, so sometimes my wife has to remind me. Mill has a naive view of human nature, perhaps generalizing from his own thoroughgoing rationality to that of all other human beings. Let me give a few examples of personal paternalism to stimulate your thinking.

When our daughter was a college senior, a crisis occurred in our family. She was unable to complete a long history paper and so would not graduate. Upon appeal, she was kindly given a one-year extension to complete the paper. She took the incomplete and moved to Washington D.C., where she got a job. Months went by, and no progress was made on the paper. My wife and I spent long hours trying to convince her that it was in her interest to complete the paper, all to no avail. She claimed that she had a writing block and saw a psychologist about it, again, to no avail. Normally a vibrant young person, she seemed depressed, suffering from low self-esteem. The day before the deadline expired, after trying to persuade her to finish the paper, I demanded that she finish it. I told her that I would type it out for her (on her typewriter, not a computer), if she would tell me what to write. Reluctantly, she complied with my order and we worked from morning to night writing it. Finally, around midnight we had completed the paper, but the process had taken a toll on our relationship. She resented my intervention. The next day she turned the paper in and graduated from college. She went on to graduate school and got a degree in international relations, which enabled her to get interesting positions in Russia and the newly independent states in Central Asia; she now writes excellent professional reports and papers. She conquered the mental block and regained her exuberance and self-esteem. For a long time, I questioned whether I had done the right thing by abridging autonomy. Would Mill have approved? If we could show that Ruth was not fully autonomous, he would have. Perhaps she was suffering under temporary psychological pressures that inhibited her doing what she really wanted to do.

If this was a justified act of paternalism, we may learn something from the conditions that made it so. I suggest that four conditions should obtain:

1. The paternalist should have intimate knowledge of the agent. If I had not been Ruth's father, perhaps I wouldn't have been justified in intervening. But I did know Ruth well, knew her values, abilities, and personality; knew she was not fully herself; and believed that she would some day be grateful for my intervention. I made a rational bet that Ruth would be better for the paternalism. I could have been wrong, but I had good evidence for my belief.
2. The agent is not functioning in a fully rational mode. My daughter appeared to be living under stress and not acting in accord with her deepest values. Mill's prohibition applies to fully rational beings, but sometimes each of us become less than fully rational.
3. The paternalist must do all he or she can to persuade the agent to consider the act in question from a rational perspective. The paternalistic act must be the act of last resort, an emergency measure, not something embarked on casually.
4. The paternalist must have reason to believe that once the agent gets through the crisis, she or he will agree that the paternalist acted correctly and will be grateful for the intervention.

If my intervention was a morally acceptable act, then paternalism is sometimes justified. How often do cases like this one occur? I don't think they are everyday happenings, but neither are they entirely rare. You prevent your friend from committing suicide or gambling with his school tuition savings or taking drugs or engaging in self-mutilation, believing that he will appreciate it when he regains possession of his faculties.

Take the following case. We are in a bar together, and while I've had a little too much to drink, I'm still rational enough to know what I'm doing. I get into a violent argument with the guy at the next table, pick a fight with him, and begin to swing. Knowing that my opponent is a world-class karate black belt who will demolish me, you intervene, hold me back against my will, and with the help of the bartender, rush me out of the bar, out of harm's way. This is an emergency situation where condition 3 doesn't apply, for there's no time to reason things out. But surely, conditions 1 and 2 apply; even if I never say thank you, I certainly ought to say it.

In both my daughter's case and the bar fight example, Mill might reply that the interventions were justified on the grounds that not only the person's own good was involved, but also the well-being of others. Our entire family was being affected by the specter of the unwritten paper, and you and my other friends would have been greatly inconvenienced in caring for my broken body if I had been allowed to fight. This only reminds us of the "no man is an island" objection to Mill. But some cases of paternalism are more justified than others.

In a famous article, "Paternalism," Gerald Dworkin argues that even by Mill's own premises, paternalism may sometimes be justified.[10] He cites Odysseus, who in the *Odyssey* asks his sailors to bind him to the mast lest he be tempted to be influenced by the melodious singing of the Sirens and drive his ship into the rocks. Sometimes adults need to be protected from their own behavior, such as getting drunk, committing suicide, risking others' lives or money, and neglecting to invest funds for the distant future; we rationally would consent to some paternalistic interventions. Many of the items listed on my original list, such as requiring people to contribute to a long-term retirement program (Social Security payments) and not gambling, may be justified on the basis of our inability to reason carefully about our future needs and desires. When we are 20, it's hard imagining being 65 and needing funds to live on. Programs such as Medicare and Social Security, which workers are required to pay into, are really rational insurance policies.

SHOULD THE STATE LIMIT FREE SPEECH?

We noted above Mill's near absolute defense of free speech, a doctrine enshrined in the First Amendment of the U.S. Bill of Rights. In an article entitled "There's No Such Thing as Free Speech and It's a Good Thing Too," Stanley Fish argues against Mill that our notion of free speech, including that specified in the First Amendment, does not exist, but is "just a name we give to verbal behavior that serves the substantive agendas we wish to advance."[11] When speech departs from our social agenda, as hate speech and racist speech do, we ought to prohibit it and punish it. In other words, we give the honorific title *free speech* to speech that fits the reigning political ideology. Fish cites contemporary Canadian law, especially the case of *R. v. Keegstra,* in which a teacher, James Keegstra, denigrated Jews and was convicted of a criminal offense. Fish hails this as a more morally reasonable decision than much contemporary American liberal and conservative thinking about free speech.

Fish argues that the conception of the good held by the community should determine what is to count as free speech. What is allowed is what is consonant with our political goals. Since we have goals of combating racism and sexism, speech that embodies those evils should not be tolerated. He notes that flag burning is a form of expression that conservatives do not tolerate. He notes that religious colleges are exempted from tolerating speech denouncing their religious doctrines. Fish argues that freedom of expression is only a prima facie principle, not an absolute one, and, as such, it can be overridden by principles that underwrite society. He would prohibit and punish hate speech and speech that offends members of minority groups.

First Amendment theorists have never held that free speech is an unqualified absolute. Speech can be a form of action and can incite to violence ("fighting words . . . likely to incite violence"). You are not allowed to cry "Fire!" in a crowded theater. Fish is correct in reminding us that speech has consequences and the right is not absolute. But there is a difference between rampant, disrespectful hate speech (against anyone, not just minorities) and academic freedom, where the truth is the alleged goal. If we are to fashion speech codes to fit our political agendas, we would be tempted to exclude the programs of minority political groups that may have agendas different from ours. The Millian principle is to realize that our agenda could be wrong, so we should tolerate great differences in viewpoint, debate all sides of an issue, and, it is hoped, come to a greater understanding of the issue. Following Fish's admonishments, academics who defended unpopular political positions have been ostracized and expelled from universities. In the 1950s, under the McCarthy witchhunts, Communist academics, like my teachers Herbert Aptheker and Sidney Finklestein, were expelled for expressing their unfashionable views. In more recent times, Arthur Jensen and Michael Levin have been attacked for expressing their views that average differences in intelligence exist between racial groups, and various groups have attempted to get them expelled from the University of California and City University of New York, respectively. Jimmy the Greek was fired from CBS for expressing the controversial, politically incorrect view that blacks are better athletes than whites, a view recently supported by considerable evidence in a book by John Entine.[12] Mill's principle is that such controversial views should be debated openly and forcefully, so that the truth has the best chance to win out—even if it conflicts with our political agenda. Sometimes, it is not free speech, but our political agenda, that should be revised.

Moral people should be respectful of others, and this includes being tactful and courteous. Teachers may not abuse their academic freedom and should be censored and even punished for proven abuses. The general rule should be: If the controversial speech (or view expressed) is relevant to the subject being studied in class, it should be tolerated and debated. If the view is not relevant to the subject, depending on the degree of its offensiveness, it may be a subject of review.

LIBERTY AND THE TRAGEDY OF THE COMMONS

Liberty can be abused; what may seem to be an exercise of freedom may turn out to be a massive catastrophe, diminishing our liberties. This process, developed in recent years by the ecologist Garrett Hardin, is called the *tragedy of the commons*.[13] Imagine a public field (a commons) where farmers have been grazing their cows for centuries. Because of the richness of the field and the poverty of the farmers, the field is never overgrazed. Now there comes a time when the carrying capacity of the field is reaching its limit. At this point it is in the short-term rational self-interest of each farmer to add one more cow to the commons in spite of its limitations. The farmer reasons that by grazing yet one more cow, he or she will be reaping a positive factor of 1 (the value brought on by the extra cow) and losing only a fraction of the negative unit 1, the loss of the field's resources, since all the farmers share that loss equally whether they participate in overgrazing or not. So it is in each farmer's interest to overgraze, but if too many farmers act in that way, it soon will be against their interest, because the pasture will be ruined. Hence, the tragedy of the commons. Complete liberty, complete disaster. The tragedy can be illustrated in other ways. A few companies dumping their refuse into the river probably won't affect the river's purity very much, but when many companies see the river as a cheap dumping spot, the whole region suffers, while the company gains an advantage and bears only a fraction of the cost. A comparable tragedy is occurring in our use of natural resources. We are in danger of depleting the world's resources through wanton overuse. Similarly, freely engaging in activities that cause greenhouse gases to be released into the atmosphere has a deleterious effect on the climate patterns. To prevent such tragedies, we must have *mutually agreed upon, mutually coercive laws* that govern matters such as population increase, overgrazing, overfishing, deforestation, pollution, and the like. Each nation must limit its liberty and manage its own commons; if one fails to do so, the logic continues, it must be left to its own misery. Benevolent intervention on the part of misguided do-gooders is only likely to increase the overall misery, as such intervention encourages continued waste and neglect, discourages needed reform measures, and only delays the massive starvation that will eventually catch up with the nation. This is known as the Rachet effect. The principle of the tragedy of the commons is consistent with Mill's harm principle, but it shows how our harm to each other may not always be direct, but indirect. Sometimes what seems to be innocent behavior, when generalized, turns out lethal and is in need of government regulation.

Russell Roberts has pointed out that a similar process goes on in government spending.[14] Take the members of Congress. They typically get elected on the basis of promising to obtain federal funds for their districts. District A is made up of farmers, so Representative A gets legislation passed to subsidize the farmers in A. Federal taxes are raised to cover the subsidy. Everyone in district A is pleased. But district B needs a new fine arts theater, so Representative B introduces a bill giving B funds for a new theater. The bill passes, the theater is built, and everyone in district B is happy. District C, because of increasing traffic congestion, could use a four-lane highway bypass, so Representative C introduces legislation to send millions of dollars to his district, and the bill passes. Everyone in district C is happy. And so representatives of all the other hundreds of congressional districts play the same game, many for very good causes, some for not-so-good causes. But the system encourages waste. Each district and its representative reasons as follows: Because we're paying only a fraction of the cost for project P, we should ask for the maximum amount of money to carry out this project. After all, the government is paying, not us. But who is the government? Because every district is thinking the same way, the result is extravagant costs and much waste. This is not an argument against helping the needy or funding worthy projects or giving emergency aid to districts that have experienced a natural disaster. But the example illustrates a problem in representative democracy, where politicians are rewarded for bringing tax dollars to their districts. Note for example, a partial list of government subsidies: sugar, tobacco, corn, peanuts, cotton, and mohair. Although these subsidies have been enacted by Congress, it's doubtful whether the programs are generally beneficial to the American people. Instead, they benefit special interest groups that are small, but powerful enough to gain the support of individual members of congress. Some defenders argue that the system is justified because it evens things out: We each give something and get something equivalent. But, even if we all did benefit, this logic overlooks the vast expenditures needed to support the intermediaries, the bureaucrats who collect the taxes and allocate the funds to the projects. Wouldn't it make more sense for the people of the district that wanted the theater or bypass to raise the funds themselves and not burden others with their wants? That way, there would be an incentive to keep costs down, because the people who benefit are paying for the project. When we all exercise our liberty in demanding more resources, the tragedy of the commons occurs, eventually bringing ruination, the total loss of liberty, to all. By siphoning off tax dollars to everyone's benefit, we end up harming everyone.

Conclusion

Mill's liberty principle, which he defends on utilitarian grounds, advocates extensive freedom for citizens and would call for significant changes in our society. We would probably legalize drugs, gambling, prostitution, and pornography, and permit high-risk behavior, including driving without seat belts and cycling without helmets. But what is often overlooked in discussions of Mill's principle is that it entails a maximum amount of personal responsibility to match the liberty. The principle applies only to mature, responsible adults. It means not harming others, including not being a burden to them. We would legalize drugs, but not provide drug rehabilitation at taxpayers' expense; we would permit motorcyclists to cycle without helmets, but refuse to pay for medical care when they are injured in accidents; we would permit automobile drivers to drive without seat belts, but increase car insurance payments from them when they have accidents. Freedom can thrive only when correlated with responsibility, and maximal freedom can thrive only with maximal responsibility. The question is, Do we really want such maximal liberty?

We examined some cases where paternalism might be justified. These cases recognize limits to our rationality. For instance, it is hard for some people to plan for the future. We also noted how liberty can be abused and result in the tragedy of the commons, so liberty must sometimes be restrained, in a manner that exemplifies an indirect version of Mill's harm principle.

We also examined Mill's ideas on free speech. His arguments, though needing qualification, seem cogent. Tolerance is an important moral value. Opponents of free speech, such as Stanley Fish, would make free speech subject to our political agendas, undervaluing the Millian principle that minority positions deserve to be heard. Academic freedom is a necessary process in the quest for truth and wisdom.

Although Mill may be mistaken in speaking as though liberty is an absolute, his reasoning about the value of personal liberty is cogent. Liberty is among our most salient values and should be protected. A heavy burden of proof rests on anyone who limits personal liberty. We will examine the relationship of liberty to justice in Chapter 5.

For Further Reflection

1.   Analyze Mill's liberty principle. How plausible is it? Should our society adopt it? Explain your answer.

2.   Examine Mill's four reasons for the utility of permitting unpopular, politically incorrect speech. Do you agree with his idea of complete freedom of expression? Can you give some examples of prohibited or politically incorrect speech that society frowns on but Mill's principle would permit?

3.   Contrast and evaluate positive and negative liberty. Are they both valid concepts?

4.   Examine Berlin's notion of agonistic liberalism. Does such a value pluralism within the context of rational inquiry make sense? What are its strengths and weaknesses?

5.   Is paternalism sometimes justified? Explain.

6.   To what extent should freedom of expression be free, and under what conditions should it be abridged? Comment on Stanley Fish's argument that all speech should be conditioned by our political goals. Is there a difference between racial (or sexual) slurs and politically incorrect discussion of race (or gender)? Apply your principles to the subject of academic freedom.

7.   Examine the idea of the tragedy of the commons. What is its message? Is it a sound argument? Explain. Can you think of other examples of the abuse of liberty that may lead to catastrophe?

8.   Can Mill's liberty principle really be defended on utilitarian grounds, as he supposed? James Fitzjames Stephen made his classic objection to Mill over 100 years ago:

> If . . . the object aimed at is good, if the compulsion employed is such as to attain it, and if the good obtained overbalances the inconvenience of the compulsion itself, I do not understand how, upon utilitarian principles, the compulsion can be bad. [see end note 2]

How strong is Stephen's criticism? How might Mill respond to the criticism?

9.   In his book *Offense to Others,* Joel Feinberg argues that some actions do not harm us but are very offensive. He invites you to imagine that you are riding on a crowded bus on the way to your job and asks you to decide whether the following offensive behaviors should be made illegal, punishable as misdemeanors. Imagine yourself on the bus, and discuss whether these behaviors should be punishable by law.

A. Affronts to the senses

Story 1. A passenger who obviously hasn't bathed in more than a month sits down next to you. He reeks of a barely tolerable stench.

There is hardly room to stand elsewhere on the bus, and all other seats are occupied.

Story 2. A passenger wearing a shirt of violently clashing orange and crimson sits down directly in your forward line of vision. You must keep your eyes down to avoid looking at him.

Story 3. A passenger sits down next to you, pulls a slate tablet from his briefcase, and proceeds to scratch his fingernails loudly across the slate, sending a chill up your spine and making your teeth clench. You politely ask him to stop, but he refuses.

Story 4. A passenger elsewhere in the bus turns on a portable radio to maximum volume. The sounds it emits are mostly screeches, whistles, and static, but occasionally some electronically amplified rock-and-roll music blares through.

B. Disgust and revulsion

Story 5. This is much like story 1 except that the malodorous passenger in the neighboring seat continually scratches, drools, coughs, farts, and belches.

Story 6. A group of passengers enters the bus and shares a seating compartment with you. They spread a tablecloth over their laps and proceed to eat a picnic lunch that consists of live insects, fish heads, and pickled sex organs of lamb, veal, and pork, smothered in garlic and onions. Their table manners leave almost everything to be desired.

Story 7. Things get worse and worse. The itinerant picnickers practice gluttony in the ancient Roman manner, gorging until satiation and then vomiting onto their tablecloth. Their practice, however, is a novel departure from the ancient custom in that they eat their own and one another's vomit along with the remaining food.

Story 8. The group's behavior now constitutes a coprophagic sequel to story 7.

Story 9. At some point during the trip, the passenger at your side quite openly and nonchalantly changes her sanitary napkin and drops the old one into the aisle.

Should any of these behaviors be made illegal and, as such, punished? If so, which? Explain your answer.

10. In May 2001, the Mormon John Green was convicted of breaking the law against polygamy. He has five wives, who voluntarily consent to live with him and have borne him 30 children. How do Mill's liberty and harm

principles apply to Mr. Green? Do you think he should be given a prison sentence for his actions?

Endnotes

1. John Stuart Mill, *On Liberty* (Hackett, 1978), p. 9. All notes and page references in the text refer to this edition.
2. James Fitzjames Stephens, *Liberty, Equality, and Fraternity* (London, 1873), p. 43.
3. Mill writes, "Genius can only breathe freely in an atmosphere of freedom" (p. 62).
4. Joel Feinberg, *Offense to Others* (Oxford University Press, 1985). For opposing views on pornography, see Ronald Dworkin, *A Matter of Principle* (Harvard University Press, 1985), and Rae Langston, "Pornography and the Oppression of Women," *Philosophy and Public Affairs* 11:4 (1990).
5. Isaiah Berlin, "Two Concepts of Liberty," in *Four Essays on Liberty* (Oxford University Press, 1969), reprinted in L. P. Pojman, ed., *Modern and Contemporary Political Philosophy* (New York: McGraw-Hill, 2002).
6. Jean-Jacques Rousseau, *Social Contract* I (7).
7. Clement Atlee's speech is quoted in *The Open University* Course Book: *Political Philosophy* (Milton Keynes, 1973), p. 54. The Labour Party defeated the Tory Party under the leadership of Winston Churchill, and Clement Atlee became prime minister.
8. Anatole France, *Le Lys Rouge* (1894).
9. See Berlin's *Four Essays on Liberty* (Oxford University Press, 1969). A good commentary on Berlin's views is John Gray's *Berlin* (Fontana, 1995).
10. Gerald Dworkin, "Paternalism," *The Monist* 56 (1972), reprinted in Pojman, op. cit. My ideas have been influenced by Dworkin's article and by John Kleinig's book *Paternalism* (Rowman & Allenheld, 1983). Discussing this matter with Tziporah Kasachkoff and my class in political philosophy helped me clarify several points. I am grateful to all these people for their help.
11. Stanley Fish, *There's No Such Thing as Free Speech and It's a Good Thing Too* (Oxford University Press, 1994), reprinted in Pojman, op. cit.
12. John Entine, *Taboo: Why Blacks Are Better Athletes than Whites and Why We're Afraid to Talk about It.* (Public Affairs, 2000).
13. Garrett Hardin, "The Tragedy of the Commons," *Science* 162 (1968), reprinted in Louis Pojman, ed., *Environmental Ethics* (Wadsworth, 1999), pp. 311–18.
14. Russell Roberts, "If You're Paying, I'll Have Sirloin," *The Wall Street Journal,* April, 1998.

3

EQUALITY

Its Nature and Value

We hold these truths to be self-evident, that all men are created equal, that they are endowed by their Creator with certain unalienable Rights, that among these are Life, Liberty and the pursuit of Happiness.
— DECLARATION OF INDEPENDENCE, 1776

There is indeed a manly and legitimate passion for equality which rouses in all men a desire to be strong and respected. This passion tends to elevate the little man to the rank of the great. But the human heart also nourishes a debased taste for equality, which leads the weak to want to drag the strong down to their level and which induces men to prefer equality in servitude to inequality in freedom.
— ALEXIS DE TOCQUEVILLE, 1835[1]

INTRODUCTION: THE MEANING OF EQUALITY

IT IS AN EMPIRICAL FACT that human beings are unequal in almost every way. They are of different shapes, sizes, and sexes; different genetic endowments; and different abilities. From the earliest age, some children manifest gregariousness, others pugnacity; some pleasant dispositions, others dullness and apathy. Take any characteristic you like, whether it be health, longevity, strength, athletic prowess, sense of humor, ear for music, intelligence, mathematical or linguistic ability, social sensitivity, ability to deliberate or do abstract thinking, sense of responsibility, self-discipline, or hormonal endowment (e.g., levels of testosterone and endorphins), and you will find vast differences among humans, ranging from very high amounts of these traits to very low amounts.

Yet it is one of the basic tenets of almost all contemporary moral and political theories that humans are essentially equal, of equal worth, and should have this ideal reflected in the economic, social, and political structures of society. (See the chapter-opening quoted passage from the

Declaration of Independence of the United States.) As Will Kymlicka has recently said, "Every plausible political theory has the same ultimate value, which is equality. They are all 'egalitarian theories'. . . Some theories, like Nazism, deny that each person matters equally, but such theories do not merit serious consideration."[2] According to Ronald Dworkin, we have reached an "abstract egalitarian plateau" on which all political discussion must now take place.[3] In the minds of many, equality has come to be identified with *justice;* inequality, with *injustice.*[4] Why is this so? And how can these opposing theses, empirical inequality and egalitarianism, be reconciled? And exactly what is equality in the first place?

Equality may have replaced liberty as the central topic of contemporary political discourse. Egalitarian theories abound. Almost every month a new book or article appears defending some version of the thesis that justice consists in treating people equally. Articles on civil rights, affirmative action, and human rights proceed from egalitarian assumptions. Welfare rights, civil rights, voting rights, and affirmative action policies; national health care proposals, legislation aimed at limiting inheritance, liberal immigration policies, and protests against capital punishment; the dismantling of apartheid in South Africa—all are typically based on egalitarian interpretations of justice. University letterheads typically announce that they are "equal opportunity/affirmative action" institutions. The notion of equality spills over into other areas of life. In a recent issue of *Bicycling,* the lead article was entitled "Egalitarian Bicycling." Much of the motivation behind politically correct language is based on the principle that everyone should feel equally good about her- or himself. Such is the pervasiveness of the concept of equality in contemporary society. People announce, "I am an egalitarian," in a manner and tone that once characterized testimonies to religious or national allegiances, to being a Catholic, a Presbyterian, an American, an Englishman.

Yet when one inquires *what* exactly should be "equalized" and what are the arguments that ground various egalitarian claims, one may be bewildered by a plethora of competing conceptions and arguments. Among the competing items to be equalized are welfare, preference satisfaction, primary goods, economic resources, social status, political power, capacity for personal fulfillment, opportunity for welfare, and opportunity for scarce resources and social positions. One is sometimes tempted to apply Hume's conclusion on competing theologies to competing egalitarian arguments: When they attack their rivals, they seem completely successful, the result being a mutual self-destruction.[5]

The internal debate among egalitarians as to which version of egalitarianism is the correct one is in full bloom, and the issue has not been decided. But there is an even more fundamental debate: the external debate between egalitarians and nonegalitarians, those who argue that equality has little or no moral significance. Despite Kymlicka's insistence to the contrary, there are two sides to this issue, both of which should be heard if we are to make progress in moral and political theory.

What is the idea of equality? Essentially, it involves a triadic relationship. Except with abstract ideas, such as numbers, there is no such thing as pure equality, equality per se. Two objects are always different in some way or other—even two table tennis balls are made up of different pieces of plastic and exist in different places. Two things A and B, if they are equal, are equal with respect to some specific property or properties. Two trees are of equal height; two baseball players have equal batting averages; two workers produce widgets at the same rate.

FORMAL EQUALITY

We can divide egalitarian theories into two types: formal and substantive. *Formal equality* states a formula or policy but includes no specific content. *Substantive equality* identifies a concrete criterion or metric by which distribution policies are to be assessed. The classic discussion of formal equality is Aristotle's notion of formal justice, that equals are to be treated equally and unequals unequally. "Injustice arises when equals are treated unequally and also when unequals are treated equally." If two things are equal in some respect, then if we treat one of them one way in virtue of that respect, the other must be treated in the same way. When applied to distributive justice, the formula of formal equality enjoins giving equals equal shares and unequals unequal shares, but it does not specify the criterion. The theory may be represented as an equality of ratios. Let A and B be two individuals and X and Y be degrees of some value-producing property P, and Q some value (or disvalue). Then

$$\frac{\text{A has } X \text{ degree of P}}{\text{B has } Y \text{ degree of P}} = \frac{\text{A should have } X \text{ degree of Q}}{\text{B should have } Y \text{ degree of Q}}$$

A's having P to degree X is to B's having P to degree Y as A's deserving Q to degree X is to B's deserving Q to degree Y. For example, if A has twice B's widget-making ability P, A should receive twice the reward Q appropriate to degree Y.

This formal notion of equality doesn't tell us anything substantive. It doesn't tell us what to put in the place of P. It could be need, desire, work, resources, strength, good genes, intelligence, effort, contribution to society, human nature, sense of humor, or any number of other things. And, of course, it also leaves Q unspecified. Almost anything can be made into a law and fit the requirements of formal equality. For example, a Connecticut law of 1650 reads: "If any man after legal conviction shall have or worship any other God but the Lord God, he shall be put to death."[6] From the Puritans' perspective, this law is perfectly egalitarian. Everyone has a right to the same true worship and will be judged by the same standard: worship of the Christian God. A person failing to do his or her rightful duty, thereby forfeits the right to life. Of course, atheists, agnostics, Jews, Muslims, and other non-Christians will probably think this kind of equality is not worth much, but that shows only how malleable the idea of equality is. It can serve any number of masters.

No substantive conclusions seem to follow from purely formal equations, yet it seems that philosophers have sometimes missed this point and tried to derive substantive conclusions from purely formal ideas. Such has been the charge against those egalitarians who argue that equality involves equal consideration of interests. The formula itself doesn't tell us how to rank competing interests or whether the scope of interests should include animals and even plants. More fundamentally, it is not obvious that interest-satisfaction is the appropriate good to be distributed. The same charge has been brought against the thesis defended by Isaiah Berlin that there is always a presumption in favor of treating people equally unless and until some relevant difference has been found. Unless we know what metric we are applying, this is an empty notion. Likewise, the idea of equality before the law may be said to be purely formal, since it just tells us that we all (or those with the specified properties) should be judged by the same laws. It doesn't tell us what those laws are or ought to be.[7]

Formal equality is simply the principle of consistency. It applies to all serious discourse. If I call the color of the piece of paper on which I am writing "white," then, on pain of contradiction, I must call anything that is the same color "white." If a black man should get a speeding ticket for exceeding the speed limit, so should a white man. All rational prescriptions, including all rules, entail this formal principle of equality: Act consistently. Don't contradict yourself. Don't act capriciously. This formula leaves a lot to be desired, for it is consistent with substantive inequality.

SUBSTANTIVE EQUALITY

The other type of egalitarianism is *substantive equality*. As Aristotle put it: "Now justice is recognized universally as some sort of equality. Justice involves an assignment of things to persons. Equals are entitled to equal things. But here we are met by the important question: Equals and unequals *in what*? This is a difficult problem."[8] This type of egalitarianism identifies some metric and argues that all relevant parties should receive equal amounts of the quality in question. As already noted, people are unequal in many ways. The first question we want to ask is, Which ways are morally indefensible? A second question is, Given that a type of inequality is morally indefensible, what, if anything, should the state do about it? Regarding the second question, socialists and liberals tend to be interventionists, calling for the state to redistribute resources where a moral case can be made for mitigating the effects of inequality. Conservatives and libertarians tend to limit the state's role here, leaving the matter of distribution to market forces or voluntary action. With regard to the first question, a few idealists, such as the French revolutionists Gracchus Babeuf and Sylvan Marechal in a famous "Manifesto of the Equals," called for the abolition of virtually all distinctions between persons:

> We declare that we can no longer suffer that the great majority of men shall labor and sweat to serve and pamper the extreme minority . . . Let there be at length an end to this enormous scandal, which posterity will scarcely credit. Away for ever with the revolting distinctions of rich and poor, of great and little, of masters and servants, of *governors* and *governed*. Let there be no other differences between people than that of age or sex. Since all have the same needs and the same faculties, let them henceforth have the same education and the same diet. They are content with the same sun and the same air for all; why should not the same portion and the same quality of nourishment suffice for each of them?[9]

Their manifesto argued for even the elimination of the arts, since they hinder "that real equality" which they would promote. The arts, of course, would reveal the difference between a Rembrandt or a Michelangelo and the rest of us. Competitive sports and academic grades would have to be abolished for the same reason. If we took Babeuf's absolute equality literally, we could not make a distinction between our treatment of criminals and of noncriminals. Certainly we could not grade students for their work, unless we gave them all the same grade.

Although not going to Babeuf's extremes, John Rawls, Stuart Hampshire, and Kai Nielsen seem to think that our intelligence, our temperament, and even our industriousness should be disregarded in matters of distribution, for they are outcomes of the natural lottery. Since we don't deserve our native endowments or our better family backgrounds, we don't deserve the results of what we do with those endowments.

However, most egalitarians acknowledge that some inequalities are morally permissible. Differences in ethnicity, interests, aptitudes, intelligence, and conceptions of the good may be innocent. Unlike Rawls and Nielsen, most other egalitarians (e.g., Ronald Dworkin, Eric Rakowski, and Richard Arneson, [and in some cases, Nielsen]) would save a place for desert. People are entitled to the fruits of their labor and should be punished for their bad acts. The question becomes, On what basis does one distinguish the morally innocent differences from the immoral differences between people? Criteria for such distinctions have not been worked out as well as one would like, but generally, they emerge from the specific theory in question.

Let us return to our earlier question: What sort of inequalities are morally wrong and should be corrected by a more equal distribution? Candidates for such qualities are primary goods, resources, economic benefits (wealth), power, prestige, class, welfare, satisfaction of desire, satisfaction of interest, need, and opportunity, among others. Some egalitarians emphasize great differences in wealth as the morally repugnant item. In most countries a small percentage of the population (the rich) owns a disproportionate amount of the wealth, whereas a large percentage (the poor) owns a small percentage of the wealth. Why should the poor suffer while the rich live in luxury? Other egalitarians emphasize political power as the item that should be equalized. Traditionally, such egalitarians have fought for universal enfranchisement, extending the vote to women in 1919 and in the South to blacks during the civil rights movement of the 1960s. The egalitarian principle opposes the American electoral college system, which enables a minority to elect a president over the votes of the majority. In the 2000 presidential election, the loser, then vice president Al Gore actually received over 200,000 more votes than the winner, President George W. Bush. The principle of political equality would seem to favor local autonomy, where each voice counts more, over broad national centralization, where each vote counts proportionately less. Yet local autonomy in the United States is often supported more by conservatives than liberals, the traditional standard-bearers of equality. Marxist and socialist egalitarians, among others, argue that the franchise is insufficient for political equality. One needs such auxiliary traits as wealth, education, and leisure to participate effectively in the political process. Marx and Engels saw that so long as a state existed, political equality was impossible, since the rulers would always control the direction and speed of power more than the individual worker-citizen. In postcapitalist society the worker owning the means of production in his or her local factory would have equal input with every other worker. Engels wrote:

> We are now rapidly approaching a stage in the development of production at which the existence of these classes has not only ceased to be a necessity, but becomes a positive hindrance to production. They will fall as inevitably as they once arose. The State inevitably falls with them. The society which organizes production anew on the basis of free and equal association of the

producers will put the whole State machinery where it will then belong—
into the museum of antiquities, next to the spinning wheel and the bronze
axe.[10]

The question is, How is complete political equality possible as long as
there is the division between ruler and ruled—even if the rule be benevolent, enlightened, and voluntarily accepted by the governed? Government
by its very nature seems to entail hierarchical chains of command, coercion, and authority of the governors over the governed. Rousseau recognized this point and so argued that political groups should be confined to
small numbers wherein everyone had an equal input. Few egalitarians espouse the kind of anarchy required for political equality, so they would
seem to opt for severely constrained political equality.

Still other egalitarians have identified equal welfare as their goal. Justice requires that social institutions be arranged so that everyone would be
as deeply fulfilled or happy as possible. But it is difficult, if not impossible,
to ensure that everyone has the same welfare level, since what is required
to provide Bill Gates with a good life is not the same as what is required to
give a Trappist monk a good life.

One important question that has often been sloughed off by partici-
pants in the debate over equality is whether or not equality of the feature
in question is an intrinsic or simply an instrumental good. Thomas Nagel
notes the importance of equality's being an intrinsic value when he writes,
"The defense of economic equality on the ground that it is needed to protect political, legal, and social equality [is not] a defense of equality *per
se*—equality in the possession of benefits in general. Yet the latter is a further moral idea of great importance. Its validity would provide an independent reason to favor economic equality as a good in its own right."[11]
While Nagel does not resolve the issue, Christopher Jencks, in his famous
report on American education, *Inequality*, writes, "Most educators and lay-
men evidently feel that an individual's genes are his, and that they entitle
him to whatever advantage he can get from them . . . for a thoroughgoing
egalitarian, however, inequality that derives from biology ought to be as *re-
pulsive* as inequality that derives from early socialization."[12] And Richard
Watson argues that equality of resources is such a transcendent value, at
least for many purposes, that if equal distribution of food were to result in
no one's getting enough to eat, we should nevertheless choose this annihilation of the human race rather than an unequal distribution.[13] Watson's prescription illustrates the problem of treating equality as an
intrinsic value, especially as an overriding one. There are three ways we
can achieve equality between people: (1) We can bring the worst-off and
everyone in between up to the level of the best-off; (2) we can bring the

best-off and everyone in between down to the level of the worst-off; and (3) we can bring the worse-off up and the better-off down so that they meet somewhere in between. No doubt, most egalitarians would like to raise everyone up to the highest level, but with regard to many qualities, that seems impossible. Even given the present technology, there is no way we can raise imbeciles to the level of Einsteins or valetudinarians to the level of optimal health, or the blind to the ability level of the sighted. Thus, the "thoroughgoing egalitarian," if equality is a transcendent value, as Jencks would have it, would have to dumb down the brilliant, infuse the healthy with disease, and blind the sighted. An instructive thought experiment on this point is Kurt Vonnegut's short story "Harrison Bergeron," in which the government inserts transmitters inside the heads of people with high IQs. These transmitters send out sharp, painful noises every 20 seconds or so to "keep [intelligent people] from taking unfair advantage of their brains." Traditionally, heavy weights were attached to the feet of fast runners and ballet dancers to keep them from outperforming the mediocre. Even if equality could be shown to be an intrinsic good, it might not be the only intrinsic good. Others, both egalitarians and inegalitarians, see equality as an instrumental good, relevant to achieve high welfare or justice. But the question remains: What is the basis of the intuition that equality is intrinsically a good thing? Is it a natural intuition constitutive of the human condition, so that those who lack it are fundamentally deficient? Is it the product of a religious system which holds that all humans are made in the image of God, with infinite value? Is it an aesthetic principle, similar to a sense of symmetry or harmony? If, for a secularist, it is bad that humans are unequal in ability, why is it not bad that humans and apes or dogs or mice are of unequal ability?

Whatever the answers to these questions, there is no doubt that the ideal of equality has inspired millions to protest undemocratic forms of government, monarchies, oligarchies, despotisms, and even republicanism. The sense that each individual is of equal worth has been the basis for rights claims from the English Civil War (1642–48) to the civil rights movements in the United States and South Africa. Who is not moved by the appeal of Major William Rainborough of Cromwell's Parliamentary Army, petitioning for political equality: "I think that the poorest he that is in England hath a life to live, as the greatest he; and therefore truly, sir, I think it's clear, that every man that is to live under a government ought first by his own consent to put himself under that government; and I do think that the poorest man in England is not at all bound in a strict sense to that government that he hath not had a voice to put himself under."[14] But the ideal of equality has dangers too. The French aristocrat Alexis de Tocqueville, in his visit to the United States in the 1830s, was astonished at the passion for and preoccupation of Americans with equality. He saw in it both the promise of the future and a great danger:

> There is indeed a manly and legitimate passion for equality which rouses in all men a desire to be strong and respected. This passion tends to elevate the little man to the rank of the great. But the human heart also nourishes a debased taste for equality, which leads the weak to want to drag the strong down to their level and which induces men to prefer equality in servitude to inequality in freedom.[15]

R. M. Hare has argued that we ought to promote equality of condition to stave off envy at great differences between people, but long before Hare, de Tocqueville warned that equality actually promoted envy:

> One must not blind himself to the fact that *democratic institutions develop to a very high degree the sentiment of envy* in the human heart. This is not because they provide the means for everybody to rise to the level of everybody else but because these means are constantly proving inadequate in the hands of those using them. Democratic institutions awaken and flatter the passion for equality without ever being able to satisfy it entirely. This complete equality is always slipping through the peoples' fingers at the moment when they believe it attained. The people grow heated in search of this blessing, all the more precious because it is near enough to be seen but too far off to be tasted. They are excited by the chance and irritated by the uncertainty of success: the excitement is followed by weariness and then by bitterness. In that state anything which in any way transcends the people seems an obstacle to their desires, and they are tired by the sight of any superiority, however legitimate . . . When inequality is the general rule in society, the greatest inequalities attract no attention. *When everything is more or less level, the slightest variation is noticed. Hence the more equal men are, the more insatiable will be their longing for equality.*[16]

Perhaps it is the multifacetedness of the ideal of equality that causes so much perplexity. On the one hand, it seems to be the means of many morally desirable goods (not to deny that it may be an intrinsic good in its own right). On the other hand, it seems to compete with other values, such as liberty, efficiency, fraternity, desert, and merit. Chapter 4 will deal with the principle of equal opportunity. In the rest of this chapter I will discuss various types of substantive equality.

Contemporary egalitarians divide on whether it is resources or welfare that is the good to be equally distributed. *Resource egalitarians,* such as John Rawls, Ronald Dworkin, and Eric Rakowski, hold that in societies of abundance, such as ours, human beings are entitled to equally valuable shares of the resources (the wealth and other primary goods). *Welfare egalitarians,* such as Kai Nielsen and R. M. Hare, go further and maintain that in such societies, people should also receive equal welfare—interpreted in terms of fulfillment or preference satisfaction. A typical expression of welfare egalitarianism is that of Kai Nielsen:

> Morality requires that we attempt to distribute happiness as evenly as possible. We must be fair: each person is to count for one and none is to count for more than one. Whether we like a person or not, whether he is useful to his society or not, his interests, and what will make him happy, must also be considered in any final decision as to what ought to be done. The requirements of justice make it necessary that each person be given equal consideration.[17]

Criticisms of resource egalitarianism have focused on two central problems: (1) the problem of differential needs and (2) the problem of slavery of the talented. The first criticism goes like this: According to Rawls and others, we are to aim at an equal division of resources, but some people have needs for much greater resources than others. Tiny Tim, who needs a wheelchair, may have to spend a large measure of his allotment just to live a minimally good life, whereas the average person will be able to use the same size allotment to satisfy nonbasic needs. This doesn't seem fair. So we should give additional resources to Tiny Tim to bring him up to the same welfare level as the average person. The "slavery of the talented" problem is this: If we are to have equal shares in all the resources of society, then, because talents are among those resources, we should be able to command the uses of the talents of the gifted. But then persons of great talent will be disadvantaged, for others will want to make use of their talents. The talented will have to bid away great sums of their other resources to preserve the use of their talents, whereas those with lesser talents (upon whom no such great demands are made) will be free to use their resources for their own welfare. But this seems unfair, so resource egalitarianism is implausible.

Welfare egalitarianism has problems of its own, one of which is the problem of external preferences. Happiness depends on many things, among which may be external preferences, desires concerning the welfare of others, either individuals or groups. The racist's happiness may consist partly in the desire that his race flourish at the expense of other races, and the sexist may desire that people of her gender flourish at the expense of the other gender. The racist and sexist would have these preferences even if they knew that they would not profit from them personally, perhaps even if these outcomes would cost them their lives. But all this seems grossly unfair. Why should we grant the racist's or sexist's preferences any weight at all—even if doing so results in an agent's lower preference satisfaction?

An application of this problem is that of double counting, whereby one person's preference gets counted twice and so outweighs another person's preference. For example, suppose Sam and Mary both desire to get a prestigious job. However, John, Mary's friend, prefers that she get the job. So Mary's preference gets counted twice, and she gets two units of welfare preference to Sam's one unit. That seems unfair to Sam.

(2) The second problem of welfare egalitarianism is that of expensive tastes. Suppose I have a taste for designer clothes, luxury cars, gourmet food, mansions, and expensive jewelry. And let us suppose these tastes are so deeply fixed in my subconscious that I cannot rid myself of them without significant withdrawal symptoms. Welfarism would enjoin us to take from the modest resources of the contented person and redistribute them to those with expensive tastes. This seems counterintuitive. Similarly, as in an example from Thomas Scanlon, just because someone "would be willing to forgo a decent diet in order to build a monument to his god" does not put a strong claim on others to aid in his project[18]—even if doing so is the only way to bring his welfare quotient up to normal. I must leave it to you to think up responses to these counterexamples.

In addition to the problems noted above, both resource and welfare egalitarianism seem to have a problem of downscaling. Suppose that a necessary condition for making everyone roughly equal is for us to make the supremely happy or talented (i.e., resourceful) less so. To make the blind equal in resources with the presently sighted, would we have to reduce everyone to blindness or transplant one eye from the sighted? Again, this response seems abhorrent, and most egalitarians refuse to carry their egalitarianism that far, asserting that there are other values besides equality. Nevertheless, the problem of downscaling seems to impose restrictions on egalitarian strategies.

R. M. Hare offers a utilitarian-welfarist defense of equality. Utilitarian equality is based on Bentham's idea "that each is to count for one, no one for more than one," and applies to all sentient creatures—humans as well as other animals. Each sentient being has an equal claim on happiness. Utilitarian equality, as Hare emphasizes, is based primarily on the economic principle of *diminishing marginal utility*, the idea that, all other things being equal, an additional unit of income, say $1, helps the pauper more than it does the rich person, so we maximize aggregate utility by transferring resources from the rich to the poor. All other things being equal, and up to a point, transfer of money from the rich to the poor probably does increase utility.

The principle of diminishing marginal utility no doubt supports redistribution of income in many cases, but two things may be said against using it as an argument for egalitarianism. First of all, it is not a principle of strict equality, but a principle for reducing poverty or reducing the gap between the rich and the poor. Plato and Aristotle, both inegalitarians, allowed the richest person to have only four or five times the wealth of the poorest. Inegalitarians, meritocrats, and utilitarians can be as much against waste, poverty, and gratuitous suffering as egalitarians. But this points to a key question: Is equality an intrinsic good, or is it merely an instrumental good? For example, do we want equality or the elimination (reduction) of poverty? If it is the former, then we should redistribute wealth even if it leaves everyone worse off, something few egalitarians advocate. If it is the latter, then it is merely a question of the best means to get there. And allowing inequalities, as Rawls recognizes, may be the most efficient way to travel.

The idea of diminishing marginal utility goes only so far. It may be that some of the affluent derive and promote more utility through their additional resources than the poor would gain if the wealth in question were distributed more equally. The gourmet with an income of $100,000 may profit from an additional $10 more than the monk who lives on grains, nuts, and goat's milk. The scholar with a thousand books would gain more from an additional book than the illiterate who owns none and wants none. We will examine the issue of economic distributive justice in Chapter 5.

THE DOCTRINE OF EQUAL HUMAN WORTH AND METAPHYSICAL EQUALITY

Metaphysical equality (or the doctrine of equal human worth) holds that all humans are of equal and positive worth because of some intrinsic property. Historically, the clearest example of this is the Judeo-Christian idea of equality. Before God, each of us is of equal (positive) worth, since we are created in God's image (Genesis 1:26). Stoics held that a divine spark was in each of us; thus, we were all related to one another in God. All humans, or all rational humans, belong to a single reference group and thus are of equal positive worth and have equal unalienable rights. This sentiment is found in the Declaration of Independence of the United States of America, quoted at the beginning of this chapter. It is also expressed in the United Nations Universal Declaration on Human Rights (1948):

> All human beings are born free and equal in dignity and rights. They are endowed with reason and conscience and should act towards one another in a spirit of brotherhood.

Kant held that by virtue of our rational nature, each of us is to be treated as an end in her- or himself and not merely as a means:

> Act so that you treat humanity, whether in your own person or in that of another, always as an end and never as a means only. Human beings qua rational have an inherent dignity and so ought to treat each other as ends and never merely as means.[19]

Each person, qua rational being, is autonomous in that one's self transcends the categories of space and time and is able to exercise free will. As such, each person is equally able to participate in moral legislation, and it is this equal ability to engage in moral deliberation that endows us with equal dignity.

There are three main problems with the idea of personal equality: (1) identifying the relevant property, (2) discovering whether we have equal amounts of it (or determining how an amount of the relevant property grants us equal worth), and (3) discovering whether a person maintains the property over time.[20] Even if we can locate the value-endowing property, a feat that seems to entail that values are objective, it is hard to see that all individuals have equal amounts of it. If there is a property that endows us all with equal positive worth, it must be grounded in a transcendent reality, one that is not discoverable apart from religious authority. But even if we could agree on what that transcendental property is, it might not be possible to discover whether different people maintained possession of it to the same degree throughout their lives.

Even if we can make sense of Kant's notion of a transcendent self, his doctrine of equality has two problems: First, why should we think that rationality—or rational autonomy—is intrinsically (rather than instrumentally) valuable? Second, if rationality is valuable, then why doesn't more of it give us more value than less of it? One interpretation of Kant is that he addresses this problem with the notion of a threshold: Having a minimum amount of X gets one into the circle of those with substantive worth. It's an all-or-nothing concept. Rawls uses this kind of method: All those who are able to deliberate and give justice are counted as equally valuable. But this seems unwarrantedly stipulative. Some are able to deliberate better than others. Shouldn't they be counted as more worthy?

Gregory Vlastos, in his celebrated article "Justice and Equality," appeals to the metaphor of a loving family to defend the notion of equal worth. If asked why we hold to equal human rights, Vlastos replies, "Because the human worth of all persons is equal, however unequal may be their merit."

> The moral community is not a club from which members may be dropped for delinquency. Our morality does not provide for moral outcasts or half-

castes. It does provide for punishment. But this takes place within the moral community and under its rules. It is for this reason that, for example, one has no right to be cruel to a cruel person. His offence against the moral law has not put him outside the law . . . The pain inflicted on him as punishment for his offence does not close out the reserve of goodwill on the part of all others which is his birthright as a human being; it is a limited withdrawal from it . . . [The] only justification [of human rights is] the value which persons have simply because they are persons: their "intrinsic value as individual human beings," as Frankena calls it; the "infinite value" or the "sacredness" of their individuality, as others have called it.[21]

Vlastos distinguishes gradable, or meritorious, traits from nongradable but valuable traits, and says that talents, skills, character, and personality belong to the gradable sort, but that our humanity is a nongradable value. Regarding human worth, all humans get equal grades. In this regard, human worth is like love. "Constancy of affection in the face of variations of merit is one of the surest tests of whether a parent does love a child." But the family metaphor, which is the closest Vlastos comes to providing an argument for his position, needs further support. It is not obvious that all humans are related to each other as members of a family. If we're all brothers and sisters, who's the parent? By virtue of what property in human beings do we obtain value? Vlastos doesn't tell us. To the contrary, if we evolved from other animals, there is no more reason to think that we are siblings to all humans than to think that we are siblings to apes and gorillas.

Note that Vlastos offers as evidence for equal worth the fact that "one has no right to be cruel to a cruel person." But surely this is not evidence for equality, for we shouldn't be cruel—without justification—to anyone, animal or human. Aristotle, certainly no egalitarian, regarded cruelty as a vice.

Nor does the gradable–nongradable distinction make a difference here because there are nongradable properties. Although all members of the set of books or cats may be equally books or cats, we can still grade members with respect to specific interests or standards and say from the point of view of aesthetic value that some books or cats are better than others. Likewise, we may agree that all Homo sapiens are equally Homo sapiens but insist that within that type there are important differences, which include differences in value. Some humans are highly moral, some are moderately moral and others are immoral. Why not make the relevant metric morality rather than species membership? The point is that Vlastos has not grounded his claim of equal worth, or any worth for that matter, and until he does, his idea of the family connection remains a mere metaphor.

Suppose a Martian were to visit Earth and inquire about our egalitarian rhetoric, asking an egalitarian like Vlastos why he uses such language of mere animals like the human animal. He invites Vlastos to consider Smith, a man of low morals and lower intelligence, who abuses his wife and children, who hates exercising and work, for whom novels are dull and art a waste of time, and whose joy it is to spend his days as a couch potato, drinking beer while watching mud wrestling, violent sports, and soap operas on TV. He is an avid voyeur, devoted to child pornography. He is devoid of intellectual curiosity; eschews science, politics, and religion; and eats and drinks in a manner more befitting a pig than a person. Smith lacks wit, grace, humor, technical skill, ambition, courage, self-control, and wisdom. He is antisocial, morose, and lazy, a freeloader who feels no guilt about living on welfare when he is perfectly able to work. He has no social conscience and barely avoids getting caught for his petty thievery. He has no talents, makes no social contribution, lacks a moral sense, and from the perspective of the good of society, would be better off dead. But Smith is proud of one thing: that he is "sacred," of "infinite worth," of equal intrinsic value as Abraham Lincoln, Mother Teresa, Albert Schweitzer, the Dalai Lama, Jesus Christ, Gandhi, and Einstein. He is inviolable—and proud of it—in spite of any deficiency of merit. From the egalitarian perspective, in spite of appearances to the contrary, Smith is of equal intrinsic worth as the best citizen in his community. We could excuse the Martian if he exhibited bemusement at this doctrine.

Contrary to egalitarian ideals, there is good reason to believe that humans are not of equal worth. Given the empirical observation, it is hard to believe that humans are equal in any way at all. We all seem to have vastly different levels of abilities. Some, such as Aristotle, Newton, Shakespeare, and Einstein, are very intelligent; others are imbeciles and idiots. Some, such as Socrates and Abraham Lincoln, are wise; others are very foolish. Some have great powers of foresight and are able to defer gratification, while others can hardly assess their present circumstances, gamble away their future, succumb to immediate gratification, and generally, go through life as through a fog. From the perspective of the moral point of view, it appears that Einstein, Gandhi, and Mother Teresa have more value than Jack the Ripper or Adolf Hitler. If a research scientist with the cure for cancer is on the same raft with an ordinary person, there is no doubt about who should be saved on the basis of functional value.

As noted at the beginning of this chapter, you can take any capacity or ability you like—reason, a good will, the capacity to suffer, the ability to deliberate and choose freely, the ability to make moral decisions and carry them out, self-control, sense of humor, health, athletic and artistic ability—and it seems that humans (not to mention other animals) differ in the degree to which they have those capacities and abilities. Furthermore, as already noted above, given the purely secular version of the theory of evolution, there doesn't seem to be any reason to believe that the family metaphor, supposed by philosophers like Vlastos and by the United Nations Declaration on Human Rights, has much evidence in its favor. If we're simply a product of blind evolutionary chance and necessity, it is hard to see where the family connection comes in. Families are egalitarian, somewhat socialistic, and based on intimacy, altruism, affection, generosity, and love—quite the reverse of relations in society at large. In the family, resources are distributed on the basis of need, not on rights, chance, or merit, the normal bases in nonfamilial relationships. The question is: Can the family metaphor be extended to the whole society, the whole nation, the whole world? It's hard to see how it can. We can respect and even feel loyalty to those who are engaged in common projects with us, say, the communal good, but it's hard to imagine that most of us would be willing to make significant sacrifices for other humans not related to us as intimately as family or friends. So social policy based on the metaphor of the family seems to lack the deep psychological attachment necessary for it to work.

Aiming to follow Kant, but without his metaphysical notions, Tom Nagel has set forth a version of a rational agency argument for equal worth in his books *A View from Nowhere* and *Equality and Partiality*. Nagel's version has been seen as more promising than other versions of the doctrine in that it centers on essential value viewed from an impersonal standpoint ("a view from nowhere"):

> You cannot sustain an impersonal indifference to the things in your life which matter to you personally . . . But since the impersonal standpoint does not single you out from anyone else, the same must be true of the value arising in other lives. If you matter impersonally, so does everyone. We can usefully think of the values that go into the construction of a political theory as being revealed in a series of four stages, each of which depends on a moral response to an issue posed by what was revealed at the previous stage. At the first stage, the basic insight that appears from the impersonal standpoint is that everyone's life matters, and no one is more important in virtue of their greater value for others. But at the baseline of value in the lives of individuals, from which all higher-order inequalities of value must derive, everyone counts the same. For a given quality of whatever it is that's good or bad—suffering or happiness or fulfillment or frustration—its intrinsic impersonal value doesn't depend on whose it is.[22]

The argument goes like this:

1. I cannot help valuing myself as a subject of positive and negative experiences (e.g., suffering, happiness, fulfillment, or frustration).

2. All other humans are relevantly similar to me, subjects of positive and negative experiences.
3. Therefore, I must, on pain of contradiction, ascribe equal value to all other human beings.

Although this may look like a promising argument, it too is defective. First of all, it is not necessary to value oneself primarily as a possessor of the capacity for positive and negative experiences. Why cannot I value myself because of a complex of specific properties—excellence of skill, ability to engage in complex deliberation, rationality, discipline and self-control, industriousness, high integrity, athletic ability, creative and artistic talent, or quickness of wit—without which I would not deem living worth the effort? I value myself more for the actual *possession* of these properties than I do for my *capacity* to suffer. These properties are what positively make up my happiness and give me a sense of worth—from the impersonal (i.e., impartial) point of view. If I were to lose any one of these properties, I, given my present identity, would value myself less than I do now. Should I lose enough of them, my present self would view this future self as lacking positive value altogether, and my future self might well agree. Should I become immoral, insane, or desperately disease-ridden, I would be valueless and I would hope to die as swiftly as possible. So it follows that I am under no obligation to value everyone, since not everyone is moral, rational, or healthy. There is no contradiction in failing to value the debauched Smith (above) or the person whose only goal in life is to get high on drugs, the rapist or child molester, the retarded or the senile, since they lack the necessary qualities in question. Furthermore, I may value people in degrees, according to the extent that they exhibit the set of positive qualities.

So, letting these positive values be called traits T, we need to revise the first premise to read: I cannot help valuing myself as the possessor of a set of traits T. But then premise 2 becomes false because all other human beings are *not* relevantly similar to me in this regard. And so Nagel's conclusion does not follow; I don't contradict myself in failing to value people who lack the relevant qualities.

There is a second problem with Nagel's argument. It rests too heavily on the agent's judgment about her- or himself ("If you matter impersonally, so does everyone"). There are three ways to invalidate this conditional. First, the conditional won't go through if you don't value yourself. If I am sick of life and believe that I don't matter, then, on Nagel's premises, I have no reason to value anyone else. Second, I may deny the consequent and thereby reject the antecedent. I may come to believe that no one else matters and then be forced to acknowledge that I don't matter either. We're all equal—equally worthless. If reflection has any force, Nagel's first premise (i.e., I cannot help valuing myself as a subject of positive and negative experiences) seems false. People cease to value themselves when they lose the things that give their lives meaning.

Third, note the consequentialist tone of the last two sentences of Nagel's statement: "at the baseline of value in the lives of individuals, from which all higher-order inequalities of value must derive, everyone counts the same. For a given quality of whatever it is that's good or bad—suffering or happiness or fulfillment or frustration—its intrinsic impersonal value doesn't depend on whose it is." We hear the echo of Bentham's "each one is to count for one, no one for more than one" in this passage. But Nagel, like Bentham before him, cannot be both a maximizer *and* an egalitarian. If it is happiness that really is the good to be maximized or suffering to be minimized, then individuals are mere placeholders for these qualities, so if we can maximize happiness (or minimize suffering) by subordinating some individuals to others, we should do so. If A can derive 10 hedons by eliminating B and C, who together can obtain only 8 hedons, it would be a good thing for A to kill B and C. If it turns out that a pig satisfied really is happier than Socrates dissatisfied, then we ought to value the pig's life more than that of Socrates, and if a lot of people are miserable and are making others miserable, we would improve the total happiness of the world by killing them.

I for one confess that I don't care whether cats thrive more than mice or whether all cats are equally prosperous. No one I know cares about this either. But from the perspective of Nagel's impersonal view from nowhere, shouldn't we care about them, since cats and mice are subjects to positive and negative experiences—pleasures and suffering? How, on Nagel's premises, are humans—themselves animals—intrinsically better than cats and mice? I can appreciate it if a religious person responds that humans are endowed with the image of God, but Nagel, not being religious, can't use this response. Why should I care that all humans are equally happy any more than I care whether all cats or mice are equally happy and as equally happy as humans? If the question is absurd, I'd like to know why. Do not misunderstand me; I don't want to harm anyone without moral justification, but I don't see any moral reason to treat all humans, let alone all animals, with equal respect.

That said, let us return to the metaphysical idea of equal worth. We may conclude that the idea of metaphysical equality may flourish within a religious community, but given secular society as we know it, this idea seems irrelevant, hence, Dworkin's quip that his theory of equality is "metaphysically unambitious." Finally, it should be pointed out that substantive conclusions do not follow from metaphysical equality. In the egalitarian early Christian Church, the idea of divinely specified functions enjoined women to defer to their husbands and slaves to be returned to their masters. At best, equal dignity leads to the idea of equal opportunity. Each of us will be judged by how well we have used the talents and opportunities we've been given. If a God exists, he can make such evaluations, but perhaps we can make rough approximations to how well we have used our talents and opportunities. We will examine the concept of equal opportunity in the next chapter.

LEGAL EQUALITY

I remember my perplexity upon first seeing the statement engraved on the United States Supreme Court building, "Equal Justice Under Law," for it occurred to me, justice has traditionally meant treating equals equally and unequals unequally. So the statement seemed pleonastic: Equally treat equals equally and unequals unequally under [our] law. I will argue that such perplexity is justified, for the use of "equality" in "legal equality" is a redundant expression.

We must all adhere to the same laws and be held accountable for our behavior. Likewise, we all have some of the same legal rights: to freedom, legal representation, and the like. This has little or nothing to do with personal or metaphysical equality, welfare, resource equality, or moral equality.

The idea of the law is to deal with people under general rules that the magistrate applies impartially. The law must be applicable to all, conferring benefits or burdens according to general prescriptions and prohibitions. Equality before the law simply means that the law should be applied impartially. If persons A and B both break law L, which carries the penalty P, A and B should (minus mitigating circumstances) pay the same penalty. What law L is, whether it is just or not, is irrelevant to the idea of equality before the law. Recall Anatole France's quip: "The law, in its majestic equality, forbids the rich as well as the poor to sleep under bridges, to beg in the street, and to steal bread."[23] A law that makes it permissible to serve only white patrons at your restaurant is just as much a law as one that prohibits you from discriminating on the basis of race. If this is so, then the idea of equality before the law can be reduced to the formal principle of treating equals equally and unequals unequally. It is not an egalitarian theory at all.

Recently, Peter Westen has developed the thesis that the principle of equality—that likes should be treated alike and unlikes as unalike—is of negative value in legal thinking, for not only is it empty of content, but it also misleads us into thinking that substantive principles can be derived from formal equality.[24] In law, it is the specific rights that do all the substantive work, the idea of equality providing only the formal constraint of consistency in application.

It has often been argued that the equal protection clause of the Fourteenth Amendment ("nor shall any State . . . deny to any person within its jurisdiction the equal protection of the laws") yields substantive rights. But Westen argues to the contrary: that "equality analysis logically collapses into rights analysis and that analyzing legal problems in terms of equality is essentially redundant."

> All legal regulation involves classification. Every state law is thus subject to scrutiny under the fourteenth amendment as a potential violation of constitutional equality—as a violation of, among other things, the constitutional norm that "likes be treated alike." In order to decide whether a state classification treats differently people who are constitutionally deemed to be "alike," however, we must first possess a constitutional standard for distinguishing those people who are alike from those who are not. We cannot find such standards in the formula that "likes should be treated alike," because the equality formula *presupposes* anterior constitutional standards for ascertaining "likeness" and "unlikeness." Yet once we ascertain the anterior constitutional standards (as we must do anyway), our substantive work is complete, and the additional and self-evident step of stating our conclusion in terms of "equals" or "unequals" is entirely superfluous.[25]

Westen illustrates this confusion with several Supreme Court decisions. In *Carey* v. *Brown* the plaintiffs engaged in peaceful picketing on the sidewalk in front of the home of the mayor of Chicago to protest the city's busing policies. They were arrested and prosecuted under a state law that prohibited picketing of private residences except "the peaceful picketing of a place of employment involved in a labor dispute." The Supreme Court overturned the judgment, holding that by treating political protesters differently from labor picketers, the statute denied the plaintiff equal protection of the laws. Westen points out that what was at issue was not really the Fourteenth Amendment. What was at issue was a First Amendment right of free speech and that all the equal protection clause added was a redundant injunction to apply principles consistently. Westen outlines the thinking of the Supreme Court this way:

1. Persons who are alike should be treated alike.
2. The state shall not deny persons the right to free speech.
3. Persons who are treated differently from others solely by virtue of regulations that violate their right of free speech are necessarily *like* the others and hence must be treated alike.

It is clear that premises 1 and 3 add nothing to the substantive aspect of the argument, premise 2 doing all the work. The equal protection clause thus collapses into a protection of a fundamental anterior right. Justice Potter Stewart has recognized this same point, saying, "the Equal Protection Clause confers no substantive rights and creates no substantive liberties."[26]

Similarly, Westen points out that the equality language of the equal rights amendment (ERA) could be better stated in rights language without reference to equality. That is, "Equality of rights under the law shall not be denied . . . on account of sex" simply means rights under the law shall not be denied on account of sex." Why did the proponents draft it in equality language? Westen speculates, "Perhaps it is because their adversaries do not perceive the tautology and, not perceiving it, are placed in the uncomfortable position of having to argue against equality."[27]

The case of the ERA illustrates the obfuscation inherent in the rhetoric of equality. It gives the false appearance that equality is a separate and independent norm, suggesting "remedies and standards all its own." Because of the emotive force of the term *equality,* we are apt to have our critical faculties lulled into making less than fully rational decisions.

Nevertheless, legal equality may well be the most plausible version of equality. We must all adhere to the same laws and be held accountable for our behavior. Likewise, we all have some of the same legal rights: to freedom, legal representation, and the like. We may designate this basic civic equality, the assurance that we will be given equal consideration under the law. Procuring true legal equality would necessitate radical changes in our legal system, assuring that every person, rich and poor, white and black, male and female, had roughly similar prospects for legal protection and representation.

Conclusion

We have examined the concept of equality in both its formal and substantive versions, and we have concluded that formal equality is without substance, and that no substantive version of equality is without significant problems, although the doctrine of diminishing marginal utility, which advocates a diminishing gap between better-off and worse-off, is a plausible principle, connecting a form of egalitarianism with utilitarianism. Both nonegalitarians and egalitarians can oppose vast differences in wealth, though for different reasons. Nonegalitarians would be inclined to support welfare for the deserving poor, but not blanket support based simply on need. We will examine this issue in Chapter 5 on justice. Furthermore, the idea of equal human worth seems plausible only within a religious context, where God is seen as the source of human value, and where all human beings are related as siblings under one Father. The most plausible concept of equality is legal equality, the idea of aiming to give each citizen the same legal rights and responsibilities. For many people, equality means equal opportunity, the concept we turn to in Chapter 4.

For Further Reflection

1.   What is equality? Is it one thing or many? If there are many concepts of equality, how are they related to one another? Are they compatible or complementary or competing?

2.   Is equality an intrinsic good, or is it just an instrumental good to some other end, or is it neither? Is it neutral, or is it actually a bad thing?

3.   What is the relationship between equality and merit (or desert)? Are they at odds? Is treating people according to their merit an inegalitarian notion, so that merit and egalitarianism are at odds? Is Rawls correct when he (apparently) denies any natural desert for a notion of institutional desert (whereas the classical notion of justice was to give people what they deserved, the Rawlsian notion is that desert is determined by what justice dictates)?

4.   What is the relationship between equality and respect? One form of egalitarianism calls on us to respect every person equally. Is this morally required? Rawls claims that self-respect is the fundamental primary good that society should help guarantee. Is it possible to give people the bases of self-respect?

5.   What is the relationship between equality and responsibility? Are people to be held equally responsible? Are people really equally responsible in their actions? Or is responsibility fundamentally unequal?

6.   What is the relationship between equality and freedom? Many egalitarians hold that these are compatible and mutually supportive concepts. Inegalitarians disagree, holding that the more we allow people to be free, the less they will be equal and vice versa.

7.   Are all humans of equal (and positive) value? If so, what are the arguments for this claim? Does equal human worth (and with it, equal human rights) rest on a theological or metaphysical doctrine, so that lacking those doctrines, the thesis is groundless? In what sense can a secularist (e.g., Kant, Nagel, and Vlastos) justify the conclusion that all people are of positive equal worth?

8.   What is the relationship of property to equality? Rousseau held that holding property was the beginning of inequality, and Marx held that

the state should own all property and each person receive according to his or her need and give according to his or her ability.

9.   Most importantly, how is equality related to justice itself? As we will soon see, Aristotle thought the two concepts were related; nearly everyone does—both egalitarians and inegalitarians. Can we distinguish formal from substantive equality? What are the theoretical implications of such a separation? (Perhaps this is the most important part of the course.) Is justice fundamentally egalitarian?

10.   Many egalitarians (e.g., Dworkin, Rakowski, and Arneson) propose that we should compensate people only for the results of brute bad luck but not for optional bad luck. They would hold people responsible for their bad choices. If Jones, a lazy good-for-nothing, will not work, neither shall he eat. But the question may be raised, What about innocent third parties? Suppose Jones begets three children. If left to Jones's resources, the children will not be treated equally with Smith's children, who are the product of a loving, industrious home where a strong self-image is produced. Should Smith, who is struggling to support his own three children, be taxed to feed and educate Jones's children? Should Jones be forced to work to support them? Or should the state require people to prove they are able to support children before it issues them a license to propagate?

11.   Examine the notion found in Vlastos's work that society or the human race is like a family where resources are distributed according to need, not desert. Do you think this is a compelling analogy? Should we regard all human beings as members of one big family?

12.   Finally, is equality in any substantive sense a morally necessary notion? Could all legitimate "equality talk" be translated into nonegalitarian discourse? That is, is the idea of equality merely an emotive expression (a positively charged "hurrah" word)? Or is there something fundamentally correct about egalitarianism that cannot be translated without loss into other forms of discourse?

Endnotes

1. Alexis de Tocqueville, *Democracy in America,* trans. George Lawrence (Garden City, NY: Doubleday, 1969), p. 57. The book was first published in 1835.
2. Will Kymlicka, *Contemporary Political Philosophy* (Oxford University Press, 1990), p. 4, and *Liberalism, Community and Culture* (Oxford University Press, 1989), p. 40.
3. Ronald Dworkin, "In Defence of Equality," *Social Philosophy and Policy* (1983), p. 24.

4. For example, Joseph P. DeMarco and Samuel A. Richmond state, "Justice requires legislation and policy that reduces the extent to which differences in inherited wealth, gender, caste, language, religion, or social status of parents determines every other inequality" ("Is Equality a Measure of Justice?" Paper presented at the American Philosophical Association, Central Division Meeting, April 27, 1995).

5. David Hume wrote:

    All religious systems, it is confessed, are subject to great and insuperable difficulties. Each disputant triumphs in his turn; while he carries on an offensive war, and exposes the absurdities, barbarities, and pernicious tenets of his antagonist. But all of them, on the whole, prepare a complete triumph for the Sceptic; who tells them, that no system ought ever to be embraced with regard to such subjects: for this plain reason, that no absurdity ought ever to be assented to with regard to any subject. A total suspense of judgment is here our only reasonable resource. And if every attack, as is commonly observed, and no defence, among Theologians, is successful; how complete must be his victory, who remains always, with all mankind, on the offensive, and has himself no fixed station or abiding city, which he is ever, on any occasion, obliged to defend? (Dialogues Concerning Natural Religion *[Bobbs-Merrill, 1947],* p. *186f.)*

6. de Tocqueville, op. cit., p. 41.

7. This is not to deny that, practically speaking, wealth can influence one's chances of profiting from the laws. The rich can hire the best lawyers to take advantage of the laws, whether they involve tax loopholes or criminal charges. Harold Laski has written that "wealth is a decisive factor in the power to take advantage of the opportunities the law affords its citizens to protect their rights . . . Broadly, there is equality before the law only when the price of admission to its opportunities can be equally paid" (*The State in Theory and Practice* [London: Allen & Unwin, 1935], p. 175).

8. Aristotle's *Ethics,* Book 5.

9. Gracchus Babeuf, quoted in Steven Lukes, "Socialism and Equality," *Dissent* 22 (1975), p. 155.

10. Friedrich Engels, *Origin of the Family, Private Property and the State* (Lawrence & Wishart, 1940), p. 194.

11. Thomas Nagel, "Equality," in *Mortal Questions* (Cambridge University Press, 1979).

12. Christopher Jencks, *Inequality: A Reassessment of the Effect of the Family and Schooling in America* (Basic Books, 1972), p. 73. Similar expressions of equality as an intrinsic value are the following: "Other things equal, it is bad if some people are worse off than others through no voluntary choice or fault of their own" (Richard Arneson, "Equality and Equal Opportunity for Welfare," *Philosophical Studies* [56:77–93 1989]. "In my view, a large part of the fundamental egalitarian aim is to extinguish the influence of brute luck on distribution . . . Brute luck is an enemy of just equality" (G. A. Cohen, "On the Currency of Egalitarian Justice," *Ethics* 99 (July 1989), p. 931. "All

inequalities resulting from variable brute luck ought to be eliminated, except to the extent that a victim of bad brute luck waived or waives his right to compensation, or someone who enjoyed good brute luck is or was allowed to retain the benefits he received by those who have or would have had a claim to some part of them" (Eric Rakowski, *Equal Justice* [Clarendon Press, 1992], p. 74).

13. Richard Watson, "World Hunger and Equality" in *World Hunger and Moral Obligation,* John Arthur and Hugh LaFollette eds. (Prentice-Hall, 1978).

14. Quoted in George Abernethy, ed., *The Idea of Equality* (Richmond, VA: John Knox Press, 1959), p. 101.

15. de Tocqueville, op. cit., p. 57.

16. Ibid., pp. 198, 673.

17. Kai Nielsen, "Ethics without Religion," *The Ohio University Review* 6 (1964).

18. Thomas Scanlon, "Preference and Urgency," *Journal of Philosophy* 72:19 (November 6, 1975), p. 659.

19. Immanuel Kant, *Foundations of the Metaphysics of Morals,* trans. Lewis White Beck, p. 46. Kant's theory of the self and equal worth are controversial notions. Robert Paul Wolff concludes, "Strictly speaking [Kant] offers no argument at all. He just begins the next paragraph flatly with the words, 'Now I say that man and in general every rational being *exists* as an end in himself, not merely as a means for arbitrary use by this or that will'" (*The Autonomy of Reason,* [Harper & Row, 1973], p. 174f).

20. For a fuller discussion of these points, see my article "On Equal Human Worth," in *Equality: Selected Readings,* L. P. Pojman and R. Westmoreland, eds. (Oxford University Press, 1997), pp. 282–99.

21. Gregory Vlastos, "Justice and Equality," in *Social Justice,* Richard Brandt, ed. (Prentice-Hall, 1962), reprinted in *Equality: Selected Readings,* L. P. Pojman and R. Westmoreland, eds. (Oxford University Press, 1997), pp. 126–27.

22. Tom Nagel, *A View from Nowhere* (Oxford University Press, 1986), and *Equality and Impartiality* (Oxford University Press, 1991), p. 11.

23. Anatole France, *The Red Lily* (1894), chap. 7.

24. Peter Westen, "The Empty Idea of Equality," *Harvard Law Review* 95:3 (January 1982), pp. 537–96. Westen credits Justice Potter Stewart with being aware of the deceptive nature of the rhetoric of equality in constitutional law and cites D. E. Browne's "Nonegalitarian Justice," *Australasian Journal of Philosophy* 56 (1978) as someone who has defended a similar thesis.

25. *San Antonio Indep. School Dist. v. Rodriquez,* 411 U.S. I, 59 (1973) (Stewart, P., concurring), quoted in Westen, supra p. 580.

26. Stewart, quoted in Westen, op. cit.

27. Westen, op. cit.

4

EQUAL OPPORTUNITY

We have also come to this hallowed spot to remind America of the fierce urgency of now. This is no time to engage in the luxury of cooling off or to take the tranquilizing drug of gradualism. Now is the time to rise from the dark and desolate valley of segregation to the sunlit path of racial justice. Now is the time to open the doors of opportunity to all of God's children. Now is the time to lift our nation from the quicksands of racial injustice to the solid rock of brotherhood . . . I have a dream that my four children will one day live in a nation where they will not be judged by the color of their skin but by the content of their character.

—MARTIN LUTHER KING, JR, "I HAVE A DREAM" SPEECH
DELIVERED AT THE MARCH ON WASHINGTON, AUGUST 28, 1963

When a society devotes resources to education and training, when it encourages individuals to believe that their life chances will be significantly related to their accomplishments, and when it provides an attractive array of choices, that is good reason to believe that individuals will be moved to develop some portion of their innate capacities. Thus, it may be argued, equality of opportunity is the principle of task allocation most conducive to the crucial element of the human good.

—WILLIAM GALSTON

INTRODUCTION

Everyone seems to be in favor of equal opportunity. But if this were really so, why would various groups continue to protest that they are not afforded equal opportunity? Are some people simply hypocritical or confused? In this chapter we shall attempt to answer those questions. On the one hand, no concept symbolizes our vision of the American way of life more complimentarily—one in which everyone, rich and poor, smart and stupid, speedy and slow, prodigy and late bloomer, is offered an equal chance to succeed in life. Abraham Lincoln, Horatio Alger, Henry Ford, Michael Jordan, Lee Iacocca, and a hundred other "rags to riches" stories or, if not to riches, to the hall of fame, all confirm this romantic vision of

America as a land of equal opportunity. University letterheads proudly announce that the institutions are equal opportunity employers, and business corporations boast that they believe in equal opportunity for all. There may be no surer way to ruin the career of a military officer than to check the "No" box alongside the question, Does the officer support equal opportunity principles?

In the 1950s and 1960s, the civil rights movement summed up its struggle in the phrase "equal opportunity for all." The goal, of ending Jim Crow laws in the South and prejudicial practices and institutions throughout America, would offer black Americans equal access to the benefits of our nation, including the voting booth, the university, public accommodations, and real estate. In *Brown* v. *Board of Education* (1954), the U.S. Supreme Court decided that the doctrine of "separate but equal" schools was inherently unequal, for it discriminated unfairly against black children. The drive toward a racially integrated society was launched in the name of equal opportunity. Integration, it was held, would spell the end to injustice, the beginning of a new world order where the children of former slaves would compete on a level playing field with the children of former slave owners. As Martin Luther King, Jr., said in his "I Have a Dream Speech" at the 1963 March on Washington, in this new America people would be judged, not by the color of their skin but by "the content of their character." A true meritocracy in the spirit of universal brotherhood was envisioned. A similar process occurred in the women's movement, opening up new job opportunities for them. Justice became defined as equal opportunity.

Many people believe that the struggle for equal opportunity in America has essentially been accomplished. Others feel we still have a long way to go. An examination of the concept of equal opportunity should shed light on the issue. I will argue that this concept is a misunderstood one, largely because it is not one simple concept; it is a complex, multifaceted notion, containing paradoxical features, features that may conflict with other values.

THE CONCEPT OF EQUAL OPPORTUNITY

The concept of equal opportunity is a compound idea, consisting of the noun *opportunity* and the adjective *equal*. An *opportunity* is a chance to get or do something—or, more accurately, a chance for an agent to attain a goal without the hindrance of an obstacle. As such, an opportunity consists of three components: the agent A to whom the opportunity O belongs; the goal G toward which the opportunity is directed; and the absence of a specific obstacle X, which would otherwise hinder A in attaining G.[1] We can symbolize it this way:

A has an O to reach G provided that no X stands in A's way.

Note the emphasis on the agent as an individual. It is not groups, but people as individuals, who should have opportunities. Groups do not have rights or personalities; they do not have souls or feel pain or pleasure, though we use the term groups to cover sets of individuals. It follows from the thesis that justice has to do with distributing goods to individuals, for the individual is the appropriate unit of value—not the group or society as a whole.

When we say that two people are equal in something, we mean that both have been measured by a common standard and the comparison shows that they are equal in the relevant manner. So applying this to the concept of equal opportunity, we may say that two people A and B have an equal opportunity to attain some goal or good G with regard to some specific obstacle X, if and only if neither is hindered from attaining G by X. For example, in eliminating the Jim Crow laws that enforced segregation in the United States, the U.S. Supreme Court removed an obstacle preventing blacks from attending many universities in the South. Relative to the obstacle of race, blacks now had equal opportunity to attend the University of Mississippi and the University of Alabama. However, obstacles such as inferior educational backgrounds, study habits, or native intelligence were not removed.

No one can have an equal opportunity with everyone else in every way to attain a goal, for there are obstacles of time and place and personal abilities that deeply distinguish us from each other. As John Schaar notes:

> [N]ot all talents can be developed equally in any given society. Out of the great variety of human resources available to it, a given society will admire and reward some abilities more than others. Every society has a set of values, and these are arranged in a more or less tidy hierarchy. These systems of evaluation vary from society to society: Soldierly qualities and virtues were highly admired and rewarded in Sparta, while poets languished. Hence, to be accurate, the equality of opportunity formula must be revised to read: equality of opportunity for all to develop those talents which are highly valued by a given people at a given time.[2]

In our society, being a highly skilled surgeon, computer programmer, or basketball player will be rewarded more than being a highly skilled organist, farmer, blacksmith, or teacher. Talents such as being the best drug dealer, thief, con artist, or murderer in the community are positively discouraged.

The doctrine of equal opportunity implies a meritocracy, the practice of appointing the best-qualified person for the position in question. Having an equal opportunity to a good implies that irrelevant traits will be excluded from the set of criteria to be used for the assessment. Skin and eye color are irrelevant for college admittance, but grade point average and SAT scores are not. Gender is irrelevant for admittance for treatment in a hospital emergency room, but not for admittance to the maternity ward.

The doctrine of equal opportunity, in its fundamental sense, is consistent with unequal results. People are very different from each other in abilities and in effort. Equal opportunity allows competition to sort out those with more talent from those with less and reward the most talented with the goods relevant to those talents. Competition is seen as a good thing, useful in challenging us to develop our potential to the fullest. It assures that we will be treated fairly, according to our achievement, not according to our prior racial or social station. William Galston argues that this vision of equal opportunity constitutes a partial definition of a good society:

> In such a society, the range of social possibilities will equal the range of
> human possibilities. Each worthy capacity, that is, will find a place within it.
> No one will be compelled to flee elsewhere in search of opportunities for
> development, the way ambitious young people had to flee farms and small
> towns in nineteenth-century societies. Further, each worthy capacity will be
> treated fairly in the allocation of resources available for individual
> development within that society.[3]

Equal opportunity assures us of a fair chance to compete for the good things of life. In this sense, it is associated with justice, which will be considered in Chapter 5.

TYPES OF EQUAL OPPORTUNITY

I turn next to discussing four varieties of equal opportunity:

1. *Arbitrary equal opportunity.*
2. *Meritocratic equal opportunity.* Napoleonic careers open to talent. Meritocracy.
3. *Procedural equal opportunity.* Each person is free (has the chance) to develop his or her talents. The state may help in providing universal education, welfare, and job training. This is the "toolbox" model of equal opportunity. Give everyone the same tools, and let them compete in the marketplace. It will result in unequal results, however.

4. *Result-oriented equal opportunity.* This type aims at equal results. We cannot have equal opportunity until everyone is equally talented, equally equipped—has a similar toolbox. The proof of equal opportunity will be equal representation of every ethnic (gender) group in every socially prized sphere.

Let us illustrate these four types of equal opportunity.

Arbitrary Equal Opportunity

In Jorge Luis Borges's, "The Lottery in Babylon," we have an illustration of what an arbitrary lottery would look like:

> Like all men in Babylon, I have been proconsul; like all, a slave. I have also known omnipotence, opprobrium, imprisonment. Look: the index finger on my right hand is missing. Look: through the rip in my cape you can see a vermilion tattoo on my stomach. It is the second symbol, Beth. This letter, on nights when the moon is full, gives me power over men whose mark is Gimmel, but it subordinates me to the men of Aleph, who on moonless nights owe obedience to those marked with Gimmel . . .
>
> I owe this almost atrocious variety to an institution which other republics do not know or which operates in them in an imperfect and secret manner: the lottery. I have not looked into its history; I know that the wise men cannot agree. I know of its powerful purposes what a man who is not versed in astrology can know about the moon. I come from a dizzy land where the lottery is the basis of reality.[4]

Once initiated into a special order, every free man participated in the sacred lottery, which "took place in the labyrinths of the god every sixty nights". The results of the drawing were unpredictable. A lucky draw could bring about one's promotion to the council of wise men or the imprisonment of an enemy or the surprise visit of a beautiful woman in his room. A bad play could bring mutilation, various kinds of infamy, death.

Every aspect of life was affected by this intensification of chance, this "periodical infusion of chaos in the cosmos". It was a type of equality, since no one had any right to expect any more from life than anyone else. The lottery decided all—equally.

But this idea can be applied to (or be seen as a subclass of) prospect-regarding equal opportunity, which Douglas Rae tells us "consists of practices under which the prospects of success are equal for all; . . . nothing about the people affects the result."[5] Examples are lotteries, drawing lots, or flipping coins.

Ending de jure segregation and ensuring equal citizenship rights are two ways we have recently tried to accomplish this type of equal opportunity. "Blacks must be allowed to enter the same schools and restaurants under the same rules of selection as whites. Blacks must be able to vote and run for office by following the same procedures as whites." In short, "Nothing about the people [may] affect" the rules under which they operate in society.[6]

The civil rights movement was in large part about this—repealing Jim Crow laws and providing blacks with equal access to education and all of life's opportunities. Its goal was to make the rules equal for all.

Meritocratic Equal Opportunity

In the 1790s Napoleon Bonaparte rose rapidly through the ranks of the French Army and, as a General, broke from the tradition of appointing officers from the nobility and opened the field to anyone with the requisite talents, knowing from his own experience that a policy of careers open to talents would produce a more effective fighting force. Impartial meritarian criteria should be used in the choice of candidates to fill positions. It doesn't matter whether you come from a wealthy or a poor family, had a private or a public school education, or belong to the upper or the lower class. All that we care about is whether you're the best-qualified person for the job. If Michael Jordan's skin had green polka dots and he was illiterate, he would still have been the most sought-after player in basketball.

Meritocratic equal opportunity, it is hoped, will lead to a convergence of the natural and the social aristocracies. Its justifications are efficiency, the fulfillment of social promises and expectations, the respect of individuals for their talents, and the intrinsic connection between practices and qualifications.

Procedural Equal Opportunity

Each person is free (has the chance) to develop his or her talents. The state may help by providing universal education, welfare, and job training. It offers each citizen a similar toolbox, which allows him or her to compete in the marketplace. But equal input of resources produces unequal prospects of success. As Jennifer Hochschild puts it:

> Activities ranging from a poker game to a high school education are
> examples of means-regarding equal opportunity. Everyone abides by the
> same rules (a full house beats 3 of a kind, grades of D or better lead to
> promotion); everyone is given the same means (7 cards; free compulsory

school attendance). The purpose of the activity is to distinguish winners from losers in ways that people deem fair because the outcome reflects relevant characteristics of the actors.[7]

In this model, providing means-regarding equal opportunity in a racial context requires more than abolishing de jure segregation and second-class citizenship. It calls for providing equal means, not just identical rules, to blacks and whites. At a minimum, schools must be desegregated and/or improved so that black children have the same academic experience as white children; employers must pay the same wages and grant similar promotions to equally qualified blacks and whites; cities must be redistricted so that electoral arithmetic favors black candidates in some places as much as white candidates in others.

The toolbox metaphor refers to the *external means* a contestant is given by society. But contestants also need a set of skills, *internal means.* Society can give the former to people without changing their personality or character, but the latter qualities do cause such changes.[8]

External means, such as better schools, improved job prospects, and redistricting, do favor the prospects of black candidates for positions. But problems arise. What constitutes a better education? Should the state coerce institutions to institute affirmative action programs, admitting blacks with lower scores (e.g., lower SAT or GRE scores) or lesser abilities? Should the state be involved in implementing job decisions? What kind? Is redistricting for purposes of increasing black political power constitutional? And how do we know whether some people decline to use some of these tools? Are unequal results between individuals and groups an indication of prejudice and unjust discrimination or simply a function of differences in human abilities?

There is a problem in turning children into undifferentiated vessels into which society pours the "right" mix of ingredients to produce identical products. (In this model, if X wants to be a car mechanic or carpenter rather than a lawyer or physician, it is evidence that he or she hasn't been given equal opportunity in terms of internal means.) Hochschild writes: "When do we declare that all children have an equal enough set of skills so that we may switch from providing equal means to encouraging their remaining differences to distinguish them in accord with the ideal of equal opportunity? As far as I can tell—bottomless swamps to be skirted around rather than plunged into."[9]

John Rawls, rejecting weak equal opportunity, seems to hold this version of equal opportunity:

[F]air equality of opportunity . . . must not be confused with the notion of careers open to talents; nor must one forget that since it is tied with the difference principle its consequences are quite distinct from the liberal interpretation of the two principles taken together. In particular I shall try to show . . . that this principle is not subject to the objection that it leads to a meritocratic society.[10]

Rawls wants to separate *equal opportunity* that promotes talent, while being mitigated by the *difference principle,* the principle that would share the economic from the *social benefits* accrued by the talented with the worst-off members of society.

Result-Oriented Equal Opportunity

The formula here is: *equal opportunity = equal results.* Some would go further than moderate equal opportunity and argue that unless and until we have equal group results in all significant life spheres, we have not achieved equal opportunity. Until we have the same average pay for all racial, ethnic, and gender groups, and an approximate equality of representation of such in each profession (lawyers, doctors, corporate executives, university professors, physicists, plumbers, electricians, and, I guess, basketball players and criminals too), we will not have achieved equal opportunity. (A few years ago a bill was passed by the California legislature requiring that University of California graduate students be in approximate proportion to their ethnic makeup in the population. The governor vetoed the bill.) The presumption of equal results: Downsize the number of Jews in law and science, the number of blacks in basketball and entertainment, the number of Asians who have earned blackbelts in karate, the number of women in nursing and child care. For meeting these kinds of goals, aggressive affirmative action programs are needed, involving reverse discrimination. The state would have to engage in intensive social engineering, intruding on personal liberty.

Of course, the equal opportunity = equal results thesis is highly controversial, denying the legitimacy of cultural differences, family autonomy, and differences in hereditary and environmental influences. But there are arguments for each of these factors, which brings the equal opportunity = equal results thesis into question. The doctrine of equal results for groups denies the individualistic component that is at the very heart of the ideal of equal opportunity, summed up in the principle of humanity. We should be judged as individuals according to our character and talents, not according to our race, ethnicity, or gender. To get a better understanding of the value of equal opportunity, we turn to arguments for and then against the thesis.

ARGUMENTS FOR EQUAL OPPORTUNITY

Traditionally, four arguments have been given in support of the justification of equal opportunity.

1. *Equal opportunity can be justified as producing efficiency.* We want the best-skilled people in positions consistent with the effective execution of social processes. We want the best political leaders to represent us in government, the best officers to lead our armies, the most-qualified airline pilots to fly our planes, the best surgeons to operate on our loved ones and ourselves, the best athletes to play on our team, the best judges in our courts, and the best teachers in our schools. All other things being equal, a business that employs merely minimally capable workers will lose out to one that employs workers with high talent. We may speak of this as *microefficiency*, the meritocratic criterion that rewards the best-qualified person for the job in question.

But overall group merit, or *macroefficiency*, may sometimes be antagonistic to equal opportunity for the individual (microefficiency). Consider this example: You and I are competing for the position of shortstop on a baseball team. You are clearly the better shortstop, though I am pretty good and am more than minimally qualified to play the position. But we also need a left fielder, and you are the best person for that position—far better than I, who have difficulty judging long, high fly balls. The team may decide that our group efficiency will be maximized if I am assigned the shortstop position and you, the position of left fielder, in spite of the equal opportunity rule that would judge on individual merit. So sometimes aggregate efficiency, a function of utility, overrides the ideal of equal opportunity, but on the whole, the principle of efficiency will support a presumption in favor of assigning positions to those most talented in the microefficiency sense.

2. *Equal opportunity is justified by a notion of desert.* There exists a deeply felt principle that people deserve to be treated in ways that follow from relevant antecedent activities. Equals should be treated equally according to their merits. Whereas the efficiency argument is teleological, forward-looking, the desert argument is deontological, backward-looking. In virtually every known culture, people think that criminals should be punished in proportion to the seriousness of their crimes and that equal work deserves equal pay. Desert implies a notion of fittingness between effort and results. It seems intuitively obvious to most people that the good should prosper and the evil should suffer, that the punishment should fit the crime. This idea is expressed in the major religions: As the New Testament states, "Whatsoever a man sows that shall he also reap" (Gal. 6:7); in Hinduism and Buddhism, the principle of Karma assures us that our actions

in this life will determine our place in the next life. This notion of desert is contained in the common expression "What goes around comes around." Kant held that people should be happy in proportion to their moral goodness.

Desert, while generally consistent with efficiency, will occasionally be antagonistic to it—as in the case of the two baseball players who were competing for the position of shortstop (discussed above). Sometimes it seems morally right to override desert claims for other considerations. If the baseball example doesn't convince you, then consider a military one. You and I are competing to be the general who leads a division across a desert landscape against the enemy. You are clearly the best person for the job, but I am also very good (suppose you are Patton and I am Montgomery). But we also have need of a general to lead a division of troops over mountainous terrain. I happen to get altitude sickness, so only you can do this effectively. Considerations of utility would tend to override individual desert claims here and assign you to the mountains and me to the desert. Suppose the mountainous mission is far more dangerous. It's simply unlucky for you that you don't get altitude sickness.

3. *Equal opportunity enables people to develop their talents to the utmost.* Galston, to repeat the epigraph at the beginning of this chapter, puts it this way:

> When a society devotes resources to education and training, when it encourages individuals to believe that their life chances will be significantly related to their accomplishments, and when it provides an attractive array of choices, that is good reason to believe that individuals will be moved to develop some portion of their innate capacities. Thus, it may be argued, equality of opportunity is the principle of task allocation most conducive to the crucial element of the human good.[11]

But, as Galston points out, this is a very general justification and is not an absolute. Sometimes personal development requires that we risk allowing the less-qualified person to have the opportunity to develop his or her skills. We might rotate leadership for the general social good rather than allow only the single best leader to govern. We put term limits on the U.S. presidency, not necessarily because we judge an incumbent unworthy in his own right, but because of considerations such as the dangers inherent in the entrenchment of power. You may be a superior artist as compared with me, but if artistic development is vital to my fulfilling my potential as a person, I should be given the resources to do so. The policy of universal basic education is based on the thesis that in modern society, numeracy, literacy, and basic critical skills are required for even a minimally adequate life.

4. *Equal opportunity promotes personal satisfaction.* By allowing people to compete for prizes and places, society promotes individual fulfillment. In this way, equal opportunity promotes excellence; if you strive for the highest achievement, you will experience deep satisfaction in attaining it. Of course, there are dangers here, for people may aim at things they have no chance of attaining and be doomed to disappointment. There is no social good without the risk of evil. Excellence, self-discipline, and commitment, which equal opportunity supports, are all good things, but they do not provide a guarantee against foolish calculations, failure, and envy in others who, by comparing themselves unfavorably with their betters, come to loathe them. But envy is a vice that can be offset by moral education and the ideal of desert. Even if you are a better student or basketball player than I am, I can be a worthy member of our society by living an exemplary moral life, fully deserving all the benefits of our society.

But, of course, the risks of equal opportunity point to some objections, which we must now examine.

OBJECTIONS TO EQUAL OPPORTUNITY

Several philosophers have attacked the idea of equal opportunity either as violating the right of free association (Nozick), as misleadingly egalitarian (Schaar), or as inherently contradictory (Fishkin). Let us briefly examine each charge:

Nozick's "Life is not a Race" Objection

Nozick attacks equal opportunity because it violates the libertarian ideal of freedom to choose, our right to freedom of association. Life is not a race with a starting line, a finish line, an umpire, and a set of talents to be measured. Rather, individuals choose activities and exchange goods and should be left alone so long as they are not engaged in force or fraud. As an employer, I have the right to hire whomever I wish, whether he or she is the most competent person or not, even as it is recognized by society that I am free to marry whomever I please (with her consent). Nozick asks us to consider this example in which 26 men and 26 women want to get married:

> For each sex, all of that sex agree on the same ranking of the 26 members of the opposite sex in terms of desirability as marriage partners: call them A to Z and A' to Z' respectively in decreasing preferential order. A and A' voluntarily choose to get married, each preferring the other to any other partner. B would most prefer to marry A'. And B' would prefer to marry A,

but by their choices A and A' have removed these options. When B and B' marry, their choices are not made nonvoluntarily merely by the fact that there is something else they each would rather do. The other most preferred option requires the cooperation of others who have chosen, as their right, not to cooperate. B and B' chose among fewer options than did A and A'. This contraction of the range of options continues down the line until we come to Z and Z', who each face a choice between marrying each other and remaining unmarried. Each prefers anyone of the 25 other partners who by their choices have removed themselves from consideration by Z and Z'. Z and Z' voluntarily choose to marry each other. The fact that their only other alternative is (in their view) much worse, and the fact that others chose to exercise their rights in certain ways, thereby having the external environment of oppositions in which Z and Z' choose, does not mean they did not marry voluntarily.[12]

Accordingly, we can have freedom to choose without having equal opportunity with other people.

Equal opportunity, like other liberal interventions, prohibits capitalist acts between consenting adults. If I want to hire my son or daughter or best friend instead of a more qualified stranger, that's my business, not the state's. We have a right to free association that is absolute.

The right to freedom of association is important, and perhaps the state does violate it in forcing some businesses to hire applicants against the wishes of entrepreneurs. It seems that as activities become more purely personal, like the choice of marriage partners or friends, personal liberty, involving the freedom of association, increases; but as the activity becomes more public, the nondiscriminatory principle of equal opportunity increases. Where agencies are functions of the state or where they receive sizable support from the government, the principle of freedom of association ought to give way to more impartial criteria; employment should be on the basis of merit alone, according to the doctrine of equal opportunity.

Galston offers the following criticism of Nozick's libertarian proposal:

Within every community, certain kinds of abilities are generally prized. Being excluded from an equal chance to develop them means that one is unlikely to have much of value to exchange with others: consider the problem of hard-core unemployment when the demand for unskilled labor is declining. To be sure, there is more than one social context, but the number is limited. In a society in which rising educational credentials are demanded even for routine tasks, exclusion from the competition for education and training—or inclusion on terms that amount to a handicap—will make it very difficult to enter the system of exchange. Equality of opportunity acknowledges these prerequisites to full participation in social competition, and it therefore legitimates at least some of the social interventions needed to permit full participation.[13]

Schaar's Communitarian Objection

From a socialist or communitarian perspective, Schaar offers a different criticism of the doctrine of equal opportunity. According to him, equal opportunity actually supports a trend to decadence and social destruction:

> The facile formula of equal opportunity quickens that trend. It opens more and more opportunities for more and more people to contribute more and more energies toward the realization of a mass, bureaucratic, technological, privatized, materialistic, bored, and thrill-seeking, consumption-oriented society—a society of well-fed, congenial, and sybaritic monkeys surrounded by gadgets and pleasure-toys. ("Equality," p. 231)

Furthermore, the policy of equal opportunity has the ironic tendency of increasing *inequalities* among people:

> In previous ages, when opportunities were restricted to those of the right birth and station, it is highly probable, given the fact that nature seems to delight in distributing many traits in the pattern of a normal distribution, and given the phenomenon of regression toward the mean, that many of those who enjoyed abundant opportunities to develop their talents actually lacked the native ability to benefit from their advantages. It is reasonable to suppose that many members of ascribed elites, while appearing far superior to the ruck, really were not that superior in actual attainment. Under the regime of equal opportunity, however, only those who genuinely are superior in the desired attributes will enjoy rich opportunities to develop their qualities. This would produce, within a few generations, a social system where the members of the elites really were immensely superior in ability and attainment to the masses. We should then have a condition where the natural and social aristocracies would be identical—a meritocracy. ("Equality," pp. 231—32)

So equality of opportunity actually increases the gap between the elites and the ordinary folk. This is bad for democracy—it will inevitably result in the elites' ruling, dominating the lives of the poor.

But here I find a problem in Schaar's analysis. He rails against equal opportunity, because it both serves the decadent ends of our decadent social order and produces a meritocratic elite. These seem quite different and opposing items. If it is the decadence of the culture he deplores, won't equal opportunity for meritocracy provide a possibility of leadership that can change the direction of society for the better? Isn't one of the problems of our democracy precisely that we often have mediocre leaders? That we lack a natural aristocracy, Plato's philosopher-king, to lead us? What is bad is the decadence, not the equal opportunity. Equal opportunity for excellence may be the only way to save us from the dangers and destruction that perennially face us. What is important is that we produce leaders who are not sybaritic (i.e., voluptuary, luxury-loving) monkeys but moral and intellectual giants. And if equal opportunity does separate the excellent from the mediocre and the ruck, why is that necessarily bad? So long as the latter are living morally and contentedly, no harm is done if they are not put in positions of power. They may still have equal protection of the law, a vote, and their basic needs met.

But Schaar thinks that our problem is deeper. He has no trouble with temporary functional inequalities, such as the authority of a teacher over his or her students, the duty of the teacher being to transmit the subject matter to the students, and thereby to become unnecessary. Competition as we have it in our society only guarantees the equal right to inequality:

> The doctrine of equal opportunity, followed seriously, removes the question of how men should be treated from the realm of human responsibility and returns it to "nature." What is so generous about telling a man he can go as far as his talents will take him when his talents are meager? Imagine a footrace of one mile in which ten men compete, with the rules being the same for all. Three of the competitors are forty years old, five are overweight, one has weak ankles, and the tenth is Roger Bannister. What sense does it make to say that all ten have an equal opportunity to win the race? The outcome is predetermined by nature, and nine of the competitors will call it a mockery when they are told that all have the same opportunity to win. ("Equality," p. 233)

What are we to make of this? One can question the basic metaphor—life is not a single race. There are many races and if we have a low probability of winning in one, there are always others. If I am not good at football, I can take up physics; if not physics, nursing; if not nursing, carpentry; if not carpentry, being a garbage collector. But suppose I am not first at any of these. Isn't it still reassuring to know that I am contributing to the commonweal, that I am a morally responsible person, doing my best and not being a drag on society? Why is it not permissible to lose in some race— say that I am person Z on Nozick's list of eligible bachelors, who must be content with marrying Z'? Z' and I, together with our progeny, may produce the best family in the community.

Schaar seems to think that winners must automatically dominate or exploit losers. Even if there is a tendency for power to corrupt, it can be offset by checks and balances, by protection of human rights, and by training the superior to be virtuous and kind.

A variation of Schaar's criticism argues that formal equal opportunity is not sufficient to ensure justice. Bernard Williams asks us to imagine a society that has been dominated for generations by a warrior class. At some point the proponents of equal opportunity win reforms; people will henceforth be chosen on the basis of competition that tests warrior skills. A procedurally fair competition is set in place, but the children of the warrior class, having had the advantage of superior training conditions, still win.[14]

The defenders of equal opportunity will respond to Williams that there is a difference between formal equal opportunity and the substantive type, which levels the playing field so that talent alone will be rewarded. Accordingly, we must aim at the latter, which may involve providing extra educational or training opportunities to the less advantaged.

But this leveling of the playing field may not be so easy. The most interesting criticism of equal opportunity along these lines, to which we now turn, is set forth by James Fishkin.

Fishkin's Trilemma

Fishkin, drawing on examples like Williams's warrior class illustration, argues that there is something contradictory about the notion of equal opportunity—at least in the form it is held by many contemporary liberals.[15] Liberals seem to want three things in their policies: (1) equal life chances for all citizens; (2) positions assigned by merit in fair competition; and (3) family autonomy. Here is Fishkin's description of these ideals:

1. *Equality of life chances.* The prospects of children for eventual positions in the society should not vary in any systematic and significant manner with their arbitrary native characteristics.
2. *Merit.* There should be widespread procedural fairness in the evaluation of qualifications for positions.
3. *The autonomy of the family.* Consensual relations within a given family governing the development of its children should not be coercively interfered with except to ensure for the children the essential prerequisites for adult participation in the society.

Fishkin then argues that given the reality of unequal abilities in individuals and unequal conditions in families, a trilemma obtains. We can satisfy two but not all three of these principles. Suppose we aim at providing children with equal life chances and also decide to distribute positions by merit. Since children receive unequal benefits in families, we will have to abolish the family to realize this sort of equal opportunity. We would have to devise a system of collectivized child rearing similar to that described in Plato's *Republic* to offset the differential investments of families in their children.

This option will no doubt seem morally unacceptable to most of us. We look upon the family as one of those institutions necessary for human flourishing. We should be allowed to invest our resources in our children, and the state should not penalize us for doing so. Suppose you decide to limit your family to 2 children and invest all your resources in their education, and suppose your neighbors choose to have 10 children and provide only minimal resources for them, spending their money on boats or gambling. If our theory of psychological development is correct—that the early years make an enormous difference in child development—there is no way that the state can make up the difference in life chances between the two sets of children. Short of abolishing the family or the practice of rewarding positions by merit, unequal life chances will result.

If the family is to be kept, we are faced with a choice: Give up either the ideal of equal life chances or the ideal of meritocracy. If we continue to hold to the ideal of equal life chances together with family autonomy, we will have to sacrifice merit-based policies and adopt policies of affirmative action for those coming from less privileged homes. But this option has serious drawbacks. For one thing, if carried out consistently, it will no doubt result in mediocrity and inefficiency. Related to mediocrity, families will lose incentive to provide a good education for their children, for parents will reason that the best way to help their children in the long run is to deprive them, so that the state will compensate the children for their disadvantage.

Finally, if we value merit and excellence for utilitarian and deontological reasons, and continue to value the family, there is no option but to give up the notion of equal life chances. But this seems a tragic choice, for the disadvantaged children are being penalized for their bad luck of being born into families with fewer resources or less ability to care.

Naturally, trade-offs are possible: We can encourage family autonomy but supplement it with universal education, including remedial education when needed, and adopt educational enhancement programs for disadvantaged children that do not penalize families who invest their resources in their children. If we are to implement affirmative action, the rule should be: the earlier the enhancement input, the better—better a Head Start program than race norming at the time of college admission. However, strong affirmative action directed at equal results violates the essence of equal opportunity, which focuses on the individual, not group membership. Justice, wearing her perennial blindfold, weighs only one's abilities, performance, and character, not one's race or gender.[16]

Drawing on Fishkin's analysis, we can conclude that there is no way to satisfy all our legitimate social concerns in devising programs for this type of equal opportunity. Society must make difficult decisions between the ideals of equal chances, merit, and family autonomy. But one more distinction must be made, which may ameliorate the matter. With regard to positions and goods, we must separate internal goods connected with these objects from external goods, especially material rewards. Galston expresses this point well:

> A fair competition may demonstrate my qualification for a particular occupation. But the talents that so qualify me do not entitle me to whatever external rewards happen to be attached to that occupation. I may nevertheless be entitled to them, but an independent line of argument is needed to establish that fact. So, for example, in accordance with public criteria, my technical competence may entitle me to a position as a brain surgeon. It does not follow that I am entitled to half a million dollars a year. Even if we grant what is patently counterfactual in the case of doctors—that compensation is determined by the market—the principle of task assignment in accordance with talents does not commit us to respect market outcomes. Indeed, the kind of competition inherent in a system of equal opportunity bears no clear relation to the competition characteristic of the market.
>
> The distinction has an important consequence. Many thinkers oppose meritocratic systems on the ground that there is no reason why differences of talent should generate or legitimate vast differences in material rewards. They are quite right. But this is not an objection to meritocracy as such. It is an objection to the way society assigns *rewards* to tasks, not to the way it assigns *individuals* to tasks.[17]

This seems, at least partly, correct. Meritocracy aims at placing excellent people in social positions, and this does not in itself entail commensurate material rewards. Unfortunately, it is hard to separate excellence from material rewards. As John Searle has said, "Money attracts talent." One of the main incentives for developing excellence is the promise of material advantage. Market forces encourage meritocracy, but merit often seeks tangible rewards. Equal life chances, as Fishkin has pointed out, become impossible if we hold to the values of merit and family autonomy. We cannot have our cake and eat it too. The best we can obtain is a workable compromise of competing ideals.

Conclusion

Our arguments for equal opportunity seem cogent in that they take the individual seriously as the basic unit of moral and political consideration.

Equal opportunity focuses on the individual's abilities and development, not on his or her race, ethnicity, or family pedigree. The problem is that there are several different conceptions of equal opportunity: arbitrary, meritocratic, procedural, and result-oriented. Arbitrary opportunity seems a violation of our rational nature, and substantive, result-oriented opportunity seems a violation of the very notion of opportunity as focusing on the individual as the basic unit of moral consideration. Fishkin's analysis, the weightiest of the objections discussed, helps us see that pure equal opportunity is impossible. The most coherent versions of equal opportunity seem to lie in the area of meritocratic and procedural policies. Taking equal opportunity seriously entails reform of our basic institutions to make them more respondent to human needs and potential, but it still distributes offices according to talent and merit. Equal opportunity is inextricably related to justice. We turn to that subject in Chapter 5.

For Further Reflection

1.   Examine the arguments for equal opportunity. Which are stronger, and which are weaker?

2.   Examine the four types of equal opportunity. Which do you think are the most justified?

3.   Examine and evaluate the objections to equal opportunity. How do they influence your view concerning this concept? Specifically, consider Nozick's analogy of choosing a marriage partner. How relevant is this analogy to the application of the principle of equal opportunity?

4.   Do you agree with Fishkin that the notion of equal opportunity is paradoxical because it involves opposing, incompatible values? Do you see a way of solving his trilemma?

5.   Assess Galston's distinction between internal and external considerations regarding merit. Compare it with Searle's view that money attracts talent.

6.   Is strong affirmative action consistent or antagonistic to equal opportunity? Explain your answer.

7.   Examine the excerpt from Martin Luther King's "I Have a Dream" speech at the beginning of this chapter, especially the sentence, "I have a dream that my four children will one day live in a nation where they will not be judged by the color of their skin but by the content of their character." What type of equal opportunity is implicit in this rhetoric? How can we best implement that dream?

Endnotes

1. Peter Westen, "The Concept of Equal Opportunity," in *Ethics* 95:9 (July 1985), pp. 837–50, reprinted in *Equality: Selected Readings*, L. P. Pojman and R. Westmoreland, eds. (Oxford University Press, 1997).
2. John Schaar, "Equality of Opportunity and Beyond," in *Nomos IX: Equality*, R. Pennock and J. Chapman, eds.(New York: Atherton Press, 1967), pp. 228–49, reprinted in Pojman and Westmoreland, op. cit. Subsequent references to Schaar's work are noted within text as "Equality."
3. William Galston, "A Liberal Defense of Equal Opportunity," in *Justice and Equality: Here and Now*, Frank S. Lucash, ed. (Cornell University Press, 1986). The discussion in the following section is based on Galston's article.
4. Jorges Luis Borges, "The Lottery in Babylon," in *Labyrinths* (New York: New Direction Books, 1964).
5. Douglas Rae et al., *Equalities* (Harvard University Press, 1981), p. 61.
6. Jennifer Hochschild, "Race, Class, Power and Equal Opportunity," in *Equal Opportunity*, Norman E. Bowie, ed. (Westview Press, 1988), p. 93.
7. Ibid., p. 94.
8. On the topic of an *equal set of skills,* Hochschild writes: "Such internal means, which change the character or personality of their recipient, could range from teaching all first-graders that reading is fun to ensuring that all adults are equally talented and ambitious. The institutional mechanisms could run from Boy Scout troops to Kurt Vonnegut's Handicapper-General. Most debates over this more extensive form of equal opportunity focus on deciding how much energy and resources the state should devote to equalizing a few critically important skills" (Ibid., p. 98).
9. Ibid., p. 99.
10. John Rawls, *A Theory of Justice* (Harvard University Press, 1971), pp. 83–84.
11. Galston, op. cit.
12. Robert Nozick, *Anarchy, State and Utopia* (New York: Basic Books, 1974), p. 263.
13. Galston, op. cit.
14. Bernard Williams, "The Idea of Equality" in *Philosophy, Politics and Society,* Series II, Peter Laslett and W. G. Runciman, eds. (Basil Blackwell, 1962), pp. 110–31.
15. James Fishkin, "Liberty Versus Equal Opportunity," *Social Philosophy and Policy* 5:1 (1978), pp. 32–48, reprinted in Pojman and Westmoreland op. cit.
16. Many people do not realize that the civil rights movement was essentially a meritocratic equal opportunity movement, and the 1964 Civil Rights Act promised not to require preferential treatment for any group. "No employer is required to grant preferential treatment to any individual or group on account of any imbalance which may exist between the total number or percentage of persons of such race, color, religion, sex, or national origin in any community, state, section, or other area" (Title VII of the *Civil Rights Act of 1964*).
17. Galston, op. cit.

5

WHAT IS JUSTICE?

Justice, [Aristotle] said, consists in treating equals equally and unequals unequally but in proportion to their relevant differences. This involves, first, the idea of impartiality . . . Impartiality implies a kind of equality—not that all cases should be treated alike but that the onus rests on whoever would treat them differently to distinguish them in relevant ways . . . That is what is really meant by the right to equal consideration—to be treated alike unless relevant differences have been proved.
—STANLEY BENN, "JUSTICE," IN *THE ENCYCLOPEDIA OF PHILOSOPHY*,
PAUL EDWARDS, ED. (NEW YORK: MACMILLAN, 1967), VOL. 3, P. 299

Remove justice and what are kingdoms but gangs of criminals on a large scale.
—ST. AUGUSTINE, *CITY OF GOD*, IV

It is only from the selfishness and confined generosity of men, along with the scanty provision nature has made for his wants, that justice derives its origin.
—DAVID HUME, *A TREATISE OF HUMAN NATURE*
(OXFORD, ENGLAND: OXFORD UNIVERSITY PRESS, 1739)

INTRODUCTION: THE CIRCUMSTANCES OF JUSTICE

PROBLEMS OF JUSTICE ARISE, as David Hume pointed out over two centuries ago, when in situations of scarcity we, as creatures of limited sympathies, seek to adjudicate between competing claims for limited goods.* Hume refers to this as the "circumstances of justice." If either we were complete altruists or goods were unlimited, questions of justice would not rise. If we had unlimited sympathies, property would not exist and no distinctions between *mine* and *thine* would obtain. If you needed the house I built, I would share it with you or move out. If your child needed the food in my garden, she would be free to take it, and my child would help himself to

---

*This refers to distributive justice, which I discuss in this chapter. Retributive and compensatory justice have different structures. I will consider retributive justice in Chapter 8.

the food you had grown. Likewise, if there were unlimited resources, we would not worry about distribution of goods. If you wanted a car like mine, you would pick one out from the innumerable ones readily available. No competition for jobs or resources would be necessary, because there would be plenty of everything for everyone. But such is not our world. We are not complete altruists, nor are resources unlimited, but the very opposite. Consider this example: Suppose 100 candidates apply for a highly desirable position (e.g., quarterback for a professional football team, university professor, chief surgeon in a medical center, airline pilot, or CEO) for which only one opening is available. What are the correct moral and legal criteria by which to decide who should get the job? Should the selection be based on merit, need, utility, previous effort, likely contribution to be made, individual need? Or should the decision be left to market forces, giving the hiring group unlimited discretion in making its choice? Should race, ethnicity, and gender be taken into consideration? If, in the past, blacks and women or the disabled have been systematically discriminated against, should affirmative action programs engaging in reverse discrimination be used, showing favor to less-qualified women and blacks over more-qualified white males (who themselves, though innocent of wrongdoing, may have profited from past favoritism)?

Or consider the use of kidney dialysis machines in a county hospital that can afford only five machines, but has a waiting list of 20 or 30 people. How should we decide which five patients should be treated? By lottery? By a process of first come–first served? By greatest need? By merit? By desert? By utility (for example, one of the candidates is the mayor of one of the towns, who has served the community well for many years)? Or should a complex set of factors (including age, contribution, responsibilities, merit, and need) be used?

The most significant and debated issue in the debate over distributive justice is that of economic justice. There are great discrepancies between the rich and the poor. What, if anything, should we do about them? Consider the statement by Tom Cottle, comparing the salaries of baseball players with those of teachers:

> Now that Robin Yount has signed a baseball contract for more than $3 million a year, he has something in common with my wife, a public school teacher. He will earn in 3 days what she earns in 9 and 1/2 months. Prior to Yount's signature, she already had this in common with Ricky Henderson and Mark Langston. Some would say this isn't fair, but at least she doesn't have to change clothes when she goes to work . . . With Kirby Puckett, my wife shares two things; First, he will earn in one year twice what she earns in 40 years. Second, they both stand less than 6 feet tall.[1]

Do you think there is something unjust about the discrepancy between the salaries of baseball stars and those of public school teachers? Which vocation is more important for society, being a baseball player or being a teacher? Many people believe teaching is more important than professional sports. If so, what should be done about such discrepancies?

How should wealth be divided up in society? Should we simply allow the free enterprise system to determine how much money and wealth people end up with, or should we redistribute wealth through some sort of income tax policy? Should there be a vigorous welfare program, ensuring that no one falls below a certain economic threshold?

In this chapter we will address these questions as we examine three theories of justice: the classical desert theory, Locke's and Nozick's classical liberal (or libertarian) theory, and Rawls's welfare liberalism.

THE CLASSIC CONCEPT OF JUSTICE AS DESERT

The symbol of justice is a blindfolded woman, holding an equally balanced scale in her hand, the metaphor pointing to the absolute symmetry between the quality of the human actions on one side and the rewards or punishments on the other. Justice is blind to all irrelevant considerations (which birth, social status, race, and gender usually are), concerned only with giving one what he or she deserves. The earliest definition of justice in Western literature is found in Book I of Plato's *Republic, suum cuique* ("to each his due"), giving to each person what he or she deserves, based on the person's character traits, including ability, virtues, and vices. If, regarding the relevant reward, you are excellent, you deserve a suitable reward. If you are vicious, you deserve punishment; if mediocre, a mediocre benefit. Plato's *Republic* was a meritocracy, made up of people in three classes, according to their abilities. But the idea of desert, focusing more on moral actions than talents, is found earlier than Plato in Eastern thought, in the doctrine of *karma,* which holds that there is a lawlike relationship between one's deeds and one's status in a future reincarnated life. Roman law was based on this classical conception of justice, as is reflected in Ulpian's *Corpus Juris:*

> Justice is a constant and perpetual will to give every man his due. The principles of law are these: to live virtuously, not to harm others, to give his due to everyone. Jurisprudence is the knowledge of divine and human things, the science of the just and the unjust.
>
> Law is the art of goodness and justice. By virtue of this [lawyers] may be called priests, for we cherish justice and profess knowledge of goodness and equity, separating right from wrong and legal from the illegal.[2]

Similar sentiments characterize Christian statements about justice.[3] The eminent cultural anthropologist George Casper Homans observes, "Men are alike in holding the notion of proportionality between investment and profit that lies at the heart of distributive justice" and "Fair exchange, or distributive justice in the relations among men, is realized when the profit, or reward less cost, of each man is directly proportional to his investment."[4] In Gilbert and Sullivan's great comic opera, *The Mikado,* the Mikado proclaims that

> My object, all sublime,
> I shall achieve in time,
> To let the punishment fit the crime,
> The punishment fit the crime.

Merit and Desert

Let us begin our examination of the desert theory by distinguishing the two related terms *desert* and *merit,* which are often used as synonyms. Although both are appraisal terms and ordinary language uses them in multifaceted and overlapping ways, sometimes, even as synonyms, they have central meanings.[5] Merit is a broader concept, the genus of which desert is the species. *Merit,* corresponding to the Greek word *axia,* is any feature or quality that is the basis for distributing positive (or in the case of *demerit,* negative) attribution, such as praise, rewards, prizes (or penalties and punishments), and grades.[6] It signifies an appraising attitude (positive or negative), such as gratitude, praise, approval, and admiration.[7] Nondeserved merit can be features that the natural lottery has distributed, such as your basic intelligence, personality type, skin color, good looks, Irish smiling eyes, good upbringing, and genetic endowments. The most beautiful dog in the canine beauty contest merits the first prize, the tallest person in the city merits the prize for being the tallest person in the city, and a black actor merits the part of playing Othello over equally good white actors, because race is a relevant characteristic for that part, even though he did nothing to deserve his blackness. In these situations, beauty, tallness, and blackness become meritorious traits, whereas ugliness, shortness, and whiteness are demerits. The formula for merit is:

> S merits M in virtue of some characteristic (or quality) Q that S possesses

where S is the subject, M is the thing that S ought to receive, and Q is the merit base, the good (or bad) quality possessed by S.

Desert, on the other hand, is typically or paradigmatically connected with action, since it rests on what we *voluntarily* do or produce. It is typically connected with intention or effort. As George Sher writes:

> Of all the bases of desert, perhaps the most familiar and compelling is diligent, sustained effort. Whatever else we think, most of us agree that persons deserve things for sheer hard work. We believe that conscientious students deserve to get good grades, that athletes who practice regularly deserve to do well, and that businessmen who work long hours deserve to make money. Moreover, we warm to the success of immigrants and underprivileged who have overcome obstacles of displacement and poverty. Such persons, we feel, richly deserve any success they may obtain.[8]

I deserve to win the race because I have trained harder than anyone else. You deserve praise for your kind act because it was a product of a morally good will. The man or woman who works hard at a socially useful job deserves more in terms of salary than the person who loafs or works half-heartedly. The Good Samaritan deserved gratitude for helping the helpless, wounded man, who was mugged on his way to Jericho. His deed deserved to be reciprocated *preinstitutionally,* but he would have deserved praise even if his efforts had failed. On the other hand, your native intelligence, reflected in a high IQ, may be merited but not deserved, since you were born with it and didn't do anything to deserve it; a prize for being the youngest person in the room is merited but not deserved, since there's nothing the person did to deserve it; and receiving an A on a test of material you mastered effortlessly was something you merited more than you deserved. Similarly, a black actor's claim on the part of playing Othello has merit, although the actor did nothing to deserve his skin color.

Some philosophers doubt that the *merit-desert* distinction is very strong.[9] But consider this: Suppose, in times gone by, a race of humans was born with wings and light bodies; thus they could fly. Such people had great social utility, for they could fly over mountains or enemy lines with important goods or information. When there was need of a secure messenger, they would typically get picked over earthbound mortals. The flyers obtained higher salaries than walkers and enjoyed great fame and social prestige—much like star athletes do today.

The flyers didn't deserve their wings, but they certainly merited the employment and honors they were given. They were the best candidates for flying to distant places—and reaching them safely and securely. Were there no need of distant communication, their wings would have had only aesthetic value. The need for a means of communicating over long distances created the institutional value of rewarding winged people.

Contrast the flyer to the person who does everything he or she can to live a virtuous life, to practice benevolence, and to contribute to the social good. This person deserves praise and honor in a way the flyer may not (let us suppose that the flyer flies almost effortlessly). One *merits* goods, whereas the other person *deserves* them. Although I cannot develop the thought here, one must be a metaphysical libertarian or (perhaps) a compatibilist to hold to rewarding desert, but even a determinist can honor merit—indeed, may be determined to do so.

Joel Feinberg calls such meritorious qualities as intelligence, native athletic ability, and good upbringing "the bases of desert," meaning that while we may not deserve these traits, they can generate desert claims. That is, while you may not deserve your superior intelligence or tendency to work hard, you do deserve the high grade on your essay, which is a product of your intelligence and effort. (Joel Feinberg "The Concept of Desert" in *Justice,* C. J. Friedrich and John W. Chapman, eds. [New York: Atherton, 1963])

The formula for desert is:

S deserves D in virtue of doing (or attempting to do) A

where S is a subject; D is the property, thing, or treatment deserved; and A is the act, the desert base for D.[10]

Desert, then, is closely connected to effort and intention, whereas merit signifies positive qualities that call forth positive response. Whereas God, knowing our inner motivations, rewards purely on the basis of desert, we fallible beings, being far less certain as to how to measure effort and intentionality, tend to reward merit, the actual contribution or positive results produced. You and I may both get the same *merit* pay bonus for producing 100 more widgets than the average worker, but I may deserve the bonus more than you do, since your superior native ability enabled you to produce them effortlessly, whereas I had to strain every ounce of strength to get the same result.

An interesting example of the conflict between desert and merit occurred recently during the Summer Olympics in Atlanta, Georgia (August 3, 1996). Carl Lewis, one of the leading United States athletes, having won his ninth gold medal in the long jump, requested that he be added to the United States men's 400-meter relay team. He argued that because of his superior ability, he merited being included. Many athletes and fans agreed with him and requested that the coach substitute Lewis for one of the other runners. Some of the other spectators and runners, including those who feared being displaced by Lewis, were outraged at his audacity. They argued that Lewis shouldn't be put on the team because he didn't deserve to be on it in spite of his great talent, for he turned down the opportunity to enter the tryouts for the team. Those who made the team had played by the rules, won their places in fair competition, and could legitimately expect to run. Here is a case where merit and desert seem to conflict, and where desert, it seems to me, wins out over merit. It wins out because we have a legitimate institution (the process of competing for a position on a team) in which those who play by the rules deserve to be rewarded with the positions that they fairly won.[11]

Finally, we may distinguish desert and merit from *entitlement,* positive rights. Even though I am a lazy bum who is undeserving of any wealth, I am entitled to the inheritance that my rich uncle bequeaths to me. For Rawls, as we will note below, all desert claims reduce to entitlements and justified entitlements are those obtaining in a society governed by the principles of justice as fairness. But desert and merit seem more fundamental qualities than rights, which are primarily products of human institutions. (We will examine the concept of rights in Chapter 7.) The desert theory is really a two-pronged theory, stating that distribution of goods should be made on the basis of desert or merit, depending on the situation.[12]

Many people think that Karl Marx is an opponent of the classic notion of justice based on desert, since he uttered the famous formula for distributive justice, "From each according to his ability, to each according to his need." But this would be to misinterpret Marx, who actually defends the classic notion. In his *Critique of the Gotha Program,* Marx attacks utopian communists such as LaSalle for uncritically adopting the needs-based motto. Distribution according to need should take place only in the ideal communist society, where all people are equally deserving, since they are all contributing according to their maximal ability. Until that time, in the socialist society, the motto must be "from each according to his ability, to each according to his contribution."[13] Indeed, Marx's condemnation of capitalism is based on the classical idea of justice as desert. His labor theory of value condemns capitalists as vampires and parasites for stealing from and exploiting the workers. Say that a worker makes a chair with a certain labor value, deriving from his skill and labor, and we give it a value of 100, translating that into monetary terms, $100. The capitalist pays the worker only a fraction of his value, say $25, keeping the rest for himself, thus growing rich on such exploitive thefts. Of course, the capitalist has a right to deduct overhead costs from the total value, the costs of the raw material and machines used, say $10, but he goes far beyond that and robs the worker of the remainder, the other $65. This is unjust, claims Marx, for the worker deserves far more than he receives. Exploitation is giving people less than they deserve, less than you owe them.

My point, of course, is not to defend Marx's labor theory of value but to indicate how widespread it was in the history of Western thought. It was held by both the father of capitalism, Adam Smith, as well as the greatest anticapitalist, Karl Marx; by both the greatest deontologist, Immanuel Kant, and the greatest utilitarian, John Stuart Mill, who thought that rewarding people according to their deserts would lead to maximal utility. The intuitionist W. D. Ross uses a thought experiment to establish the doctrine of justice as desert:

> If we compare two imaginary states of the universe, alike in the total amounts of virtue and vice and of pleasure and pain present in the two, but in one of which the virtuous were all happy and the vicious miserable, while in the other the virtuous were miserable and the vicious happy, very few people would hesitate to say that the first was a much better state of the universe than the second. It would seem then that, besides virtue and pleasure, we must recognize, as a third independent good, the apportionment of pleasure and pain to the virtuous and the vicious respectively. And it is on the recognition of this as a separate good that the recognition of the duty of justice, in distinction from fidelity to promise on the one hand and from beneficence on the other, rests.[14]

Problems with the Classic Doctrine of Justice

Today, the classic doctrine of justice is under siege. The leading political philosophers, from liberals such as John Rawls and Stuart Hampshire to libertarians such as F. H. Hayek and Robert Nozick, to communitarians such as Michael Sandel, reject it. How did this come about? Philosophers have found three significant problems with the doctrine of desert that have led many to abandon it and others to subordinate it under other ideals. They are (1) a criteria problem of determining exactly what is the appropriate desert base—contribution, performance, effort, or compensation; (2) an epistemological problem of measuring how much a person deserves; and (3) a metaphysical problem of determining whether the concept is even coherent. I will briefly examine each of these problems.

THE CRITERIA PROBLEM   This problem seeks to determine whether the relevant desert base should be one's contribution, compensation, or effort. Take a simple example of the cooperative venture of pushing a car up a steep hill. Three people are pushing the car. A is putting in the greatest effort, but B is the most effective, since he is the strongest, while C has made the greatest sacrifice to push the car, leaving her lucrative job for the afternoon to help out. How do we determine the relative values of these acts? Sometimes, particular desert bases seem intuitively fitting, such as giving grades on the basis of performance, rather than compensation or effort. The person who meets the highest standards receives the highest grade whether or not he or she made a great effort. Sometimes this problem can be solved, but at other times, it's not clear how to compare or apply desert bases.[15]

THE EPISTEMOLOGICAL PROBLEM   This problem arises because of the increasing cooperative venture involved in modern labor. Desert seems more suitable to an agrarian world where each person is responsible for his or her own plot of land (echoing the biblical notion "that whatsoever a man soweth that shall he also reap") than to the complexities of modern industry. Even Marx's labor theory of value seems misplaced, for few tables or chairs are made by single carpenters working alone; increasingly, workers labor in cooperation with each other, so it is a herculean task to measure the effort or contribution of any single individual. A hundred or more people may work on various aspects of materials in producing a final product, such as an automobile, airplane, ship, or skyscraper. How would one go about measuring who deserved what economic reward in producing the automobile's various components, let alone in designing them and the car itself? It would be almost as difficult to measure the contribution of each member of both teams in a tug-of-war.[16] As Rawls notes, even if we could figure out the ways to do the measuring, such measuring seems impracticable (John Rawls, *A Theory of Justice* [Harvard University Press, 1971]).

THE METAPHYSICAL PROBLEM   This problem of determining whether the concept of desert is even coherent is based on the increasingly naturalist interpretation of human actions, which sees our actions based in a deterministic scheme, caused by factors over which we have no control, our genetic endowment and environment. Rawls put it like this:

> No one deserves his greater natural capacity nor merits a more favorable starting place in society. But it does not follow that one should eliminate these distinctions. There is another way to deal with them. The basic structure can be arranged so that these contingencies work for the good of the least fortunate . . .
>
> It seems to be one of the fixed points of our considered judgments that no one deserves his place in the distribution of native endowments, any more than one deserves one's initial starting place in society. The assertion that a man deserves the superior character that enables him to make the effort to cultivate his abilities is equally problematic; for his character depends in large part upon fortunate family and social circumstances for which he can claim no credit. The notion of desert seems not to apply to these cases. Thus

the more advantaged representative man cannot say that he deserves and therefore has a right to a scheme of cooperation in which he is permitted to acquire benefits in ways that do not contribute to the welfare of others. (*A Theory of Justice,*[Harvard University Press, 1971] p. 104)

The British philosopher Stuart Hampshire is even more explicit about the incoherence of desert:

Is there anything whatever that, strictly speaking, a man can take credit for, or he can properly be said to deserve, with the implication that it can be attributed to him, the ultimate subject, as contrasted with the natural forces that formed him? In the last analysis, are not all advantages and disadvantages distributed by natural causes, even when they are the effects of human agency? . . . I think it would be better to think of all advantages, whether naturally acquired or conferred by men, as unearned and undeserved . . . After genetic roulette and the roulette of childhood environment, a man emerges, so equipped, into the poker game of social competition, within a social system determined by largely unknown historical forces.[17]

The argument against the notion of desert runs like this:

1. If we deserve anything, we must be the authors of our own selves (to have the kind of free will necessary to be responsible for our actions and achievements).
2. We are not the authors of our own selves.
3. Thus we do not deserve anything.

It is true that we do not deserve our genetic endowment or the early environment we inherited. But couldn't we still be said to deserve what we make of those lottery-endowed traits? No, for even the tendency to make an effort is a product of deterministic, antecedent causes.

This is the argument that has persuaded a number of philosophers to reject the notion of desert, but is this a sound argument? I don't think it is. There are a number of places to attack it, but one quick way to defeat it is to present an argument for some kind of suitable free will, either the libertarian variety, which holds that some acts are caused by the self alone rather than antecedent factors, or the compatibilist variety, which holds that so long as we act voluntarily (i.e., are not coerced by internal or external forces against our will), we are responsible for our actions, and so deserve what we get as a result. The arguments are complicated, so I cannot develop them here, but anyone who thinks freedom of the will makes sense will have reason to reject the Rawls–Hampshire argument.[18] Suffice it to say that not only does their argument defeat any notion of desert, it also destroys the notion of responsibility. If the argument against desert is sound, not only don't we deserve anything, we are not responsible for anything either. Human responsibility is an illusion. For if everything is the product of the genetic-environmental lotteries, the serial roulette wheels of fortune, how can we be held responsible for our actions, good or bad? Hitler wasn't responsible for starting the Second World War or exterminating 6 million Jews; the lotteries of life were. Timothy McVeigh wasn't responsible for blowing up the Federal Building in Oklahoma City in 1996; the roulette wheels of destiny were. So why did we execute McVeigh in June 2001? Is it all a matter of bad luck and lotteries?

Although Rawls uses the natural lottery argument, he seems to place more weight on the impracticality of making desert judgments. We must leave the discussion there for the moment and turn to the two accounts of the two criteria that have replaced desert as the material criteria of justice: rights and need. *Rights,* especially property rights, have been put forth by classical liberalism, sometimes known as libertarianism, as the content of justice. *Need* has been put forth by socialists and modern welfare liberals as the criterion of justice. We turn first to classical liberalism and the justification of property, beginning with the work of John Locke and then with his most articulate twentieth-century disciple, Harvard philosopher Robert Nozick. After this, we will examine the welfare liberalism of Nozick's teacher, the most important political philosopher of the twentieth century, John Rawls.

CLASSICAL LIBERALISM AND THE JUSTIFICATION OF PROPERTY

It is very clear, that God, as King David says, Psal. cxv. 16, "has given the earth to the children of men," given it to mankind in common . . . Though the earth, and all inferior creatures, be common to all men, yet every man has a property in his own person: this no body has any right to but himself. The labor of his body, and the work of his hands, we may say, are properly his. Whatsoever then he removes out of the state that nature hath provided, and left it in, he hath mixed his labor with, and joined to it something that is his own, and thereby makes it his property. It being by him removed from the common state nature hath placed it in, it hath by this labor something annexed to it, that excludes the common right of other men. For this labor being the unquestionable property of the laborer, no man but he can have a right to what that is once joined to, at least where there is enough, and as good, left in common for others.

—JOHN LOCKE, *SECOND TREATISE OF GOVERNMENT,* 1789, SECT. 27

Justice, according to Rawls, is the dominant concept of economically advanced societies like ours, where contract and private property are key
characteristics. Justice is not a dominant concept in primitive societies,
where duties of generosity and reciprocity reign. In many cultures taking
your neighbor's boat or weapon when you need it is not considered stealing, since the idea of property is not well defined. Societies concerned
with social justice are generally relatively stable, economically advanced
communities, where private property is a dominant institution.[19] In primitive societies the concept of justice is related more closely to partiality and
relationships than it is in our more impersonal society. For example, in a
primitive society it would be wrong not to give an important job to a close
relative, if one were a candidate, whereas in our society one would be
charged with the crime of nepotism.

All wealth is property, a word that comes from the Latin *proprietas,*
meaning "ownership." All property was once unowned, as part of nature.
This book is made up of paper that comes from wood, which comes from
trees, having an ancient pedigree in primeval forests that go back in time,
before human beings. Similarly, the bricks, stone, and steel of our buildings, molded and transformed by human labor, were once part of rock
formations and sand deposits on glacial plains. Similarly, the grapes from
which we ferment wine and the grains from which we make our bread appeared in nature long before humanity. If the earth belongs to no human,
how can human beings claim parts of it as their own? How does natural
material become owned by individual people?

John Locke's justification of property in Chapter 5 of his *Second Treatise of Government* (1789) offers the classical account of the origination and
legitimacy of property. He writes the words quoted at the beginning of this
section, that God has given the earth to all men in common, but for our
individual survival and enjoyment has allowed us to have our own property from which we can exclude others: "Whatsoever then he removes out
of the state that nature hath provided, and left it in, he hath mixed his labor with, and joined to it something that is his own, and thereby makes it
his property." Originally, all things were owned in common, which meant
that they were not really owned, in the sense that we could do whatever we
wanted with the earth's resources. But human beings had to eat or perish.
They partook of the fruits and nuts of the forest to survive. If no one ever
expropriated anything, all would die. Property acquisition is need-based.
A person may take what he or she needs to survive. Locke, as a Christian,
believed that God gave the earth to humanity to use for our survival and
enjoyment. We may take what we need and by mixing our labor with it,
make it our own. But God put two provisos on our use of nature:

For this labor being the unquestionable property of the laborer, no man but he can have a right to what that is once joined to, at least where there is enough, and as good, left in common for others. . . . (sect. 27)

    Nor was this appropriation of any parcel of land, by improving it, any prejudice to any other man, since there was still enough, and as good left; and more than the yet unprovided could use. So that, in effect, there was never the less left for others because of his enclosure for himself. For he that leaves as much as another can make use of, does as good as take nothing at all. Nobody could think himself injured by the drinking of another man, though he took a good draught, who had a whole river of the same water left him to quench his thirst: And the case of land and water, where there is enough of both, is perfectly the same. (sect. 33)

According to Locke, one must leave "enough, and as good" for others. That is, one must not hoard or greedily exclude others from the earth's bounty. And, secondly, one must not waste. We must not take more than we need for our survival and flourishing. We have right to property, extending from our own bodies to what we appropriate in nature and mix our labor with. But we are to be good stewards of the earth, not abusing it or selfishly accumulating material possessions. The basic argument goes like this:

1. I own my body and my labor.
2. In laboring with nature, I mix my labor with the object.
3. If the object is unowned, it becomes my property.

The idea is that by changing part of nature through my work, say, by turning a tree into a table or chair, I extend my body into the object. Is this true? We might point out that those who are not able to work cannot own anything in this primary way. In addition, the argument relies on a biblical account of human origins. If there is no god, it may not seem as cogent. In *Anarchy, State and Utopia* (henceforth cited as *ASU*), Robert Nozick has pointed to a problem. The argument that mixing labor with nature or land entitles you to it seems to rely on a missing premise P:

P: If I own something and mix it with something else, that is unowned, I acquire ownership of that other thing. "Ownership seeps over into the rest."[20]

But why, Nozick asks, "isn't mixing what I own with what I don't own a way of losing what I own rather than a way of gaining what I don't? If I own a can of tomato juice and spill it into the sea so that its molecules (made radioactive, so I can check this) mingle evenly throughout the sea, do I thereby come to own the sea, or have I foolishly dissipated my tomato juice?" (*ASU*, p. 175) But, funny as the counterexample is, it seems uncharitable to Locke, for dumping the can of tomato juice into the sea would not be directly mixing your labor with the sea, and presuming to gain possession of the sea in this way would violate the proviso of leaving as good and as much for others. It would be a greedy self-aggrandizement. As Nozick himself points out, it would not add value to the sea. Locke has in mind such activities as cutting down unowned trees and using the wood to build your house and fences, cultivating the land, planting corn and potatoes. Here the argument takes on an aspect of desert—"what a man sows that should he reap." By expending energy and intelligent effort, the laborer transforms a part of the forest into a farm and deserves the fruits of his or her labor, whereas the freeloader who takes the farmer's goods deserves nothing.

Once the property is yours, you may sell it or give it away, but you may not destroy it wantonly, since you are a steward of property that ultimately belongs to God. However, there is still the problem of inheritance. If the only reason you have a lot of property and I very little is because your great, great grandfather came here before my father, this seems unfair. At any rate, Locke's argument seems meant for a pioneer society, such as that of the settlers in America's Western frontier, but seems less applicable in most countries today where virtually all the inhabitable land is already owned. There simply isn't "enough, and as good" left over for others.

We can understand why Rousseau would rail against the notion of private property:

> The first man who, having enclosed a piece of ground, bethought of saying, "This is mine," and found people simple enough to believe him, was the true founder of civil society. For how many crimes, wars, murders, from how many horrors and misfortunes might not any one have saved mankind by pulling up the stakes or filling up the ditches and crying to his fellows, "Do not listen to this impostor. You will be ruined if you forget that the fruits of the earth belong to us all, and the earth itself belongs to no one."[21]

Private property in a world of scarcity and need can be challenged. P. J. Proudhon said, "Property is theft," and Marxists would abolish private property, but, as Hume argued, private property has great utility. It provides security and enjoyment that enhance our lives. Even if one does not completely accept Locke's argument, one might be persuaded by Hume's commonsense utilitarian reasoning. Even communist countries permit people to own their own private good, forbidding only ownership of the means of production.

Nozick accepts a version of Locke's theory of property and sets forth a rights-based *entitlement theory of holdings,* involving the principle of justice in acquisition and transfer of holdings. A distribution is just if everyone has that to which she or he is entitled. To determine what people are entitled to, we must understand what the original position of holdings or possessions was and what constitutes a just transfer of holdings. Borrowing from John Locke's theory of property rights, Nozick argues that we have a right to any possession so long as our ownership does not worsen the position of anyone else. His three principles are:

1. A person who acquires a holding in accordance with the principle of justice in acquisition is entitled to it.
2. A person who acquires a holding in accordance with the principle of justice in transfer, from someone else entitled to the holding, is entitled to the holding.
3. No one is entitled to a holding except by (repeated) application of 1 and 2. (*ASU*, p. 151)

Nozick later adds a principle of rectification of injustice in holdings. If a holding was acquired unjustly, justice requires that it be restored to the original owner. But the basic idea is Lockean. Nozick's entitlement theory of holdings is historical, dependent on how the acquisition came about. If the original acquisition of property came about by someone's appropriating an unowned piece of nature, that person was entitled to and could pass it down or transfer it as he or she so desired, so long as the Lockean proviso was adhered to.

Next Nozick distinguishes between patterned and nonpatterned schemes of distributive justice: "Let us call a principle of distribution *patterned* if it specifies that a distribution is to vary along with some natural dimension, weighted sum of natural dimensions, or lexicographic ordering of natural dimensions." A *patterned* principle chooses some trait or traits that indicate how the proper distribution is to be accomplished. It has the form: To each according to _____.

Socialists believe that *need* is the relevant trait. Meritocrats believe *merit* is. Utilitarians would say the trait is *utility.*[22] Classisists would put *class status* in the blank. A pluralist might put a combination of traits in the blank, depending on the type of distribution to be made.

But Nozick's theory is a *nonpatterned* scheme. There is no preordained formula it must adhere to, no pattern it must follow. If it came about justly, the holding is yours, period, and no one has a right to take it away from you.

> From each according to what he chooses to do, to each according to what he
> makes for himself (perhaps with the contracted aid of others) and what
> others choose to do for him and choose to give him of what they've been
> given previously (under this maxim) and haven't yet expended or
> transferred. (*ASU*, p. 160)

Or, to state it more succinctly, "From each as they choose, to each as they
are chosen."

Nozick's theory maximizes human liberty much in the way Mill prescribed (see Chapter 2), advocating laissez-faire capitalism. Granting people liberty to acquire and transfer property prohibits the government
from limiting what they do with their property or from taxing it.

Nozick rejects patterned types of principles, such as those of Rawls (see
below) because such attempts to regulate distribution constitute a violation of liberty. Taking liberty seriously would upset patterned distribution
schemes. He illustrates this point by considering how a great basketball
player, Wilt Chamberlain, could justly upset the patterned balance. Suppose that we have reached a patterned situation of justice based on equality. Imagine that there is a great demand to watch Chamberlain play
basketball and that people are willing to pay him an extra 25 cents per
ticket to see him play. If 1 million people pay to see him play during the
year, the additional gate receipts add up to $250,000. Chamberlain thus
takes home a great deal more than our patterned formula allows, but he
seems to have a right to this. Nozick's point is that, to maintain a pattern,
one must either "continually interfere to stop people from transferring resources as they wish to, or continually interfere to take from some persons
resources that others for some reason chose to transfer to them." A socialist or welfarist society would have to "forbid capitalist acts between consenting adults"(*ASU*, pp. 161, 163).

We might well object, "OK, Chamberlain can upset the pattern, but
only so far. We, the people, through our elected government, have a right
to tax some of that money, so we can use it for the needy." But Nozick has
a response: Taxation constitutes forced labor, a form of slavery. Consider
the following: Suppose I am charged a 25 percent income tax on my earn-
ings. I work a 40-hour week, so I am working 30 hours as a free citizen and
10 hours (25 percent of my time) as a slave to the government. Stephen
Kershnar points out that during slavery, some owners permitted slaves to
work on the shipyards and keep whatever they made beyond a specific
amount, thus providing an incentive to work harder. Taxation is a kind of
slavery within an incentive scheme, but it is still slavery, which is exploitation. The free market should be left unregulated and each person left free
to behave as prudently as he or she is able.

Of course Nozick and libertarians such as von Hayek, Milton Friedman, and John Hospers stress that they are not against private voluntary
beneficence to ameliorate the suffering of the poor and needy, who in fact
may be victims of an unrestricted free market. But there is a problem with
private charity, for some beneficent projects may succeed only if they involve large-scale coordinated programs. Consider what is sometimes called
the *assurance problem*. Suppose I am a beneficent individual who wants to
support the poor. I see an advertisement for the Voluntary Welfare Fund
(VWF), which promises to aid large numbers of the deserving poor. I am
inclined to contribute to the VWF, but I reason as follows: Either a sufficient number of others will contribute to the collective effort to make the
project successful even if I don't contribute to it, or not enough others will
contribute to it even if I do contribute to it. Since my contribution is small
relative to what is needed (though it represents a considerable sacrifice on
my part), the probability that my input will make a difference is low. But if
it is low, then it is rational for me to withhold my contribution from the
VWF. But if others are thinking this way, the worthy project, which we all
believe in, will not get the needed support, and the poor will go unaided.
So a government-enforced program of taxation may be needed to coordinate the good will of morally concerned, but rational, individuals. Adam
Smith, the father of modern capitalism and a believer in market freedom,
put the matter this way, pointing out the three duties of government:

> All systems either of preference or of restraint, therefore, being thus
> completely taken away, the obvious and simple system of natural liberty
> establishes itself of its own accord. Every man, as long as he does not violate
> the laws of justice, is left perfectly free to pursue his own interest his own way,
> and to bring both his industry and capital into competition with those of any
> other man, or order of men. The sovereign is completely discharged from a
> duty, in the attempting to perform which he must always be exposed to
> innumerable delusions, and for the proper performance of which no human
> wisdom or knowledge could ever be sufficient; the duty of superintending
> the industry of private people, and of directing it towards the employments
> most suitable to the interest of the society. According to the system of natural
> liberty, the sovereign has only three duties to attend to; three duties of great
> importance, indeed but plain and intelligible to common understandings:
> first, the duty of protecting the society from the violence and invasion of
> other independent societies; secondly, the duty of protecting, as far as
> possible, every member of the society from the injustice or oppression of
> every other member of it, or the duty of establishing an exact administration
> of justice; and, thirdly, the duty of erecting and maintaining certain public
> works and certain public institutions, which it can never be for the interest of
> any individual, or small number of individuals, to erect and maintain;

because the profit could never repay the expense to any individual or small number of individuals, though it may frequently do much more than repay it to a great society. (*Wealth of Nations*, 1776)

Libertarians like Nozick agree that government may tax us to carry out its first two duties, provide for an army and a police force to protect us from external attack and internal violence. But they sometimes forget the third duty, to which Smith draws our attention. There simply are some beneficial projects too costly for a small number of individuals to carry out successfully, which the government can and should carry out. Examples of these are a national mail service, state and federal highways, public education, a sanitation system, and pollution control. These seem reasonable, but why can't government also carry out a more extensive welfare scheme? Granted, there are numerous types of welfare schemes, many of which are not justified by good moral reasoning, so these institutions need to be carefully devised, but to preclude them in the way modern libertarians do seems unwarrantedly dogmatic. Smith's broader vision of government's duties within a free market framework seems more reasonable. Paying one's taxes can be seen as an expression of gratitude for a system that protects us from force, fraud, and pollution, and enhances our lives by providing public sanitation, basic education, and a welfare safety net for those who through no fault of their own end up unemployed or destitute.

There is another problem with Nozick's theory. If we were to take the historical acquisition premise seriously, we would probably find it doubtful whether the ownership of most or any of the property owned in the world is justified. A great deal of it was appropriated not through original mixing of labor, but by military invasion, plunder, violence, and fraud. On Nozick's principles, we would have to give much of the land in the United States back to the descendants of the native Americans who were here first and from whom much of the land was taken. It is probably wiser, let alone more moral, to have a reasonably generous policy toward land use and property, accepting our responsibility to aid those in need.

Finally, we should note that libertarians may well have a point in emphasizing the value of liberty and the dangers of governmental intervention in our lives. Governments can become oppressive by imposing heavy taxes on people. Elected representatives often remain in power by directing government revenues to local constituencies. But when every representative begins to think this way, the cumulative effect is a tragedy of the commons, where the system is endangered.

We turn now to the very opposite of libertarianism—welfare liberalism.

JOHN RAWLS'S WELFARE LIBERALISM: JUSTICE AS FAIRNESS

All social primary goods—liberty and opportunity, income and wealth, and the bases of self-respect—are to be distributed equally unless an unequal distribution of any or all of these goods is to the advantage of the least favored.

—JOHN RAWLS, *A THEORY OF JUSTICE*, 1971
(HENCEFORTH CITED AS TJ), P. 303

In our next theory, John Rawls's *justice as fairness,* we have what is probably the most important contribution to political philosophy in the twentieth century, one that both friends and foes must come to terms with. Stuart Hampshire called it "the most substantial and interesting contribution to moral philosophy since the [Second World] War [wherein] the substance of a critical and liberal political philosophy is argued with an assurance and breadth of mind that puts the book in the tradition of Adam Smith and Mill and Sidgwick."[23] Robert Nisbett calls it the "long awaited successor to Rousseau's *Social Contract,* the Rock on which the Church of Equality can properly be founded in our time." In scope and power it rivals the classics of Hobbes, Locke, and Rousseau. Deservedly, no philosophical work in the past 24 years has been quoted or debated more than this one. Fundamentally egalitarian (see quotation above), it seeks to justify the welfare state. Rawls accepts that liberal ideas of justice can be justified only where the "circumstances of justice" obtain, that is, in situations of relative affluence, like those in Westen nations.

Rawls's theory is egalitarian, distinguishing itself from utilitarian rivals by its focus on meeting individual needs rather than on aggregate or average welfare:

> Each person possesses an inviolability founded on justice that even the welfare of society as a whole cannot override. For this reason justice denies that the loss of freedom for some is made right by a greater good shared by others. It does not allow that the sacrifices imposed on a few are outweighed by the larger sum of advantages enjoyed by the many. Therefore, in a just society the liberties of equal citizenship are taken as settled; the rights secured by justice are not subject to political bargaining or the calculus of social interests. (*TJ,* p. 3)

Rawls is an egalitarian, one who believes that minimally rational human beings (sometime called "persons"), who have a conception of the good and are able to act justly, are valuable and equally so:

> It seems reasonable to suppose that the parties in the original position are equal. That is, all have the same rights in the procedure for choosing

principles; each can make proposals, submit reasons for their acceptance, and so on. Obviously the purpose of these conditions is to represent equality between human beings as moral persons, as creatures having a conception of their good and capable of a sense of justice. The basis of equality is taken to be similarity in these two respects. Systems of ends are not ranked in value; and each man is presumed to have the requisite ability to understand and act upon whatever principles are adopted. Together with the veil of ignorance, these conditions define the principles of justice as those which rational persons concerned to advance their interests would consent to as equals when none are known to be advantaged or disadvantaged by social and natural contingencies. (*TJ*, p. 19)

Justice as fairness is, in Nozick's terms, nonpatterned, in that it doesn't reward according to any specific criterion, such as desert, contribution, or need, though the latter plays an important role in the system. Rawls agrees with Nozick that patterned versions of justice are faulty and that maximal liberty is a social requirement, but he disagrees with libertarian views like Nozick's, which make negative liberty into an absolute value. Instead, Rawls presents a version of the social contract that is broadly Kantian, in which a theory of just procedures takes the place of substantive principles.

In *A Theory of Justice,* John Rawls sets forth a hypothetical contract theory in which the bargainers in the original position go behind a *veil of ignorance* to devise a set of fundamental agreements that will govern society. "Certain principles of justice are justified because they would be agreed upon in a situation of equality" (*TJ*, p. 21). Behind the metaphorical veil, no one knows his or her place in society, class, gender, race, religion, generation, social status, fortune in the distribution of natural assets and abilities, or even intelligence. They do not know their conception of the good. That is, each has a different idea of what makes life worth living, based on his or her moral or religious or aesthetic theories. The millionaire has a conception of the good different from that of the Trappist monk. This information, making up the *thick theory* of the good, could influence the contractor's deliberation, so it must be withheld. Those in the original position do have basic psychological knowledge about human nature, and have a common *thin theory* of the good. They know the *primary goods*—the liberties, opportunities, wealth, income, and social bases of self-respect. These are fundamental values, for whatever else people want, they will rationally want these basic goods. The capitalist, the monk, the dancer, the garbage collector, and the philosopher will all value liberty and self-respect and a certain amount of wealth. Parties to the contract are to act as mutually disinterested (i.e., they don't envy others for their good fortune), rationally self-interested agents, and choose the basic principles that will govern their society.

By denying individuals knowledge of their natural assets and social position, Rawls prevents them from exploiting their advantages, thus transforming a decision under risk (where probabilities of outcomes are known) to a decision under uncertainty (where probabilities are not known). To the question, Why should the individual acknowledge the principles chosen in the original position as morally binding? Rawls would answer, "We should abide by these principles because we all would choose them under fair conditions."

Rawls thinks that these conditions in the original position ensure objectivity and impartiality of judgment. If you don't know any significant facts about your particular identity, you will be less likely to be biased in your favor. You will resemble the ideal of the blindfolded justice who is committed to balancing the scales, only you are to do so from a self-interested point of view. Think of the U. S. Supreme Court justices who had to decide whether the Florida electoral vote in the 2000 presidential election, which was challenged by the Democratic constituencies, was fair. Many people believed the justices were biased in making their controversial 5-to-4 decision according to ideological lines. Suppose we had a drug that would cause people to forget their party loyalties and particular interests, but remain rational agents. We could have given it to the justices and have expected a different voting pattern. Perhaps there would have been near unanimity one way or the other rather than a narrow decision.

One further requirement of this hypothetical contract is that the contractors, as rational choosers, are to maximize the minimal position one could fall into, choosing the arrangements "as though your enemy were to assign you a place in society". Rawls calls this the *maximin* principle. He argues that the rational chooser will pick a system where, in a reasonably affluent society, you will do relatively well even on the bottom of the social-economic ladder. Putting this principle in monetary terms (to simplify), we can imagine three types of societies:

	Society 1	Society 2	Society 3
A: Income	$70,000	$50,000	$40,000
B: Income	$50,000	$ 5,000	$20,000
C: Income	$ 4,000	$35,000	$10,000

Which society would it be rational to choose? Classical utilitarians would choose society 1, for it maximizes utility, giving the highest aggregate. But Rawls thinks we will reject this, since we are concerned to maximize not aggregate utility, but the worst-off position, since we are choosing under uncertainty and have no way of ensuring that we won't end up at the bottom. So applying the maximin strategy, the rational person would choose society 3, though it has the lowest aggregate and the lowest average utility. But if you're the worst-off in society, you will be better off than if you were in societies 1 or 2. Rawls has been criticized for being too conservative here. Rational choosers might gamble and choose a society with a higher chance of doing better. One could also opt for an average utilitarian position, by calculating expected utility to be had in each society by summing up the amounts of welfare of all the people and dividing by the number. The society that offered the highest expected utility would be the one with the highest expected average utility, and thus be the one chosen. One could also follow R. M. Hare's modified utilitarian suggestion and provide a welfare safety net, ensuring that everyone's basic needs are met, but then allowing individuals to advance their economic and social positions as far beyond the mean as is possible. This is the rationale of most social systems in Western Europe. There is no ceiling on income, but the poor are assured of a minimum income below which they will not be allowed to fall. The principle of economic efficiency, pareto optimality,[24] which holds that an advancement in economic gain is optimal if no one is made worse off by it, would favor Hare's approach. It would seem to favor the notion of giving people incentives to work hard. Consider the scheme (in the table below) of distributing primary goods. If citizen B by gaining 40 more units will raise worse-off citizen A's allotment by 5 points, Rawls's maximin principle would allow B's advancement. But it would not allow B's further advancement to 100 units, since that doesn't raise A's allotment. The pareto principle would permit B's advancement, since no one is worse off and one person is better off.

UNITS OF PRIMARY GOODS	
Citizen A	*Citizen B*
10 units	10 units
15 units	50 units
10 units	100 units

It seems rational to choose a society that permits the third row of distributions to occur. Or consider a counterexample given by Russell Keat and David Miller: Suppose "a starving man has to choose which of two boxes to open, on the basis of the following information: the first contains two loaves of bread; the second may contain a single loaf, or it may be packed with food—he is told nothing about the relative likelihood of each of these outcomes."[25] Would it not seem rational to choose the second box, since it does contain at least the minimum amount to stave off starvation and may contain a great bonus?

Rawls calls his system "justice as fairness" because he seeks a contract on whose fairness all parties will agree. In effect, the parties to the contract should choose the kind of principles they could live with if their enemies were assigning them positions in society. Rawls argues that they would choose the following two principles:

1. Everyone will have an equal right to the most extensive basic liberties compatible with similar liberty for others.
2. Social and economic inequalities must satisfy two conditions:
   (a) They are to the greatest benefit of the least advantaged ("the difference principle").
   (b) They are attached to positions open to all under conditions of fair equality of opportunity. (*TJ*, pp. 302–3)

These principles are to be arranged in lexical order: first, principle 1—equal extensive liberty for all; second, principle 2(b)—equal opportunity to all positions in the society. Achieving this would require that income and resources be redistributed from those who have abundance to those who have inadequate resources. Finally, principle 2(a)—arrangements that apply the difference principle—would permit inequalities if and only if they redound to the benefit of the worst-off.

The controversial principle is 2(a), the difference principle. Rawls subsumes it under the ideal of fraternity, of "not wanting to have greater advantages unless this is to the benefit of others who are less well off" (*TJ*, p. 105). He likens fraternity to the relationship in a family where members do not wish to gain unless they do so in ways that advance the interests of the other members. You would be assured that if you ended up on the social bottom, everything was being done to arise your prospects, that your condition was a priority.

Rawls would like to distribute resources equally, but he sees two problems. First, unless a high level of goods is available in society, equality at a subsistence or mediocre level of affluence is not desirable, so we should encourage economic disparities if that will enable the bottom to rise. This notion is contained in the expression "a rising tide raises all ships." The second problem is related to Rawls' prescriptions. Socialist programs enforcing equal distributions undermine incentive. Most people will work harder if they believe they will have a more affluent life as a result. Rawls seeks to capitalize on this truth by tying economic advancement to raising the position of the worst-off members of the society.

Finally, as we noted earlier in this chapter, Rawls rejects the notion of desert as applicable to social justice:

> No one deserves his greater natural capacity nor merits a more favorable starting place in society. But it does not follow that one should eliminate these distinctions. There is another way to deal with them. The basic structure can be arranged so that these contingencies work for the good of the least fortunate . . .
>
> It seems to be one of the fixed points of our considered judgments that no one deserves his place in the distribution of native endowments, any more than one deserves one's initial starting place in society. The assertion that a man deserves the superior character that enables him to make the effort to cultivate his abilities is equally problematic; for his character depends in large part upon fortunate family and social circumstances for which he can claim no credit. The notion of desert seems not to apply to these cases. Thus the more advantaged representative man cannot say that he deserves and therefore has a right to a scheme of cooperation in which he is permitted to acquire benefits in ways that do not contribute to the welfare of others. (*TJ*, p. 104)

> The better endowed are more likely, other things equal, to strive conscientiously, and there seems to be no way to discount for their greater good fortune. The idea of rewarding desert is impracticable. And certainly to the extent that the precept of need is emphasized, moral worth is ignored . . . For a society to organize itself with the aim of rewarding moral desert as a first principle would be like having the institution of property in order to punish thieves. (*TJ*, p. 312 f)

Natural talents, in a sense, are a common asset, collectively owned.[26] Justice rejects the notion of preinstitutional desert—rewards or status that is due to us by virtue of our abilities, achievements, merit, or effort. The classic notion that justice is giving people what they independently deserve is replaced by the notion that people deserve what justice (institutionally) dictates. Rawls should say more about his rejection of desert. As I argued in the first section of this chapter, he seems to hold that since we are all determined by heredity and environmental conditions, especially our family upbringing, our talents are the result of a natural and social lottery. We can't take credit for any of our talents, virtues, or vices, so we can't take credit for what we do with our talents or virtues. At other times Rawls seems to say that it's just impracticable to take desert into account. Now that we are coming to the close of our discussion of justice, we can ask the question raised in the first section, Is it true that desert cannot function as a principle of justice? Giving up desert isn't without serious consequences for morality and autonomy, concepts Rawls surely wants to keep. But if we're autonomous agents, then don't we deserve the consequences of our actions? If I knowingly injure someone without justification or murder someone, shouldn't I be punished for it—because I deserve to be punished—not simply because punishment may deter crime? Doesn't Rawls's own system in which those who benefit the worst-off are allowed to keep their advantage of goods, depend on a notion of desert? Don't they deserve to keep their extra resources because they have benefited the worst-off, fulfilling the condition of the difference principle? Further, Rawls wants us to respect ourselves and others, but respect can't be given by fiat—it must be earned. We must believe we are worthy of respect, that we deserve it. We may disagree as to the exact place of desert in the constitution of justice, whether it can exist alone or must be balanced by the concept of need or even rights (see Chapter 7), but it is an ineliminable feature of any plausible conception of justice. That Rawls fails to appreciate these points certainly undermines his project. But his theory may be revised to incorporate a desert provision and thus survive. He makes the point that it is often impracticable to reward on the basis of desert. But even this may be an exaggeration. Don't we take desert into consideration in deciding whether the accused is guilty of the crime? We may not be able to do this with the exactness we would like, but the concept of mens rea is a well-established quality in determining guilt or innocence in criminal trials. We can often base our rewards or praise on this feature too. If a person makes every effort to obtain skills to get a job, we deem him more worthy of our help than someone who doesn't. Certainly, in close communities, we make these judgments all the time, holding people accountable for their actions. If we apply this notion of desert to the difference principle, it has the effect of modifying its application. Some of the worst-off may not deserve to be given more primary goods, so we have no obligation to them beyond minimal maintenance. Similarly, some of the needy may not deserve to be helped. We may help them out of mercy and kindness, but that is not justice, but benevolence.

What may be true is that justice doesn't consist merely in requiting desert. Need may also be a relevant canon of distribution of resources. Perhaps in a generally affluent society like ours, distributive justice consists in a combination of meeting needs and requiting desert. But the details of such a theory take us beyond the parameters of this chapter.

An Assessment of Rawls's Theory of Justice

There are many diverse criticisms of Rawls's theory besides his neglect of desert. I will briefly discuss a few of the more prominent.

Rawls has been criticized by commutarians, such as Michael Sandel, for leaving his contractors behind the veil of ignorance without personal identity, as mere abstract, thin men:

> Rawls' principles do not mention moral desert because, strictly speaking, no one can be said to deserve anything—On Rawls' view people have no intrinsic worth, no worth that is intrinsic in the sense that it is theirs prior to or independent of . . . what just institutions attribute to them.[27]

By subtracting all their contingent traits, he has left only the shell of a person. This criticism seems unfair. What Rawls is doing is setting forth an ideal condition of impartial judgment, as we expect in umpires in baseball games and referees in basketball games. This idea of impartiality, set forth in the opening quotation of this chapter by Stanley Benn, seems necessary for all rational thinking. We want to ensure fairness as well as justice, so I think Rawls can meet this criticism.

A second criticism, set forth by Wallace Matson, is that Rawls confuses fairness with justice. Rawls seems misleading in characterizing justice as a kind of fairness, for these two concepts are distinct. Fairness is comparative, whereas justice is noncomparative. A law may be unjust but fair in that it is applied consistently. I may give you a grade lower than what you deserve, say, a C instead of a B, but since I similarly downgrade all my students, I am still treating you fairly, though unjustly. It was said of the great Green Bay Packers football coach, Vince Lombardi, that he treated his players equally, treating them all like dogs. Since they were human beings, not dogs, Lombardi treated them unjustly but fairly. Similarly, the notion of a fair wage is not the same thing as a just wage. If I pay men $15 per hour for a job that I pay women only $10 per hour, I am unfair, but if I pay them both only $10 per hour when they deserve more, I am unjust, but not unfair.[28]

As we have already noted, Rawls's difference principle and its associate, the maximin principle, can be challenged. Rawls seems correct in elevating need to a canon of justice and recognizing that in an affluent society like ours, the government should do more than simply promote negative liberty. It should also redistribute some wealth to the worst-off, ensuring that their basic needs are met. Meeting needs is a controversial subject, for it's not always clear what a basic need is. Surely, having sufficient nourishment, shelter, and clothing are basic needs. In our society having a basic education is a basic need. In many communities having an automobile or a radio may be a basic need, so what counts as a basic need in many cases seems to be relative to the social context. Rawls seems correct over against Nozick and other libertarians in recognizing that justice includes meeting basic needs. He may, however, go too far in correcting for that neglect, underappreciating the need for personal responsibility and desert. Citizens must be held accountable for their actions and should be rewarded and punished accordingly. But, to reiterate, if we should give those who do evil what they deserve, why should we not give those who do good what they deserve? There is a symmetry between rewards and punishment. The good should receive appropriate good, as the evil should receive appropriate evil. It seems reasonable to suppose that contractors behind the veil of ignorance would choose to award benefits and burdens (punishments) according to desert.

One reason for Rawls's underappreciation of responsibility is his emphasis on the right over the good, that is, his concern to be neutral about the thick conception of the good. Government should be neutral on conceptions of the good, leaving that to individuals to determine on their own. But others, called *perfectionists,* hold that the state is morally required to promote an objective theory of the good. We turn to that issue in the next chapter.

Conclusion

We have noted Hume's circumstances of justice, that justice becomes salient in a situation of moderate scarcity where people have limited sympathies. We have examined several theories of justice: the notion that justice involves giving people what they deserve, Locke's and Nozick's libertarian notion of property rights, and Rawls's welfare liberalism. Although each theory has strengths, it seems reasonable to conclude that justice has something to do with both meeting people's basic needs (presuming these people are not undeserving) and rewarding people according to their desert.

For Further Reflection

1.   Examine the concept of justice as desert. What are its strengths and weaknesses?
2.   Distinguish desert from merit and rights.
3.   Examine Locke's theory of property. Is it plausible? Is there a better argument for the justification of property? Explain.
4.   Examine and evaluate Robert Nozick's libertarian theory of justice.
5.   What is the veil of ignorance? What function does it play in Rawls's theory of justice?

6. What is Rawls's difference principle? Is it a plausible principle you would choose behind the veil of ignorance?

7. Distinguish between Rawls's concepts of the thick theory of the good and the thin theory of the good.

8. Evaluate Rawls's theory of justice. What are its strengths and weaknesses?

9. What is the maximin principle? Do you agree that it would be chosen behind the veil of ignorance?

Endnotes

1. Tom Cottle, "Throwing a Curve at Our Teachers," *Boston Sunday Globe,* January 7, 1990, quoted in Stephen Nathanson, *Economic Justice* (Prentice-Hall, 1996), p. 3.
2. Ulpian, in the *Digest* of the Roman book of law *Corpus Juris,* ca. 200 A.D.
3. Witness, for example, Gal. 6:7, "Whatsoever a man sows that shall he also reap," and G. W. Leibniz's idea of justice as fitting desert in his *Theodicy:* "Thus it is that the pains of the damned continue, even when they no longer serve to turn them away from evil, and that likewise the rewards of the blessed continue, even when they no longer serve for strengthening them in good. One may say nevertheless that the damned ever bring upon themselves new pains through new sins, and that the blessed ever bring upon themselves new joys by new progress in goodness: for both are founded on the principle of the fitness of things, which has seen to it that affairs were so ordered that the evil action must bring upon itself chastisement" (Leibniz, *Theodicy,* trans. E. M. Huggard [1698]).
4. George Caspar Homans, *Social Behavior: Its Elementary Forms* (Routledge & Kegan Paul, 1961), pp. 246, 264.
5. See J. R. Lucas, *Responsibility* (Oxford University Press, 1993), for a useful, though overly simplified, version of the standard view. See Fred Feldman, "Desert: Reconsideration of Some Received Wisdom," *Mind* 104 (January 1995).
6. In Homeric culture the idea of merit is detached from intention, or our idea of moral responsibility. As A.W. Adkins writes, "The Homeric king does not gain his position on the grounds of strength and fighting ability. He belongs to a royal house, and inherits wealth, derived from the favored treatment given to his ancestors, which provides full armor, a chariot, and leisure. Thus equipped, he and his fellow *agathoi* [nobles], who are similarly endowed, form the most efficient force for attack and defence which Homeric society possesses. Should they be successful, their followers have every reason to commend them as *agathoi* and their way of life as *arete* [virtuous]; should they fail, their followers have every reason to regard this failure, voluntary or not, as *aischron* [shameful]. A failure . . . in the Homeric world must result

either in slavery or annihilation. Success is so imperative that only results have any value; intentions are unimportant" (A. W. H. Adkins, *Merit and Responsibility: A Study of Greek Values*, 1960, p. 35).

7. See David Miller, *Social Justice* (Oxford University Press, 1976), for a good discussion of appraising attitudes and their relationship to desert claims. The relevant section is reprinted in L. Pojman and O. McLeod, eds., *What Do We Deserve?* (Oxford University Press, 1999), pp. 93–100. We may note that while admiration may have as its object any value, praise (and blame) are only appropriate to desert claims.

8. George Sher, *Desert*, p. 53.

9. John Kleinig, in an Elvesier Encyclopedia entry on *desert*, writes that if there's anything to it, it's soft.

10. This is not a full characterization, since temporal indexicals need to be included. The reader can easily apply these. I leave them out to keep the discussion focused on the essential differences.

11. One may even say that they have a *right* to the spot. In this case the language of rights and desert seem to coalesce. The controversy over Lewis's participation was exacerbated by the fact that Canada unexpectedly beat the United States for the Gold Medal. Could Lewis's participation have prevented that? Should it have mattered?

12. For a more detailed defense of this position, see my article "Does Equality Trump Desert?" in *What Do We Deserve?* L. Pojman and Owen McLeod, eds. (Oxford University Press, 1998), pp. 283–97.

13. Karl Marx, *Critique of the Gotha Program*, in *Karl Marx: Selected Writings*, D. McLellan, ed. (Oxford University Press, 1977), pp. 566f.

14. W. D. Ross, *The Right and the Good* (Oxford University Press, 1930), p. 138.

15. A desert base is the criterion by which a benefit is to be bestowed. For example, the appropriate base for winning a race is the fastest time, whereas the base for moral praise is good intention. Joel Feinberg first identified the notion.

16. See David Miller, *Social Justice* (Oxford University Press, 1976), pp. 102–14, for a good discussion of this problem.

17. Stuart Hampshire, "Review of Rawls' *Theory of Justice*," *New York Review of Books* 18:3 (February 24, 1972), pp. 34–39. I am indebted to Jeff Moriarty for this quote.

18. I have defended this strategy in my essay "Free Will, Determinism and Moral Responsibility: A Response to Galen Strawson," in my book *Ethical Theory*, 4th ed. (Wadsworth, 2002).

19. For an insightful discussion of the sociological aspects of justice, see David Miller, *Social Justice* (Oxford University Press, 1976), chap. 8. Miller refers to the anthropologist E. Westermarck's observation of the behavior of Eskimos of the Bering Strait: " if a man borrows an article from another and fails to return it, the owner is not entitled to claim it back, as they consider that when a person has enough property to enable him to lend some of it he has more than he needs" (p. 260).

20. Robert Nozick, *Anarchy, State and Utopia* (Basic Books, 1974), p. 174.

21. J. Rousseau, *Discourse on the Origins of Inequality,* reprinted in L. Pojman, *Political Philosophy.*

22. Nicholas Rescher argues for a pluralist theory of justice wherein various criteria (canons)—equality, need, merit, desert-effort, contribution, and others—play a role; all fitting under the classical formula: render to each his due. The difficulty consists in how to decide which canon applies to which situation.

23. Stuart Hampshire, "A New Philosophy of the Just Society," *New York Review of Books* 18:3 (February 24, 1972).

24. A state S1 of a system is pareto optimal if and only if there is no feasible alternative state system S2, such that at least one individual is better off in S2 than in S1 and no one is worse off in S2 than in S1. Hare's suggestion is in "Rawls' Theory of Justice," in *Reading Rawls,* Norman Daniels, ed. (Blackwell, 1975). For similar points, see John Harsanyi, *Essays on Ethics, Social Behavior and Scientific Explanation* (Dordrecht, Netherlands: Reidel, 1976); Harry Frankfurt, "Equality as a Moral Ideal," *Ethics* 98.1 (October 1987).

25. Russell Keat and David Miller, "Understanding Justice," *Political Theory* 2:1, February, 1974.

26. We see then that the difference principle represents, in effect, an agreement to regard the distribution of natural talents as a common asset and to share in the benefits of this distribution, whatever it turns out to be. Those who have been favored by nature, whoever they are, may gain from their good fortune only on terms that improve the situation of those who have lost out" (*Theory of Justice,* p. 101).

27. Michael Sandel, *Liberalism and the Limits of Justice* (Cambridge University Press, 1982), p. 88.

28. Wallace Matson makes this criticism in several places, including in his "Justice: A Funeral Oration," reprinted in L. Pojman, *Political Philosophy: Modern and Contemporary Readings* (New York: McGraw-Hill, 2002). In that article, by a series of imaginative tales Matson contrasts natural justice (the authentic type) over against Rawls's paternalistic justice. The former is bottom up and based on voluntary agreements, while the latter is top down, based on the will of government. In the former, freedom is the starting point and property the necessary good; in the latter, equality is the goal and the government effectively owns all property. The mistake of paternalistic, or top down, justice is to suppose that the love and egalitarianism of the family can be extended to society at large. Matson illustrates the tension between these two motifs that exists in the philosophy of John Rawls, who with his first principle of liberty expresses bottom-up justice, but with his second, difference, principle—which distributes all inequalities in favor of the parties that are worst off—expresses top-down, paternalistic, justice.

6

STATE NEUTRALITY VERSUS
STATE PERFECTIONISM

[T]hose who care for good government take into consideration virtue and vice in states. Whence it may be further inferred that virtue must be the care of the state which is truly so called, and not merely enjoys the name, for without this end the community becomes a mere alliance.

—ARISTOTLE, *POLITICS* III.9

Political decisions must be, so far as possible, independent of any particular conception of the good life, or of what gives value to life.

—RONALD DWORKIN, *A MATTER OF PRINCIPLE*
(HARVARD UNIVERSITY PRESS, 1985), P. 127

Justice as fairness . . . [does not] try to evaluate the relative merits of different conceptions of the good . . . . There is no necessity to compare the worth of the conceptions of different persons once it is supposed they are compatible with the principles of justice. Everyone is assured an equal liberty to pursue whatever plan of life he pleases as long as it does not violate what justice demands.

—JOHN RAWLS, *A THEORY OF JUSTICE*
(HARVARD UNIVERSITY PRESS, 1971), P. 94

INTRODUCTION: THE CLASSICAL DEBATE

IN 1957 THE WOLFENDEN COMMITTEE, mandated by the British government to draw up a recommendation regarding the practice of homosexuality, issued the famous Wolfenden Report, in which it argued that there existed a realm of private morality that is sacrosanct, so that the government may not intervene. Essentially, it was a Millian position (discussed in Chapter 2), proceeding on the premise that the only legitimate grounds for criminalizing behavior was protection of the society. Where the individual alone is involved, he or she is sovereign. A distinguished British judge, Lord Patrick Devlin, took exception to the report and in 1959 gave an equally famous lecture, "Morals and the Criminal Law,"[1] in which he argued that the public/private morality distinction was bogus. Where society has deep, widespread, shared values, it should legislate them into criminal law. Just as laws against treason are necessary to protect the state from traitors, so laws against immoral private behavior are necessary to protect the community from corruption and, eventually, dissolution. Hence, since the reasonable person condemns homosexual behavior as immoral, the state has a right to criminalize such behavior. Soon afterward, the Oxford University Professor of Jurisprudence H. L. A. Hart published a sharp critique of Devlin's lecture in the British weekly *The Listener.*[2] Hart defended the Wolfenden Report, taking a Millian position and arguing that the state ought not interfere in people's private lives. This debate inaugurated the present controversy of whether the state may or should criminalize what the broader society perceives as immoral behavior. The debate has been extended by such philosophers as John Rawls, Ronald Dworkin, Robert George, and George Sher to cover the issue of pluralism regarding a vision of the good and the moral virtues in general.[3]

The Devlin argument is the following:

1. A community must have a set of rules, supported by tradition and adhered to by the majority of its people, in order to maintain social cohesion and harmony.
2. Western society contains a tradition to which the vast majority subscribe, which includes the promotion of heterosexual relations but rejects homosexual relations as an approved form of sexual expression.
3. Therefore, since we desire social cohesion and harmony, we ought to support the promotion of heterosexual relations but reject homosexual relations.

Devlin assumes, as was likely the case at the time, that a vast majority of the British public rejected explicit homosexuality as a permissible lifestyle. Devlin seems to allow for change, so that the content of the moral consensus could change over time, giving rise to acceptance of homosexual lifestyles, but until that happens, the law should reflect the majority's biases.

Recently, a child molester, who had served his time and was released on parole, began writing fiction about all the sexual things that might be done to children and circulating his writings among his fellow pedophiles. He was arrested and tried, and pled innocent of any crime, holding that writing fiction was protected by the First Amendment and was not a parole violation. The court found him guilty of such a violation and put him back in prison.[4] Devlin would very likely approve of such a judgment, arguing that writing such fiction and sharing it with pen pals undermines the communal moral fabric, even if it does not threaten anyone in particular.

There is a classical political tradition, going back to Plato, Aristotle, and Aquinas, which holds that a salient function of the state is to help citizens realize the good life, including making people virtuous. An objective theory of the good is discoverable by reason; hence the role of government is to inculcate this notion of the good in its citizens. This tradition is sometimes referred to as *perfectionism*, since it aims at using the powers of the state to make citizens as morally excellent (or near to perfect) as possible (see the opening quote from Aristotle).

This ideal has been under attack for some time. A rival to the perfectionist tradition has replaced it in the minds of many political theorists, one emphasizing liberty, autonomy, and value neutrality, together with a protectionist role for the state. While the roots of this theory are found in Kant's ideal of autonomy, it was John Stuart Mill who, in his classic work *On Liberty*, argued that the role of government is to protect citizens from being harmed by others. They should be left alone to do whatever they want, so long as they do not unjustifiably harm others. This modern theory is referred to at the *protectionist* model of government as opposed to the ancient Greek *perfectionist* model. Although the debate really gets a jumpstart with the Devlin–Hart exchange, an earlier and perhaps more powerful defense of protectionism is that of Karl Popper's *The Open Society and Its Enemies*, vol. I (1944), in which he attacks Plato's perfectionism as a kind of fascism (comparing it to Nazism, a brand of perfectionism that in the name of perfect justice created a perfect hell of injustice, *summum justicia, summa injuria*).[5] Rather than imposing a rigid straight jacket, a single vision of morality, onto the world, it is more fitting that the state see its function as protecting people from harm and allowing them to work out their own visions of the good. The assumption here is that there are many types of the good life, a plurality of visions of the good, so the perfectionist model not only deprives people of their legitimate autonomy, but falsely supposes that it has the only correct theory of how life should be lived. For Popper, the very notion of secular democracy entails pluralism. Perfectionism is simply a euphemism for intolerance, tyranny, coercion, and oppression.

This protectionist neutralist model has been developed by contemporary liberal political philosophers, such as John Rawls (see the quotation at the beginning of this chapter), Ronald Dworkin, Bruce Ackerman, Charles Larmore, and Jeremy Waldron, under the name of *neutralism*.[6] That is, the state should be neutral concerning particular theories of the good. Governments ought to provide stability and minimal order in society so that individual self-determination can flourish. Government and its laws ought to remain neutral between rival conceptions of the good life for human beings, and the government ought to be forbidden to impose any one particular moral outlook.

Ronald Dworkin explicitly represents this liberal neutralist position: "Political decisions must be, so far as possible, independent of any particular conception of the good life, or of what gives value to life." But the most celebrated neutralist theory is that of John Rawls, who, in his magnum opus *A Theory of Justice* (1971; discussed in Chapter 5) argues in the spirit of Kant and Mill that justice as fairness requires that each citizen have maximal liberty to pursue his or her own notion of the good life, so that behind the *veil of ignorance* the individual does not even know his or her conception of the good. Rawls seems to reject perfectionism for two reasons: (1) because it violates the autonomy of citizens and (2) because it lacks a comprehensive rational defense. The second criticism seems ambiguous —between a skeptical argument and a relativistic argument about the good. With that in mind, let us examine the four major arguments against perfectionism: (1) the argument from relativism, (2) the argument from skepticism, (3) the argument from tyranny, and (4) the argument from autonomy. Later in the chapter, I will distinguish legal from moral perfectionism and outline a version of moderate perfectionism.

The Argument from Relativism

Rawls says, "A community is simply an arena in which individuals each pursue their own self-chosen conception of the good life, and political institutions exist to provide that degree of order which makes such self-determined activity possible." Rawls seems to imply that everyone and every subculture can choose their own values.

One argument for state neutrality regarding the good, which Rawls may be embracing, is moral relativism, the theory (which we discussed in Part Two of the Introduction of this book), that there is neither objective moral good nor universal moral truth. All moral principles are relative to culture, so we cannot impose our moral values on anyone. Reason cannot justify a general core conception of the good. "Goodness," as I've heard students proclaim, "is in the eye of the beholder—or at least of his or her culture. Everything, including morality, is relative." But we want to ask, Is this really so? Is slavery just as morally justified as freedom? The oppression of women as morally justified as a society with equal rights for all? Nazi culture as justified as that of a group of peace-loving altruists such as Gandhi, Mother Teresa, Albert Schweitzer, Jesus Christ, and Martin Luther King, Jr.? If ethical relativism is true and the majority is always right, reformers are always wrong—including the ones mentioned in the previous sentence. But aren't the reformers sometimes right and society wrong? If morality is about promoting welfare and human flourishing, some moral systems would seem to be better than others. Why oppose injustice or oppression or even culturally approved terrorist acts if there is no objective right or wrong?[7]

But if there is a common human nature, and the goal of morality is to promote human flourishing, then doesn't it seem obvious that we'll need certain definite rules, such as don't kill innocent human life, don't steal or cheat, don't lie or break your promise, don't cause unnecessary suffering, help those in need, and cooperate with others? Doesn't the success of Rawls's own contract theory depend on the contractors' being faithful to the contract chosen behind the veil of ignorance?

I think many people think that they are moral relativists because they identify moral objectivism with moral absolutism, the view that some principles may never be overridden. One who believes in objective morality (in moral truth) typically holds that moral principles are universally binding but prima facie principles. They are universally valid, but may conflict with other moral principles, and sometimes be overridden by them. Also, the objectivist doesn't say that all moral principles are universally valid. Some, like sexual mores, may be relative to circumstances and culture. Although some sexual mores may be relative to culture, principles such as honesty and respect for others are not. Consider someone with a sexually transmitted disease such as HIV concealing that fact from the person with whom he is about to have unprotected sex. Ironically, Devlin, whose essay sparked this whole debate regarding neutralism, appears to have been a moral relativist, holding that a community's moral beliefs should be enshrined in law. In fact, this usually happens, but the philosophical question is, Are the community's beliefs true and morally justified? Just because a community is homophobic does not mean that homosexual relations are immoral. A principle of tolerance may enjoin us to expand our ideas of what is morally permissible.

If the arguments offered in the Introduction are sound, moral relativism is false and there is at least a minimal core morality that constitutes a conception of the good, one that every society will need if it is to flourish. Indeed, some contemporary liberal neutralists, such as Dworkin and Waldron, accept the notion of an objective core morality but still fear the undermining of autonomy and the danger of an oppressive tyranny inherent in the perfectionist's vision. As the quotation at the head of this chapter indicates, Rawls thinks that society needs a minimal level of tolerance and respect for others, but within the scheme of justice, individuals must be left alone to develop their own particular theory of the good life.

The Argument from Skepticism

As we noted in the previous chapter, Rawls says that behind the veil of ignorance no one knows his or her conception of the good. So we cannot give any particular conception of the good special status. Hence, the state must be neutral regarding the good. But, as Jeremy Waldron has noted, neutralists should be careful of demanding neutrality about values, for neutrality itself is a value, a normative position, "a doctrine about what legislators and state officials ought to do."[8] Indeed, Rawls's admission that we have basic knowledge of human nature seems to entail that we have knowledge of the core morality, those principles that may be included in the set of primary goods, those goods that we would want, whatever else we might want. We would want some primary goods for our children, our fellow citizens and, it is hoped, ourselves. These primary moral goods would include the cardinal virtues of honesty, fidelity, benevolence, discipline, nonmaleficence, respect, and tolerance for others. Rawls prizes autonomy, but, then, isn't autonomy part of our conception of the good? All these things seem constitutive of the good life and the good community, relevant to any society, and Rawls actually seems to presuppose them in his notion of compliance with the basic ideas of his theory of justice as fairness.

I suspect Rawls, Dworkin, Popper, and others are motivated in their rhetoric of neutrality by a concern to protect society from religious authoritarianism and fanaticism, such as might come about through the influence of fundamentalist Islam, Hinduism, Protestantism, and Roman Catholicism, and which might gain widespread power if a majority chose such theories of the good, perhaps leading to homophobia, prohibition of alcohol and cigarettes, and the suppression of women, if not to outright persecution of minority points of view. The concern to protect minority rights is salutary, but we don't have to give up a basic core conception of the good to safeguard the tolerance of nonconformity. Tolerance itself is a moral value, part of our conception of the good.

Perhaps we could make a distinction between a general theory of the good (part of Rawls's idea of the thin theory of the good, discussed in Chapter 5) and particular theories of the good (the very thick theory of the good), including religious and other ideological worldviews. The general theory would include the core morality discussed above, including integrity, fidelity, honor, benevolence, discipline, tolerance, and nonmalevolence, all of which can be defended by reason. The particular theories would include religious and ideological doctrines, which must be held by faith or aesthetic preference.

If contractors in the original position would choose the liberty principle and the difference principle, why shouldn't we suppose they would choose those moral principles necessary for the flourishing of the just society? After all, don't we have to be people who keep our commitment to make the just society work? Isn't a certain core morality presupposed in the very idea of justice as fairness or any other kind of flourishing social system? Similarly, Dworkin's rights system is based on equal concern for people. But isn't mutual concern a virtue that must be encouraged by the society as a whole? Isn't mutual concern part of a general theory of the good, which the government ought to be concerned to inculcate in its citizens?

The Argument from Tyranny

> We see here that Plato recognizes only one ultimate standard, the standard of the interest of the State. Everything that furthers it is good and virtuous and just; everything that threatens it is bad and wicked and unjust. Actions that serve it are moral; actions that endanger it, immoral. In other words, Plato's moral code is strictly utilitarian; it is the code of the collectivist or political utilitarian. *The criterion of morality is the interest of the state.* Morality is nothing but political hygiene.[9]

Karl Popper condemns the perfectionist society advocated by Plato in his *Republic* as oppressive—even fascist. Poetry and the arts are censored, and people are regimented in a vast, undemocratic police state. Whether or not Popper's criticism of Plato is fair, he points to a danger of power corrupting its possessors and using their conception of the good to oppress others who disagree with it. But totalitarianism is not a necessary corollary of perfectionism. Aristotle and Aquinas certainly thought the state should serve the individual and promote virtue at all levels, excluding oppression. Moreover, as Michael Rosol has pointed out, neutralism is no guarantee against oppression. Since neutralism is itself a value, it could be used to persecute those who promote a conception of the good that opposed neutralism.[10] Since most forms of moral perfectionism value liberty, they would be less likely to lead to tyranny than some forms of neutralism. But if neutralism values liberty, it seems to be a version of perfectionism. The rational ideal aimed for by moral perfectionists is one wherein progress and criticism are part of the rational program, so that diversity and difference are permitted and celebrated within the context of a comprehensive theory of the good. A moderate perfectionist can be a pluralist about individual choice and worldviews without surrendering a core objective morality. A lively, educated democracy can combat the danger of monolithic tyranny without surrendering a general theory of the good.

Furthermore, the state need not adopt a monolithic legal perfectionism. In fact, it need not put all its principles, such as benevolence, into law at all. It may use education rather than the coercive power of the law to change people's hearts and minds.

The Argument from Autonomy

One of the sharpest attacks on perfectionism is based on the principle of autonomy, which neutralists claim perfectionists undermine. Autonomy is the trait of being a rational law unto oneself, of using reason, not authority, to govern one's actions. We examined Robert Paul Wolf's defense of autonomy against authority in Chapter 1. Some philosophers, such as Douglas Rasmussen and Douglas Den Uyl, recognizing that autonomy is an important value, argue for state neutralism combined with social perfectionism:

> Freedom, then, is a necessary condition of a virtuous society, not only because the high likelihood is that the standard imposed on men with the power of the state would not in fact be virtuous standards, but also because, even if they were virtuous, to impose them upon individual persons would immensely reduce their ability to act virtuously at all and absolutely destroy their potential for active, creative, positive, virtue.[11]

First of all, autonomy, important as it is, is not a moral absolute, but an objective moral principle (a prima facie principle) that may sometimes clash with other moral principles. If I can save your life by preventing you from jumping off the Empire State Building, I may be justified in doing so. Autonomy may be relative; few of us may be completely autonomous about certain things. Just as we train children to virtuous living by habituating them to following rules before they fully understand them, moral education may be vital in helping us all inculcate good moral habits.

Actually, far from detracting from autonomy, perfectionist policies aim to enhance autonomy, by providing the kind of moral education necessary for liberating citizens from narcissism and slavish self-indulgence, so that they may have a greater possibility of reaching their potential as human beings in a caring community. A commitment to the good needs autonomy to be successful in reaching the good, and part of the goal of reaching the good is to produce autonomous individuals.

Conclusion

Summing up, neither the arguments from relativism or skepticism, nor those from tyranny or autonomy, work against moral perfectionism. Perfectionism, feared by so many liberal political philosophers, may actually be an important means for moral education and the good society.

Liberalism may have failed us in failing to recognize its importance. Sher puts his criticism of liberal neutrality this way:

> I am ambivalent toward contemporary liberalism. On the one hand, I believe that many of today's liberal thinkers are waging a necessary and courageous battle on behalf of certain vital but embattled Enlightenment attitudes—attitudes that include a willingness to abstract away from differences of background and culture to defend universally applicable standards of fairness and right; a commitment to such liberal values as civility, toleration, and respect for others; and, most important, a confidence in the power of reason to resolve our disagreements.
>
> But at the same time, contemporary liberal thought has taken a turn I find deeply problematic. For some important reason . . . many liberals have concluded that reason's scope is drastically limited. Though still confident about our ability to reach universally applicable conclusions about justice and rightness, these thinkers are much less sanguine about the prospects for reaching conclusions about goodness or value.[12]

Sher's ambivalence is characteristic of many political philosophers who see a core morality inseparable from a theory of the good. The same objective reasoning that would lead us to support tolerance and justice as universal moral norms would seem to support a principle of honesty, including rational assessment of the evidence, a principle of promise keeping, a principle of beneficence, and a principle of sobriety and self-discipline. Perhaps some issues are simply matters of taste or free choice, such as the kind of music or art one prefers, one's sexual orientation, the decision to marry or to remain single, one's religious preference, and the decision to be a risk taker or a cautious player of life's game. But underlying these options, it seems, there ought to be a common denominator of integrity and self-control (*sophrosune*), necessary for the good life and the good society.

A few years ago *The New York Times* reported the story of a high school girl in upstate New York who found $1,000 in a wallet. She searched out the owner and returned the money to him. Her fellow students, upon hearing of her act, mocked her as a fool. After arguing about the matter, they went to their teacher, asking for her judgment. The teacher responded, "I cannot tell you what I think. That would be imposing my values on you." Instead of using this as an opportunity for moral education, or supporting the moral integrity of the isolated girl, the teacher opted for moral neutrality, which is really *amoralism.* But then, is it any wonder that individuals are losing their moral bearings in a society barraged by media messages of instant gratification, egregious egoism, and conspicuous consumption? Moral perfectionism holds that morality is the glue that holds our society together, so we must encourage virtue in every walk of life.

MORAL VERSUS LEGAL PERFECTIONISM

We must also make a distinction between moral perfectionism, in which the state has an obligation to make people morally better, and legal perfectionism, in which the state has an obligation to make people better by instituting laws imposing sanctions on immoral behavior and, perhaps, rewarding virtuous behavior. It is not always easy to tell which kind of perfectionism a philosopher is advocating. Aristotle, Aquinas, Devlin and, to some degree, George seem to be advocating legal and moral perfectionism. On the other side, philosophers such as Rawls, Hart, and Dworkin hold that the state should not get into the value question, but let individuals determine their own conception of the good. In the moral and legal zone, the state must remain neutral. George, defending both moral and legal perfectionism, puts the matter this way:

> I defend the proposition that, though there are indeed global principles of justice and political morality (principles whose existence enables us to speak meaningfully of fundamental human rights), no such principles exclude the legal enforcement of true moral obligations. I shall argue that someone who has good reasons to believe that a certain act is immoral may support the legal prohibition of the act of protecting public morals without necessarily violating a norm of justice or political morality.[13]

George doesn't say that the perfectionist must support a legal prohibition against an immoral act. He uses our present antidrug legislation as an example, where a perfectionist may hold that drug use is a bad thing but should not be made illegal. Similarly, many people think that smoking, eating junk foods, and consuming pornography are bad things but would not want to make them illegal. On the other hand, there is no absolute injunction against making immoral or harmful behavior illegal. In many states smoking in public places (which may not be immoral, but is harmful) is prohibited. In the future, we might come to realize that wasting and polluting water is so deleterious to the human good that we might legislate against it. In doing so, we would be adopting a minimal or moderate position of perfectionism.

AN OUTLINE OF A MODERATE PERFECTIONISM

What would a reasonable, moral perfectionism look like? It would recognize certain goods constitutive of human life, and it would promote those goods, which would be inculcated essentially by noncoercive means. Various suggestions on the makeup of a coherent conception of the good appear in the literature. The intuitionist W. D. Ross states: "Four things . . .

seem to be intrinsically good—virtue, pleasure, the allocation of pleasure to the virtues, and knowledge."[14] The Oxford University philosopher of law John Finnis lists knowledge, play, aesthetic experience, sociability, practical reasonableness, and "religion" (apparently signifying a meaningful worldview).[15] Derek Parfit set forth what he calls "the objective list theory" of universal goods: "The good things might include moral goodness, rational activity, the development of one's abilities, having children and being a good parent, knowledge, and the awareness of true beauty."[16] Finnis's criterion for selection is self-evidence. The items on the list are simply obvious upon reflection and do not require further defense. Sher's criterion of judging which goods constitute a general conception of the good consists in their being universally accepted and necessary, or "near inescapable."[17] He defends a version of Parfit's general list. My own suggestion, overlapping with the above theories, is that the conception of the good should consist of two tiers. First-tier goods include health, love, and friendship (especially family relationships); education (including knowledge and wisdom); development of one's talents; and aesthetic enjoyment.[18] These are nearly universal, self-evident goods (on reflection), which meet Sher's requirement of being nearly unavoidable. That is, upon understanding them, we cannot help wanting these goods. Who would want to be unhealthy and suffer disease, ignorant, or loveless, or have his or her talents go unfulfilled? Who would prefer ugliness to beauty? I must leave it to you to reflect on these items. But then there is a second tier, of one overarching good in the general theory of the good, that of moral virtue. It doesn't have the same self-evident lucidity as the first-tier values, but upon reflection, we see that moral virtue is the glue that holds the first-tier goods together into a workable, coherent whole. Without fidelity and integrity, love dissipates and families are pulled apart. Without good moral habits, including self-control, health (both physical and mental) is undermined and our bodies and minds become weakened or diseased. With moral concern for others, we can promote education and the development of each other's talents in a mutually advantageous manner. Consider the fact that the Surgeon General has just issued a report stating that 65 million Americans have sexually transmitted diseases (STDs). Isn't it proper for the state to promote a comprehensive health education program, helping people understand the facts about sexuality, to enable them to protect themselves from STDs? The government is already doing this, albeit somewhat ineffectually, regarding the dangers of smoking and drug use.

We might add that self-respect would emerge as the result of such a two-tier theory. Rawls states that the just society should provide people with the "bases of self-respect." He doesn't elaborate on this, but omits to note that self-respect is not something you can give to people. They must earn it by the way they live. The general theory of the good explains how self-respect is achieved, through being responsible for one's own personal development, by inculcating both tiers of goods into one's life. Governmental programs cannot give people self-respect, but through education, through the media, it can encourage a culture of integrity that will better enable people to understand that the good is good for them, that moral virtue is a social necessity for self-respect and the good life in general.

I should mention that this account of the good is pluralistic. Each person has different talents and abilities and should be free to develop them or a subset of them in his or her unique manner. Similarly, each of us needs love, but so long as it is exercised within the bounds of moral integrity, many forms are possible. Marriage and family will be attractive to most of us, but remaining single and devoted to friends and/or children or even animals is a viable option. A wide variety of options exist.

My aim has been not to give a complete general theory of the good, but to argue that we already have an intuitive idea of such a theory and that the state should support it. This should be done in as noncoercive, indirect manner as possible, through education and special programs, such as a national youth corps (mirroring the Peace Corps), which would encourage young people to serve their country, especially the poor and needy. Exactly how the state can walk the tightrope of edification without falling off on one side by becoming oppressive and tyrannical (as Devlin's own views may do) or falling off on the other side by becoming neutral with regard to a conception of the good (as some of Devlin's opponents may do) is the challenge of the modern enlightened state.

Conclusion

We have examined the debate between state neutrality and perfectionism and have concluded that the arguments against perfectionism, especially moral perfectionism, are unsound, though some may be important danger signs, illustrating the perils of trying to improve the world through state action. The state is a powerful institution whose power can corrupt. A religious or political ideology may become inordinately powerful and become tyrannical. The Roman Catholic Church may contain important truth, but the Crusades and the Inquisition showed how its power could be corrupted. Marxism may have contained some good ideas, but, if so, Stalin certainly abused them, transforming socialism into a diabolical tyranny. And certain forms of Islamic fundamentalism may abuse the idea of perfectionism. However, just because good ideas can be abused is no reason to prohibit implementing them. Their opposites are often amoralist anarchy. We must not throw out the baby with the dirty bath water. Study of the history of the abuse of good ideas must serve as a warning against corruption, humbling us to check for error and distortions, but should not prevent us from striving to improve our society. There are good reasons for supporting a moderate, pluralist general theory of the good in which the state recognizes constitutive attributes of the good life and encourages their inculcation in society. With all due modesty and caution, we should pursue the good with all our strength, minds, and wills.[19]

For Further Reflection

1. Review the arguments for and against perfectionism. Evaluate them and give your own assessment of the issues regarding state neutrality versus perfectionism.

2. What is the difference between moral and legal perfectionism?

3. Evaluate the quotations at the head of this chapter by Aristotle (385–325 B.C.), Ronald Dworkin, and John Rawls. Why do you think contemporary liberals such as Dworkin and Rawls differ so much from the ancient Greek philosopher Aristotle?

4. What values, if any, do you think would be promoted by a perfectionist government? Explain your answer.

5. What do you make of Devlin's claim that the state ought to put into law the community's deeply held moral beliefs? Devlin used this principle to oppose the Wolfenden Report, which recommended decriminalizing homosexual relationships. Can you think of some issues on which our society criminalizes behavior, not because it has a strong moral argument, but because of deeply held feelings? Discuss the case of the paroled pedophile who wrote about his sexual fantasies.

6. Should the government embark on health education programs to help young people prevent sexually transmitted diseases? Is this a minimal form of moral perfectionism or simply a protective measure?

Endnotes

1. Patrick Devlin, "Morals and the Criminal Law," *Proceedings of the British Academy* 45 (1959).

2. H. L. A. Hart, "Immorality and Treason," *Listener* (July 30, 1959).

3. See references in the Bibliography.

4. I am indebted to Stephen Kershnar for this story.

5. Karl Popper, *The Open Society and Its Enemies*, vol. 1, (London: Routledge & Kegan Paul, 1944).

6. See references in the Bibliography.

7. For a fuller discussion of these issues and a defense of moral objectivism, see my *Ethics: Discovering Right and Wrong* (Wadsworth, 2002).

8. Jeremy Waldron, "Legislation, Morality and Neutrality," in *Liberal Rights* (Cambridge University Press, 1991).

9. Popper, op. cit., p. 107. Popper is probably unfair to Plato, but the quotation illustrates Popper's criticism of perfectionism.

10. In his unpublished senior thesis (see endnote 19).

11. Douglas Rassmussen and Douglas Den Uyl, *Liberty and Nature, An Aristotelian Defense of Liberal Order* (Open Court Press, 1991), pp. 211–12. I am indebted to Michael Rosol for directing me to this work.

12. George Sher, *Beyond Neutrality* (Cambridge University Press, 1997), p. ix. This chapter has benefited from Sher's brilliant book.

13. Robert George, *Making Men Moral* (Oxford University Press, 1994), p. viii.

14. W. D. Ross, *The Right and the Good* (Oxford University Press, 1930), p. 140. I am indebted to Sher's work for this section.

15. John Finnis, *Natural Law and Natural Rights* (Oxford University Press, 1980), chaps. 3 and 4.

16. Derek Parfit, *Reasons and Persons* (Oxford University Press, 1984), p. 499.

17. Sher, op. cit., p. 239.

18. I don't claim that my list is complete. I suspect that items such as doing useful work and, contributing to the flourishing of the community should be added. Perhaps play and recreation also should be added.

19. In writing this chapter, I have benefited greatly from the senior thesis of my student at the U. S. Military Academy, Cadet Michael Rosol, "Towards a Pluralist Perfectionism: Concepts of the Good and State Action" (2001). I am also indebted to Stephen Kershnar and the writings of Robert George in working through these issues.

7

RIGHTS

We hold these truths to be self-evident, that all men are created equal, that they are endowed by their Creator with certain unalienable Rights, that among these are Life, Liberty, and the pursuit of Happiness.
—DECLARATION OF INDEPENDENCE OF THE
UNITED STATES OF AMERICA, JULY 4, 1776.

Natural rights is simple nonsense: natural and imprescriptible rights, rhetorical nonsense,—nonsense upon stilts . . . Right is a child of law; from real laws come real rights, but from imaginary law, from "laws of nature," come imaginary rights. . . . A natural right is a son that never had a father.
—JEREMY BENTHAM, "ANARCHICAL FALLACIES,"
THE WORKS OF JEREMY BENTHAM, VOL. 2 (1843)

INTRODUCTION: THE NATURE AND VALUE OF RIGHTS

HUMAN RIGHTS HAVE BEEN the centerpiece of political theory for over two centuries. They were the justification for the American and French Revolutions in the eighteenth century and for a succession of revolutions for political independence in the nineteenth and twentieth centuries, as well as the motivation for the civil rights movement in the 1960s and the women's movement in the 1970s.

Natural rights are said to be the moral basis of positive law and the grounds for welfare rights and foreign aid, but the exact set of such universal rights varies. During the past century a proliferation of rights occurred. Women won the right to vote. Workers won the right to organize, and unions claimed the right to strike. Blacks claimed the rights to vote and to have equal access to public accommodations. Women claimed the right to choose to have an abortion, and patients claimed the right to sue their physicians for malpractice. Many people advocate special children's rights and a separate set of parents' rights. Others claim a special set of rights for homosexuals, gay rights. Article 24 of the United Nations

156

Declaration on Human Rights states, "Everyone has the right to rest and leisure, including periodic holidays with pay." Nonsmokers claimed the right to a smoke-free environment. Animal rights advocates claim that animals have a right to life; some "deep ecologists" and environmentalists claim that ecosystems and the wilderness have a right to be left inviolable. During the 1960s male students at my university claimed the right to have all their needs satisfied, including their need for sex. Others rallied for laws against sexual harassment, claiming the right not to be sexually harassed in the workplace. The poor were awarded welfare rights. Terminally ill people claimed the right to die. Hospitalized patients were given a patient's bill of rights. In the 1960s members of minority groups were given the right to preferential treatment. Currently, Harvard law professor Charles Ogletree and the lawyer Johnnie Cochrane are putting together a lawsuit seeking reparations for the descendants of slaves, claiming that African Americans have a right to be compensated for the evils of slavery. A couple in Montclair, New Jersey (Warren and Patricia Simpson), declared that they're not very good at child rearing and don't much like it, so they're exercising their *right* to retire from it. "Between the crying and the fighting and asking for toys, it was getting to be very discouraging," Mrs. Simpson said. "We're both still young, and we have a lot of other interests." They've put their three small children up for adoption, and after seven years of parenting, they "are moving on."[1] No doubt many of these rights claims are warranted, but their very proliferation as claims for being fundamental moral entities may be causing an inflation, devaluing the currency of rights.[2] Groups extend rights to animals, to corporations, and to forests. Nevertheless, almost all rights systems grant human beings the rights of life, liberty, property, and the pursuit of happiness.

Rights are important to our lives. They provide a normative advantage in protecting vital interests against incursion. As such, we are ready to defend them, to demand their recognition and enforcement, and to complain of injustice when they are not complied with. We use them as vital premises in arguments that proscribe courses of action (for example, Please stop smoking in this public place, for we nonsmokers have a right to clean air). Eventually, when we receive no redress for violations of our rights, we even consider civil disobedience.

It is because of their protective importance that we need to ask: What precisely are rights? Where do rights come from? Are there any natural rights, rights that do not depend on social contract, prior moral duties, utilitarian outcomes, or ideals?

Although there is a great deal of variation in defining *rights* in the literature, for our purposes we can say that a *right* is a claim against others that at the same time includes a liberty on one's own behalf.[3] J. L. Mackie captures this combination when he writes, "A right, in the most important sense, is a conjunction of a freedom and a claim-right. That is, if someone, A, has the moral right to do X, not only is he entitled to do X if he chooses—he is not morally required not to do X—but he is also protected in his doing of X—others are morally required not to interfere or prevent him."[4] Rights are typically *relational,* in that we have them against other people: If I have a right against you regarding X, you have a duty to me regarding X. For example, if you have promised to pay me $10 for cutting your lawn and I have done so, I have a right to that $10 and you have a duty to pay up.

As already noted, rights give us a normative advantage. If you have a right, then others have obligations toward you. They are put at a normative disadvantage. They require special justification for overriding or limiting your right; conversely, if you have a right, you have a justification for limiting the freedom of others in regard to exercising that right.

TYPES OF RIGHTS AND THEIR JUSTIFICATION

Next we should distinguish among the basic types of rights that we will encounter in this part of our work:

1. *Natural rights.* Those rights, if any, that humans (or other beings) have simply by nature of what they are. According to John Locke and the U.S. Declaration of Independence, God bestows these rights upon us.
2. *Human rights.* This is an ambiguous term. Sometimes it means natural rights, at other times it means rights that humans have, and at still other times it means moral rights.
3. *Moral rights.* Those rights that are justified by a given moral system. They may be derivative of duties or ideals or consequentialist goals.
4. *Positive rights.* Those rights that society affords its members, including legal rights, such as the right of a woman to have an abortion, the right to a fair trial with a jury of one's peers, or the right to vote.
5. *Prima facie rights.* Presumptive rights that may not necessarily be actual rights in a given situation. My right to hear loud music may be overridden by your right to peace and quiet.
6. *Absolute rights.* Rights that cannot be overridden. For example, for those who hold that justice is an absolute right, my right to fair treatment may not be overridden by utilitarian considerations.

Which types of rights do we have and how can we justify them—or are rights simply "nonsense," as Bentham claimed? Many take natural rights for granted. In his book *Taking Rights Seriously,* even so capable a philosopher as Ronald Dworkin simply assumes that we have rights, without argument:

> Some philosophers, of course, reject the idea that citizens have rights apart from what the law happens to give them. Bentham thought that the idea of moral rights was "nonsense on stilts." But that view has never been part of our orthodox political theory, and politicians of both parties appeal to the rights of the people to justify a great part of what they want to do. I shall not be concerned, in this essay, to defend the thesis that citizens have moral rights against their governments.[5]

Nowhere in Dworkin's much celebrated book does he attempt to justify rights, nor the basic right to equal respect, which figures prominently in his work. He seems to hold an intuitionist policy on rights. But intuitionism seems unsatisfactory. While Dworkin may find certain claims intuitively obvious, others, say, Nietzsche or MacIntyre, might not. Intuitions are sometimes merely indications of our upbringing or group prejudice. So Dworkin's attitude seems philosophically unsatisfying. We want to know what the nature of rights is, whether we have any human rights, and what they are. We want, as philosophical beings, to have a justification for our rights claims. Consider, for instance, two claims: (1) I have a right to smoke wherever I please, and (2) I have a right to be treated justly. What distinguishes (2) from (1)? Why do at least most of us accept (2), but not (1), as a valid right? Are all rights simply legal rights? Or are rights simply relative to cultural tastes? Consider Arthur Danto's view that they are simply what our peers will let us get away with:

> In the afterwash of 1968, I found myself a member of a group charged with working out disciplinary procedures for acts against my university. It was an exemplary group from the perspective of representation so urgent at the time: administrators, tenured and nontenured faculty, graduate and undergraduate students, men and women, whites and blacks. We all wondered, nevertheless, what right we had to do what was asked of us, and a good bit of time went into expressing our insecurities. Finally, a man from the law school said, with the tried patience of someone required to explain what should be plain as day and in a tone of voice I can still hear: "This is the way it is with rights. You want 'em, so you say you got 'em, and if nobody says you don't then you do." In the end he was right. We worked a code out which nobody liked, but in debating it the community acknowledged the rights.[6]

But this seems unsatisfactory, making rights language more like a con game or a successful public relations gimmick. Apply this reasoning to

Gangster Gus, who extorts protection money from all the local businesses, claiming that he has a right to do so. When challenged, he quotes Danto: "This is the way it is with rights. You want 'em, so you say you got 'em, and if nobody says you don't then you do." He might just as well have said, "Might makes right." The law professor's logic is flawed; since it makes everyone's acquiescence a necessary condition for having a right, all it takes is one person to say "you don't" to defeat a right claim. But that leads to a vicious kind of ethical relativism. Rights need a better justification than group acquiescence. We should be able to do better than this or else drop rights language altogether.

We must first consider what is meant by *natural rights* and by what is often used as its synonym, *human rights.* By a natural right, we mean a right that is ours simply by the nature of things, independent of any other reason or moral duty or ideal. This notion, which may be traced back to the Stoics and was explicit in the late Middle Ages, became prominent in the seventeenth century with the works of Hugo Grotius (1583–1645) and John Locke (1632–1704). For Locke, humans possess rights by nature (namely, life, liberty, and property) that society must recognize if it is to be legitimate. They are bestowed on us by God. Because these rights are a gift of God, they are "inalienable" or "imprescriptible"; that is, we do not give them to people, nor can we take them away or even give our own rights away (for example, we cannot give away our right to freedom by selling ourselves into slavery). They become the proper basis of all specific rights, such as the right to vote, to be protected by the law, to sell property, to work, and to be educated. Let us call this position the natural law theory of rights. Here is the way the French philosopher Jacques Maritain expresses this theory:

> The human person possesses rights because of the very fact that it is a
> person, a whole, master of itself and of its acts, and which consequently is not
> merely a means to an end, but an end, an end which must be treated as such.
> The dignity of the human person? The expression means nothing if it does
> not signify that by virtue of natural law, the human person has the right to be
> respected, is the subject of rights, possesses rights. These are things which are
> owed to man because of the very fact that he is man.[7]

Most philosophers who deny natural rights do not deny that we have rights. They simply deny that they are in the nature of things, as natural law theorists affirm. These nonnaturalists state that all rights are derivable from something else, such as law, moral duty, utilitarian outcomes, or ideals. These are called *positive rights,* as opposed to *natural rights.* Let us look at each of these possibilities:

1. *Positive versus Natural Rights.* Some philosophers, including the legal positivist John Austin, Jeremy Bentham, and Alasdair MacIntyre, argue that all rights (as well as their correlative duties) are institutional in the way that legal rights are. MacIntyre says that there are no natural rights, "and belief in them is one with belief in witches." These are positive rights, those actually invented by organized society. As MacIntyre writes:

> [C]laims to the possession of rights . . . presuppose the existence of a socially
> established set of rules. Such sets of rules only come into existence at
> particular historical periods under particular social circumstances. They are
> in no way universal features of the human condition . . . [T]he existence of
> particular types of social institutions or practices is a necessary condition for
> the notion of a claim to the possession of a right being an intelligible type of
> human performance.[8]

Natural rights, as a part of natural law, hold that rights are inalienable and part of a natural order, but it is hard to see how this natural law could exist without a supreme lawgiver and enforcer, such as God. Natural law philosophers Locke and Jefferson, indeed, held that God created us with such rights, but it is controversial whether God exists, so it cannot be the basis of secular society. But even if God did bestow a system of law and rights onto us, it would not be a natural, but a supernatural conventional system.

2. *Contract-based ethical theories.* Hobbes held that rights proceeded from a social contract in which we each give up our liberty to do what we please in the state of nature to procure security in a civil society. Rawls, as we noted in Chapter 5, holds that rights originate through a hypothetical contract. For all contractualists, rights are the results of agreements between contracting parties. The problems with contractualism are the following: (1) As Dworkin points out, a hypothetical contract is not just a pale contract, but no contract at all, which as such cannot generate rights and duties; (2) contractual rights are relative, depending on the contingencies of the contracting parties, but what we need when we claim to have a right is something objective and universally valid; (3) once, having become dissatisfied with the contract I've made, because it didn't turn out to be favorable to me, why should I continue to adhere to it? This problem of compliance seems to presuppose at least one noncontractual objective moral principle: We have a duty to keep agreements made. This need for an extracontractual norm leads to the next two types of theories.

3. *Duty-based (deontological) ethical theories.* Theories such as those of Kant, Ross, or Frankena hold that rights are simply entailments of moral obligations. Since I have a duty to pay you back the money I borrowed,

you have a corresponding right to the money. However, some duties do not generate rights. For example, I may have a duty to share my abundance with the poor and needy, but no one poor or needy person has a right to it. If you are poor, you cannot properly demand $50 from me, for there may be others equally poor to whom I choose to give the money. It is duty that is primary to the moral system, and rights are but correlates to duties. To have a right means simply that one is the beneficiary of someone else's duty. For this reason, it is misleading to speak of human rights as a separate subject apart from a duty-based moral system.

4. *Goal-based theories.* Theories such as the utilitarianism of John Stuart Mill or L. W. Sumner's consequentialist systems argue that rights are derivable from our understanding of the good, ideal goals, such as utility.[9] We will all be happier if we have certain of our interests protected, especially our interest in noninterference. Goal-based systems generally turn into duty-based ethical systems, such as rule-utilitarianism, specifying a general duty to maximize happiness, welfare, and so forth. Mill puts in this way:

> Though society is not founded on a contract, and though no good purpose is answered by inventing a contract in order to deduce social obligations from it, every one who receives the protection of society owes a return for the benefit, and the fact of living in society renders it indispensable that each should be bound to observe a certain line of conduct towards the rest. This conduct consists, first, in not injuring the interests of one another; or rather certain interests, which, either by express legal provision or by tacit understanding, ought to be considered as rights; and secondly, in each person's bearing his share (to be fixed on some equitable principle) of the labors and sacrifices incurred for defending the society or its members from injury and molestation. These conditions society is justified in enforcing, at all costs, to those who endeavor to withhold fulfillment. (*On Liberty*, p. 73)

In a goal-based system, rights are prima facie features that have presumptive force, but are not absolute and can be overridden for consequentialist reasons. My right to privacy may be overridden if your violating it would likely lead to the saving of a life. But most deontologists would agree that rights are only objective, not absolute.

5. *Ideals.* A variation on this theme is the view of Kurt Baier and Richard Brandt that rights are those claims and liberties that would be included in an ideal moral system, which need not be a utilitarian one, but could be one chosen by an ideal observer, omniscient, omnibenevolent, and absolutely impartial. They are moral features that should be assigned to us even though they may be presently missing. Hence, we may assert that blacks had a right to freedom from slavery before the Emancipation

Proclamation, even though the majority of people in the southern United States, as well as the law, failed to recognize that right. It is in this light that we may interpret some of the rights enumerated in the United Nations Universal Declaration of Human Rights, such as the right to free education and paid holidays. These are ideals that we should strive to realize, not absolute human rights. But other rights seem necessary for a normal life. These would be the right to security (not to be harmed unjustly) and subsistence, the right to have one's fundamental survival needs met. No minimally adequate social system should omit them. They seem so basic as to place claims on the rest of the world to protect.[10] The problem with ideal rights is that they seem to depend on ideal conditions, which may not be practicably realizable, or on the perfect judgment of an ideal observer, which is a sheer fiction. We don't know any such beings and can't be certain what he or she would decide. Such a being seems like God, which reduces the system to a religious one. When we try to modify the notion of rights as ideals, we seem to end up with a goal-based system (as described on page 162).

HOHFELDIAN CLASSIFICATION OF RIGHTS

To philosophers who hold to natural rights, antinaturalist views seem like a profanation of rights, an undermining of rights' power and presence. To counter this tendency to treat rights as second-class citizens in our moral repertoire, Joel Feinberg uses a thought experiment in which he asks you to imagine a place, Nowheresville, that is quite nice but lacks rights. Having all the other benefits a good society could offer except this one thing, Feinberg argues, leaves Nowheresville in bad shape, for rights are logically connected with claims. In Nowheresville people cannot make moral claims, and in this way they are deprived of a certain self-respect and dignity. Rights are valid moral claims that give us inherent dignity:

> Having rights, of course makes claiming possible, but it is claiming that gives rights their special moral significance. This feature of rights is connected in a way with the customary rhetoric about what it means to be a human being. Having rights enables us to "stand up like men," to look others in the eye, and to feel in some fundamental way the equal of anyone. To think of oneself as the holder of rights is not to be unduly but properly proud, to have that minimal self-respect that is necessary to be worthy of the love and esteem of others. To respect a person then, or to think of him as possessed of human dignity, simply is to think of him as a potential maker of claims."[11]

As such, rights are necessary to an adequate moral theory.

A useful analysis of rights is that of the legal philosopher Wesley New-comb Hohfeld (1879–1918), who identified four types of legal rights, which have been extended to cover moral rights as well.[12] Hohfeld identifies four basic types of rights: claim rights, liberty rights, power rights, and immunity rights, all of which are relational (i.e., implying a relationship of one subject to another):

1. *Claim right.* Person X has a (legal or moral) claim against some person Y that Y perform some action A if and only if Y has a (legal or moral) duty to do A to X. For example, Y has contracted to repair X's car, so X has a right to Y's repairing his car.
2. *Liberty right.* X has a (legal or moral) liberty in the face of some person Y to perform some action A if and only if X has no duty to Y not to do A. For example, X has a liberty right to park her car in a public parking space if she arrives there before Y does.
3. *Power right.* X has a power over some second party Y to bring about some legal or moral consequence C for Y if and only if some voluntary action of X would be legally or morally recognized as having this consequence for Y. Our notion of authority is allied to this concept. For example, a physician has the power (or authority) to treat patients and dispense drugs to them since she is licensed by law to do so. Similarly, X has the power to give his property to Y, thus bringing about a new state of affairs, that of Y's having property that once belonged to X. Powers are second-order counterparts of liberties. Just as my liberty specifies something I am permitted to do, so a power indicates something it is possible for me to do.
4. *Immunity right.* X has a legal or moral immunity against some party Y from some specific legal consequence if and only if Y lacks the legal or moral power to do any action that would be recognized by X as having the consequence C for X. For example, before leaving office President Clinton pardoned the fugitive from justice Marc Rich and some convicted criminals, thus making them immune from a criminal trial and prison sentence. Similarly, a soldier in battle surrenders his immunity right not to be killed, whereas noncombatants have an immunity right against soldiers, protecting them against being directly harmed.

We could represent the logical relations (including the relationship of rights to duties) of the Hohfeldian normative scheme in the following manner. The rows represent correlative relationships, the columns (and diagonals) give opposites. Let X and Y be persons and A some act.[13]

X has a liberty in relation to Y to A	Y has no claim against X that X not A
X has a duty to Y not to A	Y has a claim against X that X not A

For example, if Xavier has a liberty right to sleep in, rather than get up early and jog, no one else (Y) has a claim on him that he get up and jog. But if Xavier has promised Yolanda that he would get up early and jog with her, Yolanda has a claim right against Xavier that he get up early and jog with her.

Elaborating on the notions of a power and an immunity, we can treat a power as an ability or authority and an immunity as an exemption. Hohfeld treats them in terms of liabilities and disabilities. If I, as a doctor, have a power over you to dispense drugs, you have a liability with regard to my power. You do not have the authority to interfere with my action. If you have an immunity against me regarding my charging fees for my services (because I have failed to fulfill the terms of your contract), I have a disability with respect to you regarding such fees. I don't have the authority to charge you for my services.

Suppose I offer to buy your car for $10,000. In virtue of my offer, you have the power to impose a duty on me to pay you the $10,000, which you can experience by accepting my offer. But while I have a duty to you regarding the sum, I have an immunity against a third party imposing the duty on me, but no immunity against you. But while you have a power to enforce your claim that I pay you the $10,000, you have the immunity right to absolve me of my obligation.

We can apply Hohfeldian distinctions to the discussion of both moral and legal rights. For instance, there is a debate whether soldiers, in joining the army, give up their right to life. Some military ethicists, such as Paul Christopher, say they do, whereas others, such as Daniel Zupan, say they don't. By using Hohfeld's distinctions, we can say that as human beings, soldiers do not give up a claim right to life, but in combat they do give up an immunity right not to be the target of violence, a right noncombatants retain even in war. But the most important kind of right is the claim right. You and I can claim the right to have others keep promises to us, to pay their debts to us, and not to infringe on our liberty.

Although Hohfeld's categories have been widely accepted, the schema has been criticized for being purely directionally relational, applying to two-party relationships, rather than universal ones. Rights theorists such as Henry Shue want a system of universal rights, applying to everyone.[14]

It is helpful in this regard to compare rights with desert. When people deserve some good from us, we mean that there is a fittingness in our giving it to them in virtue of their accomplishments or efforts. This fittingness is weaker than that derived from our having promised them the good thing or from meeting an official standard, such as coming in first in a contest. In these latter cases they have a right to the good. They are in a position to demand it as their due. The fittingness between the action and reward is, in Feinberg's words, more like that between "humor and laughter or good performance and applause." It is less stringent than the fittingness of giving someone a good because it is her or his right.

We say, for instance, that equal work deserves equal pay, but the person who does the equal work may not have a right to equal pay. If you can get me to repair your broken-down car for less than the going rate, no right need have been violated. I may deserve more than I have agreed to take, but I have no claim on you to pay me more than we agreed on. If I do a superb job, and actually improve your car so that it is in better shape than it was before the accident, I certainly deserve your gratitude and perhaps a tip or some special favor, but I have no basis to claim more money than agreed on in our original transaction.

A CRITIQUE OF RIGHTS LANGUAGE

However important rights are in promoting a sense of self-respect, one can place too much importance on them. In some cases, as Elizabeth Wolgast has argued, rights language can distort the moral domain. The language of rights tends to transform every relationship into a legalistic one. For example, there is a current political move to devise a patient's bill of rights, presumably to protect the patient from harm, enabling him or her to sue the medical establishment for malpractice if things go seriously wrong. But this is often inappropriate. What a patient needs most may not be rights, but to be cared for as a person with needs in a relationship of trust, which the emphasis on rights obscures. In many cases the disease may so affect a patient to the point where he or she may not be a fully autonomous agent, the equal of the physician. Since medicine is not a science, as some researchers might have us believe, but an art, the more we can inculcate a personal relationship of openness and care, the better our medical system is likely to become. The language of rights suggests that the same self-interested model that governs consumer relationships (of impersonal economic forces) governs all our relationships, turning us into economic atoms, rather than recognizing the special place of personal fiduciary relationships. Wolgast points out that the language of rights also distorts the peculiar status of women as mothers. Affording them the *right* to maternity leave treats childbearing as a disease, like cancer or heart disease, which men may have, to justify giving mothers time off. A more communal, less atomistic society would recognize the uniqueness of maternity and treat the need for rest and baby nurturing as a special need.[15] When we have to formalize behavior into a legal right, we have passed from a situation of communal and personal trust to an impersonal, bureaucratic, and legalistic society. Take the issue of noise in a neighborhood. In a caring community, such as the neighborhood I knew in the 1950s, if a person were bothered by a neighbor's loud party (or a dog's barking), he or she would go to the neighbor's home and mention the problem. Invariably, the noise level would reduce. Now in many neighborhoods, when there is a noise problem, people call the police and then file a complaint, claiming a right to a noise-free environment. The police make an official visit to the home and get the problem corrected, but the neighbors probably don't get to know each other. The relationship is entirely impersonal and legal. If the noise problem continues, the neighbors are brought to court, where they may meet each other for the first time, thanks to their lawyers. In the name of rights, we are in danger of losing a basic civility and sense of trust in many of our communities.

Wolgast's analysis corrects Feinberg's emphasis on the importance of rights. Feinberg holds that rights are fundamental; hence all duties are derived therefrom. We have a right to life; hence murder is wrong. We have a right to property; hence we have a duty not to steal. We have a right to liberty; hence coercion is wrong. But this analysis may not be correct. Duties may be the foundation of moral obligation and rights. As I noted above, I may have a duty even though no one in particular has a corresponding right. According to Kant's idea of imperfect duties, I have a duty to contribute to the amelioration of suffering, but there are innumerable ways I can do this; thus no particular sufferer can claim a right to my care unless I have a special relationship with that sufferer (say, I caused the suffering unjustly or am a close relation to the sufferer). It seems to me that Kant, Mill, and Ross are correct here. Morality is centered in our duties to carry out the moral law or promote the human good, and some of these duties entail specific rights on the part of others.

A further argument for the priority of duties over rights is found in examining the *posterity problem*, the thesis that we have duties to future generations.[16] Rights theory requires that we have identifiable individuals as the bearers of rights, but most of us sense that we have obligations to future generations, to people not yet born. At least we have a duty not to deplete the environment to the extent that it will not be fit for prosperous human habitation in the future. But if the rights-priority thesis is correct, our intuition is misguided. We have no such duty and the environmental movement, oriented as it is to duty to future generations, is misguided. If we have obligations to leave the world (the environment) in as good shape as we found it, then duties are prior to rights, for the particular future bearers of rights do not yet exist.

Another argument in favor of the priority of duties is the question of our relationship to animals (other than humans). If rational self-consciousness is a requirement for having a right, then many animals do not have rights. But we may well have a duty not to unnecessarily harm them or cause them death or suffering. This duty flows from a general duty not to cause unnecessary suffering rather than from a focus on the rights of animals.

Everyone prefers rights to duties, for rights give us things, making others responsible for our welfare, whereas duties are onerous because they hold us accountable for our actions and demand things of us, sometimes at considerable sacrifice. But a society emphasizing our duties to each other fosters responsible behavior, whereas one emphasizing rights tends to foster impersonal, social atomism; adversarial relations; and litigation, whereby lawyers, but not necessarily the people, come out ahead. So although rights have a place in our moral repertoire, serving as correlatives to duties, they should not become the central focus of our moral and political discourse. The very proliferation of rights in our society probably is a symptom of a growing anonymity and anomie, where the adversary relationship replaces informal discussion, personal trust, and a sense of a public self, where each of us recognizes his or her social responsibility and loyalty to the society at large. We don't want to live in Nowheresville, but neither do we want to live in Litigationville, with its rights-dominated orientation, one that our society is in danger of approximating.

Conclusion

Rights are nice; they give us things that we want. But duties are onerous; they make claims on us. We need both, but duties seem to be basic, and if we are virtuous, living in a community of virtuous fellow citizens, not really so onerous after all.

Rights, then, seem to be derived from duties or goals, and not vice versa. We can have duties without rights, but not rights without duties. It is because life itself is a basic core value that we seek to protect, and we have a moral rule to the effect that murder is wrong, that we say we have a right to life; because property is a fundamental human value that we see that stealing is wrong and we acknowledge a right to property; because promise keeping is a fundamental duty that we have a right to have promises made to us kept; because we value liberty as a necessity for carrying out our projects that we recognize a right to liberty.

Fundamental human rights, to life, liberty, property and the pursuit of happiness, including basic civil rights, reflect our deepest moral values and should be protected, but there is a danger in extending the concept of rights too widely to cover activities that should be handled informally by common sense and a caring community of reasonable, responsible citizens. An inflation of rights paradoxically leads to a devaluing of its currency.

For Further Reflection

1.   What are rights? What kinds of rights are there? What kinds of rights should there be?

2.   Do you agree that in the past 50 or 60 years there has been a proliferation of rights? If so, how has this come about? What are its good and bad points?

3.   Does rights language result from an adversarial, litigious context that tends to endanger civility and social harmony in our society?

4.   Examine Article 24 of the United Nations Universal Declaration of Human Rights, which states: "Everyone has the right to rest and leisure, including periodic holidays with pay." Does this mean that a society before the industrial age was unjust and immoral since these rights were unknown before the twentieth century?

5.   Discuss these questions: Which are more basic—rights or duties? Which tend to increase a sense of personal responsibility?

6.   Why do you think rights are so popular in society today?

7.   Examine the question discussed at the end of this chapter: Are rights or duties more fundamental? How do the posterity problem and our obligations to animals affect our answer to this question?

8.   What are Hohfeld's four types of rights, and how can they help us distinguish various types of rights claims?

9.   Are there universal human rights, such as the right to security and subsistence, that make claims on the whole world?

Endnotes

1. Michael Rubiner, "Retirement Fever," *New York Times* op-Ed, February, 1996.

2. See Carl Wellman, *The Proliferation of Rights* (Westview, 1999) for a penetrating, balanced discussion of these points. I have been aided by Wellman's work.

3. For a more comprehensive treatment of the nature of a right, see Carl Wellman, *A Theory of Rights* (Rowman & Allanheld, 1985); L. W. Sumner, *The Moral Foundation of Rights* (Oxford University Press, 1987); and James Nickel, *Making Sense of Human Rights* (University of California Press, 1987).

4. J. L. Mackie, "Can There Be a Right-Based Moral Theory?" *Midwest Studies in Philosophy* 3 (1978).

5. Ronald Dworkin, *Taking Rights Seriously* (Harvard University Press, 1977), p. 184.

6. Arthur Danto, "Constructing an Epistemology of Human Rights: A Pseudo Problem?" in *Human Rights*, E. Paul, F. Miller, and J. Paul, eds. (London: Blackwell, 1984), p. 30.

7. Jacques Maritain, *The Rights of Man* (London: Scribner's, 1944), p. 37.

8. Alasdair MacIntyre, *After Virtue* (University of Notre Dame Press, 1981), p. 64 f.

9. L. W. Sumner, *The Moral Foundation of Rights* (Oxford University Press, 1987), chap. 6.

10. Henry Shue, *Basic Rights: Subsistence, Affluence and U.S. Foreign Policy* (Princeton, NJ: Princeton University Press, 1980).

11. Joel Feinberg, "The Nature and Value of Rights," *Journal of Value Inquiry* (1970), reprinted in L. Pojman, *Political Philosophy: Modern and Contemporary Readings* (New York: McGraw-Hill, 2002), pp. 460–8.

12. For a more comprehensive treatment of Hohfeld's fourfold meaning of rights, see Wellman, op. cit., chap. 2.

13. I am indebted here to Sumner, op. cit., pp. 27–31.

14. Shue, op. cit.

15. Elizabeth Wolgast, *The Grammar of Justice* (Cornell University Press, 1987), op. cit.

16. The posterity problem haunts many ethical theories. Egoists fail to provide a solution to this problem, asking, Why should I care about posterity? What has posterity ever done for me? Kantians too fail to address it, for they require rational agents as the objects of our duties, but future people aren't identifiable because they don't exist. Consequentilist doctrines such as utilitarianism seem to have the best solution: We have a duty to create general welfare, including the conditions of welfare for those not yet born.

8

PUNISHMENT

What kind and what degree of punishment does public justice take as its principle and norm? None other than the principle of equality in the movement of the pointer of the scale of justice, the principle of not inclining to one side more than to the other. Thus any undeserved evil which you do to someone else among the people is an evil done to yourself. If you rob him, you rob yourself; if you slander him, you slander yourself; if you strike him, you strike yourself; and if you kill him, you kill yourself.

—IMMANUEL KANT[1]

INTRODUCTION

On June 11, 2001, at 8:14 A.M. Timothy McVeigh, a Gulf War veteran, was executed for a crime he committed six years earlier. On April 19, 1995, McVeigh blew up the Alfred P. Murrah Federal Building in Oklahoma City, killing 168 people. McVeigh expressed no remorse for his deed, but regretted that 19 children died. "They were collateral damage," he said. Was McVeigh's execution morally justified?

The National Center of Health Statistics has reported that the homicide rate for young men in the United States is 4 to 73 times the rate of other industrialized countries. In 1994, for example, 23,330 murders were committed in the United States. Whereas killings per 100,000 by men 15 through 24 years old in 1987 was 0.3 in Austria and 0.5 in Japan, the figure was 21.9 in the United States and as high as 232 per 100,000 for blacks in some states. The nation ranked closest to the United States was Scotland, with a 5.0 homicide rate. In some U.S. central-city areas, the rate is 732 times that of men in Austria. In 1997, the rate was 21.8 per 100,000 for blacks and 3.3 for whites.[2] The number of homicides in New York City broke the 2,000 mark in 1990. Black males in Harlem are said to have a lower life expectancy than males in Bangladesh. Although some improvement has been made, escalating crime has caused an erosion in the quality of urban living and is threatening the fabric of our social life.

Homo sapiens is the only species in which it is common for one member to kill another. In most other species, when there is a conflict between individuals, the weaker party submits to the stronger through some ritual gesture and is then permitted to depart in peace. Only in captivity, where the defeated animal cannot get away, will it be killed. Only human beings deliberately kill other individuals and groups of their own species. Perhaps it is not that we are more aggressive than other species but that our drives have been made more lethal by the use of weapons. Weapons such as guns or bombs, allow us to harm or kill without actually making physical or even eye contact with the victim. Likewise, someone who sends a letter bomb through the mail may never have even laid eyes on the victim. The inhibition against killing is undermined by the trigger's power, a point to be kept in mind when discussing gun-control legislation. We are a violent race whose power of destruction has increased in proportion to our technology.

The subject of punishment is receiving increased attention, as are the social causes of crime. As a student activist in the 1960s, I once opposed increased police protection for my neighborhood in Morningside Heights, New York City, arguing that we must get to the causes of crime rather than deal only with the symptoms. I later realized that this was like refusing firefighters the use of water hoses to put out fires because they dealt only with the symptoms rather than the causes of the fire.

The truth is that we do not know the exact nature of the causes of crimes of violence. Males commit a disproportionate number of violent crimes in our country, over 90 percent, with young, black males (between the ages of 15 and 24) constituting the group with the greatest tendency toward committing violent crimes.[3] Why is this? Many people in the United States believe that poverty causes crime, but this is false. Poverty is a terrible condition and surely contributes to crime, but it is not a necessary or sufficient condition for violent crime. The majority of people in India are far poorer than most of the American poor, yet a person, male or female, can walk through the worst slum of Calcutta or New Delhi at any time of the day or night without fearing molestation. As a student, I lived in a poor neighborhood in a city in England, which was safer than the Midwestern working-class neighborhood in which I grew up. The use and trafficking of illegal drugs contributes to a great deal of crime, and the turn from heroin to crack as the drug of choice has exacerbated the matter, but plenty of crime occurred in our society before drugs became the problem they now are. We leave the subject of the causes of crime for psychologists and sociologists to solve and turn to the nature of punishment.

To be responsible for a past act is to be liable to praise or blame. If the act was especially good, we go further than praise. We reward it. If it was especially evil, we go further than blame. We punish it. To examine the notion of punishment, we first need to inquire under what conditions, if any, criminal punishment is justified. We will examine three approaches to this problem: the retributivist, the utilitarian, and the rehabilitationist.

Even though few of us will ever become criminals or be indicted on criminal charges, most of us harbor deep feelings about the matter of criminal punishment. Something about crime touches the deepest nerves of our imagination. Take the following situations, which are based on newspaper reports from the mid-1990s:

> A drug addict in New York City stabs to death a vibrant, gifted, 22-year-old graduate student who has dedicated her life to helping others.
> A sexual-pervert lures little children into his home, sexually abuses them, and then kills them. Over 20 bodies are discovered on his property.
> A man sends his wife and daughter on an airplane trip, puts a time bomb into their luggage, and takes out a million-dollar insurance policy on their lives. The money will be used to pay off his gambling debts and for prostitutes.

What is it within us that rises up in indignation at the thought of these atrocities? What should happen to the criminals in these cases? How can the victims (or their loved ones) ever be compensated for these crimes? We feel conflicting emotional judgments of harsh vengeance toward the criminal and, at the same time, concern that we don't ourselves become violent and irrational in our quest for revenge.

THE DEFINITION OF PUNISHMENT

We may define *punishment*, or more precisely *institutional or legal punishment*, as an evil inflicted by a person in a position of authority upon another person who is judged to have violated a rule.[4] The definition can be broken down into five concepts:

1. *An evil*: To punish is to inflict harm, unpleasantness, or suffering (not necessarily pain). Regarding this concept, the question is: Under what conditions is it right to cause harm or inflict suffering?
2. *For a violation of a rule:* The violation is either a moral or a legal offense. The pertinent questions are: Should we punish everyone

who commits a moral offense? Need the offense already have
been committed or may we engage in prophylactic punishment
where we have good evidence that the agent will commit a crime?

3. *Done to the offender:* The offender must be judged or believed to be
guilty of a crime. Does this rule out the possibility of punishing
innocent people? What should we call the process of "framing"
the innocent and "punishing" them?

4. *Carried out by a personal agency:* The punisher must be a rational
agent, rather than a natural phenomenon, such as an earthquake
or disease.

5. *Imposed by an authority:* The agent who punishes must be justified
in carrying out the evil.

Let us spend a moment examining each of these points and the questions
they raise.

1. *Punishment is an evil.* It may involve corporal punishment, loss of
rights or freedom, or even loss of life. These are things we
normally condemn as immoral. How does what is normally
considered morally wrong suddenly become morally right? To
quote H. L. A. Hart, former Oxford University Professor of
Jurisprudence, What is this "mysterious piece of moral alchemy in
which the combination of two evils of moral wickedness and
suffering are transmuted into good"?[5] Theories of punishment
bear the burden of proof to justify why punishment is morally
required. The three classical theories have been retribution,
deterrence, and rehabilitation which, we shall examine below.
These theories attempt not only to justify types of punishment,
but also to provide guidance on the degrees of punishment to be
given for various crimes and persons.

2. Punishment is administered for an offense, but must it be for a
violation of a legal statute or may it also be for any moral failure?
While most legal scholars agree that the law should have a moral
basis, it is impractical to make laws against every moral wrong. If
we had a law against lying, for example, our courts would become
cluttered beyond their ability to function. Also, some laws may be
immoral (e.g., antiabortionists believe that the laws permitting
abortion are immoral), but they still are laws, carrying with them
coercive measures.

   Whether we should punish only offenses already committed or
also crimes that are intended is a difficult question. If I know or
have good evidence that Smith is about to kill some innocent

child (but not which one), and the only way to prevent this act is by incarcerating Smith (or killing him), why isn't this punishment morally acceptable? Normally, we don't have certainty about people's intentions, so we can't be certain that Smith really means to kill the child. But what if we do have strong evidence in this case? Nations sometimes launch preemptive strikes when they have strong evidence of an impending attack (e.g., Israel, in the Six-Day War in 1967, acting on reliable information that Arab nations were going to attack, launched a preemptive strike that probably saved many Israeli lives). Although preemptive strikes are about defense, not punishment per se, could the analogy carry over? After all, part of the role of punishment is defense against future crimes.

3. *Punishment is done to the offender.* No criminologist justifies punishing the innocent, but classic cases of framing the innocent to maximize utility do exist. Sometimes Caiaphus's decision to frame and execute Jesus of Nazareth is cited: "It were better that one man should die for a nation than that the whole nation perish" (John 10:50). Utilitarians seem to be vulnerable to such practices, but every utilitarian philosopher of law eschews such egregious miscarriages of justice. Why this is so is a point I will discuss below.

   This stipulation "done to an offender" also rules out other uses of the word *punish*, as when, for instance, we say that boxer Mike Tyson punished his opponent with a devastating left to the jaw. Such metaphorical or nonlegal uses of the term are excluded from our analysis. Similarly, although the law allows for the quarantine of confirmed or potential disease carriers, we would not call this imposed suffering punishment, for our intention is not to cause suffering but to prevent it, and the carrier is innocent of any wrongdoing.

4. *Punishment is carried out by a personal agency.* Punishment is not the work of natural forces, but of people. Lightning may strike and kill a criminal, but only people (or conscious beings) can punish other people.

5. *Punishment is imposed by an authority.* Punishment is conferred through institutions that have to do with maintaining laws or social codes. This stipulation rules out vigilante executions as punishments. Only a recognized authority, such as the state, can carry out legal punishment for criminal behavior.

We turn now to the leading theories of punishment.

THEORIES OF PUNISHMENT

Retributivist Theories

Retributivist theories make infliction of punishment dependent on what the agent, as a wrongdoer, deserves, rather than on any future social utility that might result from the infliction of suffering on the criminal. That is, rather than focusing on any *future* good that might result from punishment, retributivist theories are *backward-looking*, assessing the nature of the misdeed. The most forceful proponents of this view are Immanuel Kant (1724–1804), C. S. Lewis (1898–1963), and Herbert Morris. Here is a classic quotation from Kant, which deserves to be quoted at length:

> Juridical punishment can never be administered merely as a means for promoting another good either with regard to the criminal himself or to civil society, but must in all cases be imposed only because the individual on whom it is inflicted *has committed a crime*. For one man ought never to be dealt with merely as a means subservient to the purpose of another, nor be mixed up with the subjects of real right. Against such treatment his inborn personality has a right to protect him, even though he may be condemned to lose his civil personality. He must first be found guilty and *punishable* before there can be any thought of drawing from his punishment any benefit for himself or his fellow-citizens.
>
> The principle of punishment is a categorical imperative, and woe to him who creeps through the serpent-windings of utilitarianism to discover some advantage that may discharge him from the justice of punishment, or even reduces its amount by the advantage it promises, in accordance with the Pharisaical maxim, "It is better for *one* man to die than for an entire people to perish" [John 10:51]. For if justice and righteousness perish, there is no longer any value in men's living on the earth.
>
> But what kind and what amount of punishment is it that public justice makes its principle and standard? It is the principle of equality, by which the pointer of the scale of justice is made to incline no more to the one side than the other. It may be rendered by saying that the undeserved evil which any one commits on another, is to be regarded as perpetrated on himself. Hence it may be said, "If you slander another, you slander yourself; if you steal from another, you steal from yourself; if you strike another, you strike yourself; if you kill another you kill yourself." This is the *law of retribution (jus talionis)*—it being understood, of course, that this is applied by a court as distinguished from private judgment. It is the only principle that can definitely assign both the quality and the quantity of a just penalty. All other standards are wavering and uncertain; and on account of other considerations involved in them, they contain no principle conformable to the sentence of pure and strict justice.
>
> But what does it mean to say, If you steal from someone, you steal from yourself? Whoever steals makes the property of everyone else insecure and therefore deprives himself (by the principle of retribution) of security in any possible property. He has nothing and can also acquire nothing; but he still

wants to live, and this is now possible if others provide for him. But since the state will not provide for him free of charge, he must let it have his powers for any kind of work it pleases (in convict or prison labor) and is reduced to the status of a slave for a certain time, or permanently if the state sees fit. If, however, he has committed murder he must *die.* Here there is no substitute that will satisfy justice. There is no similarity between life, however wretched it may be, and death, hence no likeness between the crime and the retribution unless death is judicially carried out upon the wrongdoer, although it must still be freed from any mistreatment that could make the humanity in the person suffering it into something abominable. Even if a civil society resolved to dissolve itself with the consent of all its members—as might be supposed in the case of a people inhabiting an island resolving to separate and scatter themselves throughout the whole world—the last murderer lying in prison ought to be executed before the resolution was carried out. This ought to be done in order that every one may realize the desert of his deeds, and that bloodguiltiness may not remain upon the people; for otherwise they will all be regarded as participators in the murder as a public violation of justice.[6]

This is a classic expression of the retributivist position, for it bases punishment solely on the issue of whether or not the subject in question has committed a crime and punishes him accordingly. All other consideration—eudaemonistic or utilitarian—are to be rejected as irrelevant. For example, Kant considers the possibility of a capital criminal allowing himself to be a subject in a medical experiment as a substitute for capital punishment in order to benefit the society, but he rejects the suggestion. "A court would reject with contempt such a proposal from a medical college, for justice ceases to be justice if it can be bought for any price whatsoever." I have heard the phrase "that bloodguiltiness may not remain upon the people" interpreted as implying utilitarian consideration, signifying that the people will be cursed in the future. Perhaps a more charitable interpretation is that failure to punish constitutes an endorsement of the criminal act and thus a kind of criminal complicity after the act.[7]

Kant and the classic retributivist position in general have three theses about the justification of punishment:

1. Guilt is a necessary condition for judicial punishment; that is, *only* the guilty may be punished.
2. Guilt is a sufficient condition for judicial punishment; that is, all the guilty must be punished. If you have committed a crime, morality demands that you suffer an evil for it.
3. The correct amount of punishment imposed on the morally (or legally) guilty offender is that amount which is *equal* to the moral seriousness of the offense.

There are various ways of arguing for these theses. One is to argue, as Kant does, that in lying, stealing, or unjustly striking or killing another, the offender lies, steals, or unjustly strikes or kills himself. That is, by universalizing the maxim of such acts, the offender wills a like action on himself. This is the law of retaliation (*jus talionis*): "the undeserved evil which any one commits on another, is to be regarded as perpetrated on himself." The criminal need not consciously desire the same punishment, but by acting on such a principle, for example, "murder your enemies," the offender implicitly draws the same treatment on himself. He deserves to suffer in the same way he has harmed another. Or, at least, the suffering should be equal and similar to the suffering he has caused. This is the *strict equality* (sometimes called the *lex talionis*) interpretation of retributivism.

The weakness of the equality interpretation is that it is both impractical and impossible to inflict the very same kind of suffering on the offender as he or she has imposed on others. Our social institutions are not equipped to measure the exact amount of harm done by offenders or repay them in kind. We rightly shrink from torturing the torturer or resuscitating the serial murderer so that we can "kill" him a second, a third, a fourth time, and so forth. How do you give a trusted member of the FBI or CIA who betrays his or her country by spying for the enemy an equivalent harm? Our legal systems are not equipped to punish according to the harm inflicted but, rather, according to the wrong done, measured against specified statutes with prescribed penalties.

A second way, of arguing for the theses, following Herbert Morris and Michael Davis, is to interpret them in terms of social equilibrium.[8] The criminal has violated a mutually beneficial scheme of social cooperation, thereby treating law-abiding members of the community unfairly. Punishment restores the scales of justice, the social equilibrium of benefits and burdens. We might put the argument this way:

1. In breaking a primary rule of society, a person obtains an unfair advantage over others.
2. Unfair advantages ought to be redressed by society if possible.
3. Punishment is a form of redressing the unfair advantage.
4. Therefore, we ought to punish the offender for breaking the primary rule.

Punishment restores the social equilibrium of burdens and benefits by taking from the agent what he or she unfairly got and now owes, that is, exacting his or her debt. This argument, like the Kantian one above, holds that society has a duty to punish the offender, since society has a general duty to redress unfair advantages if possible. That is, we have a prima facie duty to eliminate unfair advantages in society, even though that duty may be overridden by other considerations, such as the high cost (financially or socially) of doing so or the criminal's repentance.

Whereas the Kantian interpretation focuses on the nature and gravity of the harm done by the offender, Morris's *unfair advantage* or *fair play argument* focuses on the unfairness of the offense—the idea of unfair advantage that ought to be repaid to society. Although it is not always the case that the criminal gains an advantage or profits from crime, he or she does abandon the common burden of self-restraint to obtain criminal ends. While the rest of us are forgoing the use of unlawful and immoral means to obtain our goals, while we are restraining ourselves from taking these shortcuts, the criminal makes use of these means to his or her ends. Thus, we have been unfairly taken advantage of, and justice requires the annulment of the unfair advantage. The criminal must repay his or her debt to society. He or she need not be punished in the same way as his or her offense, but the punishment must fit the crime, that is, be a proportionate response.

It is not clear, however, that Morris's and Davis's interpretation can do all the work. For one thing, it is modeled on the act of stealing (or cheating), getting an unfair advantage over others. The criminal may obtain an unfair advantage over others by cheating on exams or taxes, by killing a rival for a job, or by stealing another's purse, but this model of unfair advantage doesn't work as well with sadistic crimes, which may leave the criminal psychologically worse off than the victim. The successful rapist may be worse off, not better off, than before his crime. The terrorist who detonates a bomb on the crowded bus he is riding doesn't gain any advantage over others, for he no longer exists. Furthermore, we do not punish all instances of unfair advantage, as when someone lies. Daniel Farrell has objected to the fair play argument, pointing out that even before we enter into a social contract, even in a Lockean state of nature, the concept of just desert holds, and we should intervene on behalf of an innocent victim who is being attacked by an aggressor, a malicious rapist, or a killer.[9] Moreover, we think someone is deserving of punishment even when he or she only *attempts*—with malice aforethought—to harm others, when the intention to do evil is unsuccessful. This is sometimes referred to as mens rea: having a guilty mind.

DESERT   Both the strict equality (*lex talionis*) and the fair play interpretations of retributivism have some validity, but both partially misfire. Strict equality of punishment is not practical or necessary for retributive justice. On the other hand, the fair play argument overemphasizes the advantage gained by the criminal, fails to account for evil intentions (or mens rea), and tends to treat punishment as restitution. But both theories correctly point to the broader, underlying ground for punishment: that the criminal deserves suffering in a way fitting his or her crime. Farrell correctly points to this salient feature—desert, which exists even in a Lockean state of nature (a precontractual state). While it is not practical, let alone necessary, to punish the criminal in a manner equal to the gravity of the crime, we can punish him or her in a manner proportionate to the seriousness of the offense. So we should modify the third premise of the strict equality interpretation to read:

> 3. The correct amount of punishment imposed on the morally (or legally) guilty offender is that amount which is *proportionate* to the moral seriousness of the offense.

The concept of desert is connected with our notion of responsibility. With free agents who can choose, a moral universe would be so arranged that we would be rewarded or punished in a manner equal to our virtue or vice. As the biblical adage puts it, "Whatsoever a man sows, that shall he also reap" (Galatians 6:17). Those who sow good deeds would reap good results, and those who choose to sow their wild oats would reap accordingly. Given a notion of objective morality, the good should prosper and the evil should suffer—both in equal measure to their virtue or vice. This idea is also reflected in the Eastern concept of karma: You will be repaid in the next life for what you did in this one. The ancient Greek philosophers and the Roman jurists, beginning with Cicero, define justice as giving to each his due, *suum cuique tribuens.* Jesus may be seen as adumbrating the same principle in his statement, "Render unto Caesar that which is Caesar's and unto God that which is God's" (Luke 20:25). In the Christian tradition, the idea is reflected in the doctrine of heaven and hell (and purgatory). The good will be rewarded according to their good works, and the evil will be punished in hell—which they have chosen by their actions.

It would seem that eternal hell is excessive punishment for human evil and that eternal bliss is excessive reward, but the basic idea of *moral fittingness* seems to make sense. G. W. Leibniz refers to the principle that Kant, as noted above, calls the principle of equality, a sort of symmetry between input and output in any endeavor. We get a hint of this symmetry in the practice of gratitude. We normally and spontaneously feel grateful for services rendered. Someone treats us to dinner, gives us a present, teaches us a skill, rescues us from a potential disaster, or simply gives us directions. A sense of gratitude wells up inside us toward our benefactor; we feel indebted and sense that we have a duty to reciprocate in kind. On the other hand, if someone intentionally and cruelly hurts us, deceives us, or betrays our trust, we feel involuntary resentment. We want to reciprocate and harm that person. The offender deserves to be harmed, and we have a right to harm him or her. If the offender has harmed someone else, we have an instinctual duty to harm the offender. Henry Sidgwick argued that these basic emotions are, in fact, the grounds for our notion of desert: Punishment is resentment universalized and rewards—a sort of positive retribution— are gratitude universalized.[10] Whether such a reduction of desert to resentment and gratitude completely explains our notion of desert may be questioned, but it lends support to two theses: first, that there is natural, preinstitutional desert and, second, that desert creates obligations.

These theses wee defended in Chapter 5. I will only add that the notion of desert as creating obligations underlies our revulsion regarding prejudicial discrimination. We object to racist and sexist practices because they treat people unfairly; they make irrelevant features, such as race and gender, rather than desert or merit, the criteria for social goods. We have a duty not to harm people unjustly, but to treat them positively according to their moral dignity. Similarly, children who have been afflicted with life-threatening diseases deserve to be compensated by society so that their underserved suffering is mitigated. Such desert claims create prima facie obligations on all of us who have the means to aid in meeting them. This principle seems to be one that is intuitively recognized by people everywhere in their everyday practices. The sociologist George Caspar Homans has noted that in economic relations, people in every culture "are alike in holding the notion of proportionality between investment and profit that lies at the heart of distributive justice" and have a notion that "fair exchange . . . is realized when the profit, or reward less cost, of each man is directly proportional to his investment."[11]

DESERT AND UTILITARIANISM   Utilitarian considerations can partially explain our belief in the propriety of rewarding and punishing people according to the nature of their acts. Rewarding good works encourages further good works, whereas punishment has a deterrent effect. By recognizing and rewarding merit, we promote efficiency and welfare. We want the very best generals to lead our sons and daughters to battle, the most outstanding basketball and football players to play on our team, and excellent surgeons, airline pilots, and judges to serve our needs. A superior teacher can teach twice or thrice as effectively as a minimally competent one. We want the best car for our money, not just an average car. While some tasks have thresholds beyond which it is not necessary to improve on (e.g., I'm satisfied with our slow mail delivery, though getting the mail a few hours earlier would be better), some tasks—those mentioned above— crucially depend on high efficiency. So a utilitarian defense of meritocracy is possible. In general, we can say that a society that has a fitting notion of rewarding those who contribute to its well-being and punishing those who work against its well-being will survive and prosper better than a society lacking these practices. But, of course, utilitarian considerations can be used to override considerations of merit.

Utilitarian considerations are important, but I doubt that they are the whole story behind the long-standing, universal history of our faith in meritocracy. One would like to have a nonutilitarian, deontological argument to ground our intuitions that regarding any good and useful function X, the good (at X) should prosper and the bad (at X) should suffer. W. D. Ross argues that meritocracy is a fundamental intuition, offering, as evidence for this thesis, the following thought experiment. After identifying two intrinsically good things—(1) pleasure and (2) virtue—Ross asks us to consider a third:

> If we compare two imaginary states of the universe, alike in the total amounts of virtue and vice and of pleasure and pain present in the two, but in one of which the virtuous were all happy and the vicious miserable, while in the other the virtuous were miserable and the vicious happy, very few people would hesitate to say that the first was a much better state of the universe than the second. It would seem then that, besides virtue and pleasure, we must recognize (3), as a third independent good, the apportionment of pleasure and pain to the virtuous and the vicious respectively. And it is on the recognition of this as a separate good that the recognition of the duty of justice, in distinction from fidelity to promise on the one hand and from beneficence on the other, rests.[12]

I think that most people would agree with Ross that it is intuitively obvious that the appropriate distribution of happiness and unhappiness should be according to virtue and vice. Even if we could produce more aggregate happiness or welfare by making the vicious better off, would we not prefer a world where people get what they deserve to one of utility? Part of what makes the world good consists in giving people what they deserve. It seems to be exactly the intuition that motivated Kant's dictum that conscientiousness or the good will, being the single desert base, is the only moral basis for happiness: "An impartial spectator can never feel approval in contemplating the uninterrupted prosperity of a being graced by no touch of a pure and good will, and that consequently a good will seems to constitute the indispensable condition of our very worthiness to be happy."[13]

Consider again Farrell's example concerning an aggressor who is attacking an innocent victim in the state of nature. Would we not intervene on behalf of the victim if we thought we could safely make a difference in the outcome? Would we not think it better that the aggressor die than that the victim die? And if two aggressors attacked one victim, so that twice as many *dolors* (units of suffering) were incurred by killing both aggressors in saving the life of the innocent party, would we not prefer this than that the victim die (with the result that half as many dolors resulted)? If the correct answer to these questions is yes, then not only is desert preinstitutional (contra Rawls and company), but it is a valid concept apart from utilitarian outcomes. If this is so, desert trumps utility.

Desert also trumps equality. What we object to in inequalities, I think, is that they so often are undeserved. We don't morally object when the better quarterback is chosen as a starter over ourselves; or when a superior student, who works equally hard, gets a higher grade than ourselves; or when an enterprising entrepreneur succeeds in establishing a socially useful business and thereby makes more money than her lazy brother who spends his days surfing off the California coast. What we may object to is the lazy brother's inheriting vast sums of money from his enterprising sister, and what we certainly do object to is the lazy brother's stealing the money from his sister, for the lazy surfer doesn't deserve his gains.

Our concept of justice includes notions of responsibility, reciprocity, and desert that are preinstitutional and deontological, so that perpetrators of evil deserve to suffer and virtuous people deserve a level of well-being corresponding to their virtue. Since we have a general duty to strive to bring about justice in the world, it follows that we have a duty to try to bring it about directly or indirectly, through just institutions, by which, wherever possible, the virtuous are rewarded with well-being and the vicious with suffering, inclining them to repentance.

This is not to argue that we must always give people what they deserve. There may be grounds for mercy, forgiveness, and rehabilitation: Mitigating circumstances may be taken into consideration to lessen the severity of the punishment. But the aim is to bring about moral homeostasis, a just social order where the good are rewarded and the bad are punished in proportion to their deeds.

Although we have indirectly addressed it, let us say a word about the revised third thesis of retribution, stated earlier:

3. The correct amount of punishment imposed on the morally (or legally) guilty offender is that amount which is proportionate to the moral seriousness of the offense.

An attempt at proportionality seems to be universal. As Émile Durkheim noted, "There is no society where the rule does not exist that the punishment must be proportioned to the offense."[14] We have a general idea of *ordinal* orderings of crimes according to their gravity, for example (1) murder, (2) rape, (3) theft, (4) perjury. But it is difficult, if not impossible, to give them absolute rankings: for example, theft must always be visited with 1 year in prison; burglary with breaking and entering, with 5 years; perjury with six months, and so on, for it is hard to compare crimes. How much worse is rape than assault? Well, different rapes are of different magnitudes of severity, and likewise with assaults and murders and perjuries and so forth. Some relativity applies to our perceptions of the seriousness of crimes; thus if legal punishment is perceived as excessive, juries will fail to convict; and if legal punishment is perceived as too lenient, private vengeance will emerge. In either case, the law is subverted. So even if it were the case that rapists deserved castration (as Jefferson advocated) or being raped themselves, if the public perception is that these punishments are too brutal, then the penal system is forced to impose lesser or, at least, different punishments. Complete punitive justice, even if we knew what it was, might not be possible in an imperfect world.

None of this is meant to deny in the least the general thesis that the punishment should fit the crime, that the criminal deserves punishment commensurate with the gravity of the crime. The discussion is meant to urge caution and restraint, to impart a sense of our fallibility, and to foster a realization that an insistence on perfect justice is counterproductive (*summum justicia, summa injuria*—the demand for nothing less than *perfect* justice results in perfect injury). On the other hand, we must seek to respect the demands of impartial justice, inflicting punishments that correspond to the gravity of the crime. Someone who takes another's life in cold blood (mens rea) deserves to die; someone who maliciously blinds another deserves blindness or something equivalent; someone who steals from another deserves to lose his or her possessions or—if he or she has gambled or spent them—to be punished in a manner deemed suitable by the judicial system. Roughly equivalent punishments satisfy the notion of symmetry or fittingness inherent in our notion of desert. But not all crimes (e.g., embezzlement and perjury) lend themselves to this symmetry model. In these areas, practical wisdom, what the Greeks called *phronesis*, is needed. A uniform schedule of penalties for various crimes attempts to provide standardized punishments, removing arbitrariness from the penal system; but the weakness of this system is that it also removes discretion, *phronesis*, from the sentencing process.

Finally, we must separate retributivism from vengeance. Vengeance signifies acts that arise out the victims' desire for revenge, for satisfying their anger at the criminal for what he or she has done. The nineteenth-century British philosopher James Fitzjames Stephen thought vengeance was a justification for punishment, arguing that punishment should be in-

flicted "for the sake of gratifying the feeling of hatred—call it revenge, resentment, or what you will—which the contemplation of such [offensive]
conduct excites in healthily constituted minds."[15] The *lex talionis*—"an eye
for an eye, a tooth for a tooth, a life for a life" (Exod. 21–23)—set forth by
Moses in the Old Testament was actually a gesture of restraint on the passion for vengeance, which might otherwise demand life for an eye or a
tooth, two lives for the life of one member of my family. Thomas Jefferson
was one of the earliest Americans to set forth a system of proportionality
of punishment to crime:

> Whosoever shall be guilty of rape, polygamy, sodomy with man or woman,
> shall be punished, if a man, by castration, if a woman by cutting through the
> cartilage of her nose a hole of one half inch in diameter at the least. [And]
> whosoever shall maim another, or shall disfigure him . . . shall be maimed, or
> disfigured in the like sort: or if that cannot be, for want art, then as nearly as
> may be, in some other part of at least equal value.[16]

But retributivism is not based on hatred for the criminal (though a feeling
of vengeance may accompany the punishment); it is the theory that the
criminal *deserves* to be punished and deserves to be punished in proportion to the gravity of his or her crime—whether or not the victim or anyone else desires it. We may all deeply regret having to carry out the
punishment.

Although the retributivist theory has broad intuitive appeal, it is not
without problems. One problem is to make sense out of the notion of balancing the scales of justice. The metaphor suggests a cosmic scale that is
put out of balance by a crime, but such a scale may not exist, or if one does,
it may not be our duty to maintain it through punishment. That may be
God's role. Furthermore, retributivism seems unduly retrospective. If we
can restore the repentant criminal to moral integrity through rehabilitative
processes, then to insist on a pound of flesh seems barbaric. Nevertheless,
although retributivism needs to be supplemented by other considerations,
it still provides the core idea of justice as distribution on the basis of desert.

Utilitarian Theories

Utilitarian theories are theories of deterrence, reform, and prevention.
The emphasis is not on the gravity of the evil done, but on deterring and
preventing future evil. Their motto might be, "Don't cry over spilt milk."
Unlike retributive theories, which are *backward-looking* and based on *desert*,
utilitarian theories are *forward-looking*, based on *social improvement*. Jeremy
Bentham (1748–1832) and John Stuart Mill (1806–1873) are classic utilitarians. Their position can be broken down into three theses:

1. Social utility (including reform, prevention, and deterrence) is a necessary condition for judicial punishment.
2. Social utility is a sufficient condition for judicial punishment.
3. The proper amount of punishment to be imposed on the offender is that amount which will do the most good (or least harm) to all those who will be affected by it. Stanley Benn puts it well: "The margin of increment of harm inflicted on the offender should be preferable to the harm avoided by fixing that penalty rather than one slightly lower."[17]

Punishment is a technique of social control, justified so long as it prevents more evil than it produces. If there is a system of social control that will give a greater balance (e.g., rehabilitation), then the utilitarian will opt for that. The utilitarian doesn't accept draconian laws that would deter because the punishment would be worse than the crime, causing greater suffering than the original offense. Only three grounds are permissible for meting out punishment: (1) to prevent a repetition; (2) to deter others—the threat of punishment deters potential offenders; and (3) to rehabilitate the criminal (this need not be seen as punishment, but it may involve that).

The threat of punishment is everything. Every act of punishment is to that extent an admission of the failure of the threat. If the threat were successful, no punishment would be needed, and the question of justification would not arise.

One problem with the utilitarian theory is simply that it goes against our notion of desert. It says that social utility is a necessary condition for punishment. But I would be in favor of punishing at least the most egregious offenders even if I knew they would never commit another crime. Suppose we discovered Adolf Hitler living quietly in a small Argentine town and were sure that no good (in terms of deterrence or prevention) would come of punishing him. Shouldn't we still bring him to trial and punish him appropriately?

A further problem is that utilitarianism would seem to enjoin punishment for prospective crimes. If the best evidence we have leads us to believe that some person or group of people will commit a crime, we are justified in applying punitive measures if our actions satisfy a cost-benefit analysis.

The main weakness of utilitarianism is that it seems to allow the punishment of the innocent if that will deter others from crime. We want only criminals punished, but utilitarians focus on results, not justice. If we can frame an innocent bum for a rape and murder to prevent a riot, the utilitarian will be tempted to do so. This violates the essence of justice.

Some philosophers, namely, Anthony Quinton, Stanley Benn, and R. S. Peters, have rejected this criticism as missing the point of what punishment is. They contend that punishment is logically connected with committing a crime, so that the one punished must be presumed guilty.[18] But this "definitional stop" only moves the problem to a different dimension without solving it. Suppose we call "punishment" punishing the guilty and give another name, such as "telishment" (Rawls's suggestion), to judicially harming the innocent for deterrent purposes. Now the question becomes, Should we ever telish people? The utilitarian is committed to telishment—whenever the aggregate utility warrants it.

While these criticisms are severe, they do not overthrow utilitarianism altogether. One surely admits that penal law should have a deterrent effect. The point seems to be that utilitarian theories need a retributive base on which to build (a point I will comment on later).

Rehabilitative Theories

According to rehabilitative theories, crime is a disease, and the criminal is a sick person who needs to be cured, not punished. Such rehabilitationists as B. F. Skinner, Karl Menninger, and Benjamin Karpman point to the failures and cruelties of our penal system and advocate an alternative of therapy and reconditioning. "Therapy not torture" might be said to be their motto, for criminals are not really in control of their behavior, but are suffering personality disorders. Crime is by and large a result of an adverse early environment, so what must be done is recondition the criminal through positive reinforcement. Punishment is a prescientific response to antisocial behavior. At best, punishment temporarily suppresses adverse behavior, but, if untreated, Skinner argues, the behavior will resurface as though the punishment had never occurred. It is useless as a deterrent. Rehabilitationists charge that retributivists are guilty of holding an antiquated notion of human beings as possessing free wills and being responsible for their behavior. We, including all our behavior, are all products of our heredity and, especially, our environment.

Menninger sees rehabilitation as a replacement for the concept of justice in criminal procedure:

> The very word *justice* irritates scientists. No surgeon expects to be asked if an operation for cancer is just or not. No doctor will be reproached on the grounds that the dose of penicillin he has prescribed is less or more than *justice* would stipulate . . . It does not advance a solution to use the word *justice*. It is a subjective emotional word . . . the concept is so vague, so distorted in its application, so hypocritical, and usually so irrelevant that it offers no help in the solution of the crime problem which it exists to combat but results in its exact opposite—injustice, injustice to everybody.[19]

We need to confine criminals for their own and society's good, but a process of positive reinforcement must be the means of dealing with criminals and their "crimes." Karpman, one of the proponents of this theory, puts it this way:

> Basically, criminality is but a symptom of insanity, using the term in its widest generic sense to express unacceptable social behavior based on unconscious motivation flowing from a disturbed instinctive and emotional life, whether this appears in frank psychoses, or in less obvious form in neuroses and unrecognized psychoses . . . If criminals are products of early environmental influences in the same sense that psychotics and neurotics are, then it should be possible to reach them psychotherapeutically.[20]

Let me begin my criticism of the rehabilitation theory by relating the Good Samaritan story (Luke 10: 29–37). You'll recall that a Jew went down from Jerusalem to Jericho and fell among thieves who beat him, robbed him, and left him for dead. A priest and a Levite passed by him, but an outcast Samaritan came to the beaten man's rescue, bringing him to an inn for treatment and paying for his care.

A contemporary version of the story goes like this: A man is brutally robbed and left on the side of the road by his assailants. A priest comes by but regrets having to leave the man in his condition to avoid being late for the church service he must lead. Likewise, a lawyer passes by, rushing to meet a client. Finally, a psychiatrist sees our subject, rushes over to him, places the man's head in his lap and in a distraught voice cries out, "Oh, this is awful! How deplorable! Tell me, sir, who did this to you? He needs help."

Not all psychiatrists fit this description of mislocating the victim, but the story cannot be dismissed as merely a joke in poor taste. It fits an attitude that substitutes the concept of sickness for moral failure. Let me briefly note some of the problems with the whole theory of rehabilitation as a substitute for punishment. First, this doctrine undermines the very notion of human autonomy and responsibility. Individuals who are not mentally ill are free agents whose actions should be taken seriously as flowing from free decisions.[21] If a person kills in cold blood, he or she must bear the responsibility for that murder. Rehabilitation theories reduce moral problems to medical problems.

Furthermore, rehabilitation doesn't seem to work. Rehabilitation is a form of socialization through sophisticated medical treatment. Although humans are malleable, there are limits to what socialization and medical technology can do. Socialization can be relatively effective in infancy and early childhood, less so in late childhood, and even less effective in adulthood. Perhaps at some future time when brain manipulation becomes possible, we will make greater strides toward behavior modification, even being able to plant electrodes in a criminal's brain and so affect the cerebral cortex that he or she "repents" of the crime and is restored to society. The question then will be whether we have a right to tamper with someone's psyche in this manner. Furthermore, would a neurologically induced repentance for a crime really be repentance, or would it be an overriding of the criminal's autonomy and personality? And won't that tampering itself be a form of punishment?

APPLICATION TO THE DEATH PENALTY

Probably the most controversial aspect of punishment revolves around the issue of the death penalty or capital punishment. Retentionists, who seek to retain the institution of capital punishment argue that it is justified on the basis of either retributivism or deterrence. Abolitionists, who seek to abolish the institution, claim that the death penalty does not deter and is not necessary for retributive justice. A long prison sentence would do as well. They may also add that our judicial system is vulnerable to error and prejudice, so that a disproportionate number of minority members and some innocent people are executed, while the rich can hire the best lawyers to escape the electric chair. While this is not the place to definitively decide the matter, it should be briefly discussed and the relevant issues clarified.[22]

One can separate the theoretical from the practical issue of capital punishment. On the theoretical side, we must ask whether the death penalty is ever morally permissible. Do murderers like Timothy McVeigh and Ted Bundy, who is reported to have raped and murdered over a hundred women, deserve to be executed by the state. If we review the nature of retributive justice, it is likely we will conclude that such cold-blooded murder deserves capital punishment. But if life in prison turns out to be just as effective, retributivism may not decide the issue one way or the other.

The crucial issue may turn out to be utilitarian, depending on whether we have evidence that capital punishment does or does not deter would-be murderers from killing other people. Sometimes students argue that the evidence proves that the death penalty does not deter, but this is incorrect. The statistical evidence is ambiguous and does not prove either that capital punishment does or does not deter would-be murders. We can imagine a situation where the death penalty did deter rational agents bent on murder. Imagine that every time someone intentionally killed an innocent person he or she was immediately struck down by lightning. When Ted Bundy slashed the throat of the girl he and his confederates just raped, lightning struck Ted. His companions witnessing his corpse would doubtless think twice before they duplicated Ted's act. When burglar Bob pulls out his pistol and shoots bank teller Betty through her heart, lightning levels Bob in the midst of his fellow robbers and the bystanders. Do you think that the evidence of cosmic retribution would go unheeded?

Of course, we do not have such swift and sure retributivism, but the question is, whether we could improve our penal system to approximate it to a sufficient degree to justify use of the death penalty. Can we sometimes have sufficient evidence to apply the death penalty for a murder, say in the cases of McVeigh and Bundy, and apply it in a public manner that causes prospective murderers to refrain from murdering innocent people? I must leave the difficult issue for you to decide.

Conclusion

Let me close by suggesting that there are elements of truth in all three theories of punishment. Rehabilitationism, insofar as it seeks to restore the criminal to society as a morally whole being, has merit as an aspect of the penal process, but it cannot stand alone. Retributivism is surely correct to make guilt a necessary condition for punishment and to seek to make the punishment fit the crime. Its emphasis on desert is vital to our theory of rewards and punishment, and with this it respects humans as rational, responsible agents, who should be treated in a manner fitting to their deserts. But it may be too rigid in its *retrospective* gaze and in need of mercy and *prospective* vision. Utilitarianism seems correct in emphasizing this prospective feature of treatment with the goal of promoting human flourishing. But it is in danger of manipulating people for the social good— even of punishing the innocent or punishing the guilty more than they deserve (to serve a social purpose). One way of combining retributivism and utilitarianism has been suggested by John Rawls in his classic essay, "Two Concepts of Rules," in which he attempts to do justice to both the retributive and the utilitarian theories of punishment.[23] He argues that there is a difference between justifying an institution and justifying a given instance where the question Why are we applying the law in the present situation in this mode? Applied to punishment, (1) Why do we have a system of punishment? and (2) Why are we harming John for his misdeed? are two different sorts of questions. When we justify the institution of punishment, we resort to utilitarian or consequentialist considerations: A society in which the wicked prosper will offer inadequate inducement to virtue. A society in which some rules are made and enforced will get on better than a society in which no rules exist or are enforced. But when we seek to justify

an individual application of punishment, we resort to retributivist considerations; for example, when someone commits a breach against the law,
that person merits a fitting punishment.

We can operate on two levels. On the second-order (reflective) level,
we accept rule utilitarianism and acknowledge that the penal law should
serve society's overall good. To accomplish this goal, we need a retributive
system—one that adheres to common ideas of fair play and desert. So rule
utilitarianism on the second-order level yields retributivism on the first-
order level. As we have noted, some have interpreted this process to entail
that there is no preinstitutional or natural desert or justice, but that these
things come into being only by social choice. It is more accurate to say that
there is a primordial or deontological idea of desert that needs social
choice to become activated or institutionalized for human purposes. It is
not as though society could rationally choose some other practice, but
that, if it is to choose rationally—to promote its goals of flourishing and
resolving conflicts of interest—it must choose to reward and punish according to one's desert.

For Further Reflection

1.   Examine the theories of punishment discussed in this chapter.
Which seems the best justified? Or do you think a combination of theories
is best justified?

2.   Reflect on Rawls's split level theory discussed at the end of the
chapter, which aims at differentiating between justifying an institution and
justifying a given instance where the institution is applied. Does it make
good sense?

3.   Apply your thoughts on punishment to the institution of capital
punishment. Is the death penalty ever justified? Explain your answer.

Endnotes

Some of the material in this chapter is adapted from my part of *The Death
Penalty: For and Against* written with Jeffrey Reiman (Rowman & Littlefield,
1998).

1. Immanuel Kant, *The Metaphysics of Morals*, trans. E. Hastie (Edinburgh,
1887), p. 155. This book was originally published in 1779.

2. Statistics are from the National Center of Health Statistics and are available
from the Centers for Disease Control. The National Center for Injury
Prevention and Control reports that 8,116 young people aged 15 to 24 were
victims of homicide in 1994, or an average of 22 youth victims per day in the

United States. This homicide rate is 10 times higher than Canada's, 15 times higher than Australia's, and 28 times higher than those of France and Germany. In 1994 a total of 102,220 rapes and 618,950 robberies were reported in the United States.

3. The FBI's 1994 *Uniform Crime Reports* states that 1,864,168 violent crimes occurred that year; 25,052 offenders were listed. "Of those for whom sex and age were reported, 91% of the offenders were males, and 84% were persons 18 years of age or older . . . Of offenders for whom race was known, 56% were black, 42% white, and the remainder were persons of other races" (p. 14).

4. For the following analysis, I am indebted to Anthony Flew, "Justification of Punishment," *Philosophy* (1954); Joel Feinberg, "Punishment," in *Philosophy of Law*, 2nd ed., Joel Feinberg and Hyman Gross, eds. (Wadsworth, 1980); and Herbert Morris, "Persons and Punishment," *The Monist* 52 (October 1968). See also Tziporah Kasachkoff, "The Criteria of Punishment: Some Neglected Considerations," *Canadian Journal of Philosophy* 2:3 (March 1973).

5. H. L. A. Hart, *Punishment and Responsibility* (Oxford University Press, 1968), p. 234.

6. Kant, op. cit., pp. 155–56.

7. I am grateful to Jeffrey Reiman for pointing this out to me.

8. Morris, op. cit. See also Michael Davis, "Harm and Retribution," and *Philosophy and Public Affairs* 15:3 (Summer 1986).

9. Daniel Farrell, "Justification of General Deterrence," *Philosophical Review* 44:3 (July 1985).

10. Henry Sidgwick, *Methods of Ethics* (Hackett), Book 3, chap.5.

11. George Caspar Homans, *Social Behavior: Its Elementary Forms* (Routledge & Kegan Paul, 1961), pp. 246, 264.

12. W. R. Ross, *The Right and the Good* (Oxford University Press, 1930), p. 138.

13. Immanuel Kant, *Groundwork of the Metaphysic of Morals*, trans. H. J. Paton (Hutchinson University Library, 1948); p. 59. For a fuller defense of the thesis that desert creates obligations, see my "Merit: Why Do We Value It?" (*Journal of Social Philosophy*, 1997).

14. Émile Durkheim, *The Rules of Sociological Method*, (Oxford University Press, 1952), quoted in Ernest van den Haag, *Punishing Criminals: Concerning a Very Old and Painful Question* (Basic Books, 1975), p. 194.

15. James Fitzjames Stephen, *Liberty, Equality, Fraternity* (Cambridge University Press, 1967), p. 152.

16. Thomas Jefferson, *Bill for Proportioning Crime and Punishments* (1779), quoted in Ernest van den Haag, op. cit., p. 193.

17. Stanley Benn, "Punishment," in *The Encyclopedia of Philosophy*, Paul Edwards, ed. (Macmillan, 1967), vol. 7, pp. 29–35.

18. Anthony Quinton, "Punishment," in *Philosophy, Politics and Society*, P. Laslett, ed. (London: Routledge & Kegan Paul, 1959). Stanley Benn and R. S. Peters admit that "if utilitarianism could really be shown to involve punishing the innocent, or a false parade of punishment, or punishment in anticipation of

an offense, these criticisms would no doubt be conclusive. They are, however, based on a misconception of what the utilitarian theory is about. We said at the beginning of this chapter that 'punishment' implied in its primary sense, not the inflicting of *any* sort of suffering, but inflicting suffering under certain specified conditions, one of which was that is must be for a breach of a rule" ("The Utilitarian Case for Deterrence", p. 98).

19. Karl Menninger, *The Crime of Punishment* (Viking Press, 1968), pp. 17, 10–11. The passage is remarkable for its apparent denial and assertion of the objective reality of justice.
20. Benjamin Karpman, "Criminal Psychodynamics," *Journal of Criminal Law and Criminology* 47 (1956), p. 9. See also B. F. Skinner, *Science and Human Behavior* (Macmillan, 1953), pp. 182–93.
21. I am assuming that the case for free will and responsibility is cogent. For a good discussion, see the readings by Harry Frankfurt, Gary Watson, and Peter van Inwagen in *Moral Responsibility*, John Martin Fischer, ed. (Ithaca, NY: Cornell University Press, 1986).
22. See my and Jeffrey Reman's, *The Death Penalty: For and Against* (Rowman & Little Field, 1998).
23. John Rawls, "Two Concepts of Rules," *Philosophical Review* (1955).

9

COSMOPOLITANISM, NATIONALISM, AND WORLD GOVERNMENT

In order that society should exist and, a fortiori, that a society should prosper, it is necessary that the minds of all the citizens should be rallied and held together by certain predominant ideas; and this cannot be the case unless each of them sometimes draws his opinions from the common source and consents to accept certain matters of belief already formed.

—ALEXIS DE TOCQUEVILLE[1]

Nationalism "is the measles of mankind."

—ALBERT EINSTEIN[2]

When anyone asked him where he came from, [Diogenes] said, "I am a citizen of the world."

—DIOGENES LAERTIUS, ON DIOGENES THE CYNIC

INTRODUCTION: AN OVERVIEW OF GLOBAL ANARCHY

IF ANARCHY IS THE FIRST challenge to government in general, threatening chaos and leading to the invention of the state as the answer to that chaos, on an international plane, anarchy is the ultimate challenge to the collection of governments, threatening global chaos through revolution and war, and thereby creating the need for the invention of an international governing body to promote peace and stability. Each state tends to act on the global scene in a manner analogous to the individual in a state of anarchy (a tacit war of all against all), each being vulnerable to attack and destruction at the hands of its neighbors. Any nation, so long as it is strong enough, can make a promise when it is advantageous to do so and break it with impunity when it is advantageous to do so. Treaties are essentially unenforceable, and laws without binding sanctions mere documents of convenience. Essentially, might makes right. And war, whether cold or hot, is the constant companion of every corporate body. Whereas the state can enforce its laws and treaties among its members, no international body exists that can enforce laws and treaties among its member states. In international affairs we are in a Hobbesian state of nature, a state of war (a war of all against all), not necessarily hot, but where the threat of aggression and violence is imminent. History amply illustrates the Hobbesian doctrine.

During the Peloponnesian War in the fifth century B.C.E., the Athenians asked the inhabitants of Melos, hitherto neutral, to acknowledge their lordship. The envoys met and held a debate, which Thucydides recorded in full, and which, for sweet reasonableness of its form, stood out in candor and eloquence. The Melians demurred and said that they refused to be slaves. They appealed to the gods for help. The Athenian general replied: "The powerful exact what they can and the weak grant what they must. Of the gods we believe and of men we know that by a law of nature, wherever they can rule, they will. This law was not made by us, and we know that you and all mankind, if you were as strong as we are, would do as we do. So much for the gods; we have told you why we expect to stand as high in their good opinions as you."[3] Thereupon the Athenians put to death all who were of military age and made slaves of the women and children. They then colonized the island, sending thither 500 Athenian settlers. The Greeks gave us the notion of *realpolitik*—kill or be killed; conquer or die. War is seen as a mechanism for survival and power in which the *Brazen Rule* predates the Golden Rule—Do it to others *before* they get a chance to do it to you.

Political realists, as they are called, from the Athenian generals through Machiavelli (who advocated that the ruler survive at all costs, including the use of deception, betrayal, and murder) and from Hobbes to the twentieth-century political theorists Hans Morganthau and George Kennan (former U.S. ambassador to the U.S.S.R.), all hold that morality has no application in international relations. Machiavlli held that it is foolish to apply morality to politics:

> There is such a gap between how one lives and how one ought to live that anyone who abandons what is done for what ought to be done learns his ruin rather than his preservation: for a man who wishes to make a vocation of being good at all times will come to ruin among many who are not good. Hence it is necessary for a prince who wishes to maintain his position to learn how not to be good, and to use this knowledge or not use it according to necessity.[4]

Machiavelli advocated deception by the ruler even over his subjects. Most contemporary realists confine the deception and fraud to external relations (and where the truth to its own citizens would compromise its external or international prospects). Morganthau writes, "The state has no right to let its moral disapprobation . . . get in the way of successful political action, itself inspired by the moral principle of national survival."[5] Dean Acheson, secretary of state under President Truman, speaking about the government's discussion of foreign policy, confessed, "Our discussions centered on the appraisal of dangers and risks, the weighing of the need for decisive and effective action against considerations of prudence . . . Moral talk did not bear on the issue."[6] And the eminent ambassador Kennan laments that "morality as a general criterion for determination between states has no place. Here other criteria, sadder, more limited, more practical, must prevail."[7] Realism announces that while morality is very important for self-contained societies, it has no rational place in the interaction between states, where it will result only in deserved defeat of the gullible: Nice guys finish last. In personal relations, we might follow Jesus and turn the other cheek, but states do not have cheeks, and to pretend they do is to betray one's duty to promote the survival and interests of one's own nation–state.

The history of Western Europe in the nineteenth and twentieth centuries amply illustrates the realist thesis, that nations break treaties and aggress others when they perceive it is in their interest to do so. For example, Germany invaded France in 1870, seeking to add Alsace-Lorraine to its state; Germany and its allies attacked Belgium and France in 1914 because of the absence of an arbiter of disputes; Germany broke the Treaty of Versailles and invaded and annexed Czechoslovakia in 1939, and because that appropriation was tolerated by its neighbors, proceeded to invade Poland, Belgium, the Netherlands, Denmark, and France. Hitler signed the Ribbentrop Treaty with Russia to buy time for rearmament, then broke the treaty with impunity, invading Russia in 1941 under the pretext of *lebensraum,* the need for more land.

The geopolitics of the world has been transformed in the past decades. Instead of the cold war, threat of a global nuclear explosion, the trend in the past decades has been a geopolitical implosion of internecene atrocities, as the inhabitants of the former Yugoslavia revive the deadly ghosts of a former age; Hutu carry out a virtual holocaust against their ethnic relatives, the Tutsi, in Rwanda; Tamil rebels kill Sinhalese in the name of nationalism in Sri Lanka, while nationalist Catholic Irish engage in mutual murder with nationalist Protestants who are still fighting the Battle of the Boyne of 1690 in Northern Ireland, their nationalism trumping their common Christian heritage.

These atavistic exhibitions of violence raise the claim that a global organization creating institutions and enforcing laws is desirable to promote peace, assure compliance with contracts and treaties, and prevent international anarchy by promoting orderly processes, international morality, and reliable expectations. A universal set of laws with fixed penalties that are impartially enforced by a central policelike agency could be a catalyst for peace, the protection of human rights, and environmental wholeness. This last function is a modern one, having to do with the fact that air and water pollution tend to spread, impervious to political boundaries. For example, contaminated air from the nuclear explosion at Chernobyl wafted westward to Sweden and Switzerland. An increasingly depleted ozone layer over the Antarctic makes all people vulnerable to cancer-causing ultraviolet radiation. Greenhouse gases that originate in specific locales have global effects, changing climate patterns throughout the world. Recent international conferences on global warming and environmental policy, such as the Kyoto Accords in 1998, though they failed to reach universal agreements with strong sanctions, further demonstrate the need for an authoritative global body. As Hobbes wrote in 1651, "Covenants without swords are just words."

Add to these factors the modern development of an increasingly global economy, free trade, international transportation and communication systems (from the Boeing 777 to the Internet), and growing global consciousness (CNN and other new's networks beam the latest Asian uprising or African coup into our living rooms, sometimes before the government is aware of it).

We are living in a world that is becoming increasingly interdependent. In Seattle, Washington, workers are building the Boeing 777 with parts manufactured in 12 countries: 60 percent of the Sony workforce is now outside Japan. A reaction to globalism is also arising. Workers' wages are insecure, rising here and falling there. Overall, organized labor is losing control over the market and the terms of employment. Labor is relatively fixed, while capital has wings and flies off to more lucrative fields whenever it finds the labor conditions unsatisfactory. Labor perceives free trade as a threat and has shown resentment at what it perceives as dangerous economic policies and corporate globalism, especially passage of the North American Free Trade Agreement (NAFTA) between the United States, Canada, and Mexico. A coalition of antiglobalists has vigorously protested (and even rioted) during the World Trade Organization (WTO) conferences in Seattle and Toronto in 2000 and 2001. Labor's fears are not altogether without basis. Multinational corporations are the brains and brawn of the new world order, designing gargantuan worldwide networks and threatening to replace the nation–state as the dominant force in the global revolution. Fifty-one of the world's top economies are multinational corporations. They have assets greater than the gross domestic product (GDP) of most nations. General Motors has revenues roughly the same size as those of Ireland, New Zealand, and Hungary combined, larger than those of Turkey or Denmark. Ford has revenues more than those of South Africa; Toyota and Exxon, more than those of Norway or Poland. Microsoft's revenues are reported to exceed the GDP of France. The top five corporations double the GDP of all of South Asia.[8] International economics is contributing to vast waves of migration, as workers from all over the globe, often at considerable risk, gravitate to where jobs are, resulting in new configurations of ethnic diversity and the alteration of centuries of stable cultural patterns, as is occurring in Scandinavia, France, Germany, and the Netherlands. At the same time, progress has been made in joining the nations of Western Europe into a corporate European Union with a common currency. A similar movement is under way in Africa, the African Union. Combine these factors, and we get a picture of growing pressures for the eroding of national boundaries and national sovereignty and in favor of globalism, perhaps even some form of international government.

Thomas Friedman has argued that a globalized system of informal relations has replaced the cold war as the dominant social-economic-political fact of our time. It consists of free market capitalism, through free trade and international competition, producing more efficient and private uses of wealth. Individuals, corporations, and nation–states are able "to reach around the world farther, faster, deeper and cheaper than ever before, and in a way that is also producing a powerful backlash from those brutalized or left behind by this new system."[9] Globalization is occurring in virtually every country in the world. Unlike the great nations and empires of the past, this supernational organization has no geographical capital, no center of power. No one nation or corporation can control it. Rapidly expanding, fluid, penetrating each segment of the globe, it is ushering in a new democratic revolution. The symbol of the cold war system was the wall, which divided everyone. The symbol of the global system is the World Wide Web, which unites everyone—well, not quite everyone. The Indian peasant, the Bhutan nomad, and the poor of Afghanistan are as isolated and as bad off as ever. Rapid change, technological advances, and corporate tentacles spreading into every part of the world are also creating greater distances between the older, more atavistic or primitive cultures and the new ones budding in their midst. Friedman describes an automobile assembly plant outside Tokyo where 310 robots, supervised by a few human beings, are building the world's greatest luxury car, the Lexus. While witnessing this technological miracle, he received a report on his cell phone from Jerusalem, where Palestinians and Jews were fighting over who owns which olive tree. "It struck me," he writes, "that the Lexus and the olive tree were actually pretty good symbols of this post-Cold War era: half the world seemed to be emerging from the Cold War intent on building a better Lexus, dedicated to modernizing, streamlining, and privatizing their economies in order to thrive in the system of globalization, and half the world—sometimes half of the same country—was still caught up in the fight over who owns which olive tree."[10]

We are all intertwined in an interdependent global web in other ways as well. A German businessman, while making a deal in Pakistan, picks up a virus that originated somewhere in Africa. He gets on a plane for Frankfurt, infecting the entire planeload of passengers, who spread the disease throughout Europe. An infected American tourist brings the virus with her on a flight from Frankfurt to the United States, where the virus spreads over the country. For good and bad, and in between, globalization is spreading, eroding prevailing national borders and creating a new informal network of relationships. It is the most significant political fact of our age. The world is becoming a global village. New worldwide regulations and behavior patterns are called for to deal with this new reality. A prima facie case may even exist for international government or, at least, for a sovereign body to enforce international laws, to safeguard the rights of individuals and individual nations against unjust incursions and exploitation. Perhaps the United Nations, which is really, as its name suggests, only a union of states, ineffectual as it is at present, is the precursor of a coming global governing body, and the World Court in The Hague, a precursor to a world system of law.

THE COSMOPOLITAN SPIRIT

For the cosmopolitan idealist, nationalism is just another vicious prejudicial ideology, like racism and sexism. Why prefer your own nation to nations elsewhere? From the third century B.C.E., an alternative ideal of the world citizen has been a live option for many. Diogenes the Cynic is alleged to have been the first cosmopolitan, calling himself a world citizen. The Stoics followed his doctrine, becoming the first people to reject the narrow provinciality of particular loyalties and to identify themselves as cosmopolitans. But the vision of a peaceable kingdom was set forth even earlier, by the Hebrew prophet Isaiah in the sixth century B.C.E.:

> The wolf shall dwell with the lamb,
> and the leopard shall lie down with the kid,
> and the calf and the lion and the fatling together,

and a little child shall lead them.
The cow and the bear shall feed;
their young shall lie down together;
and the lion shall eat straw like the ox.
The suckling child shall play over the hole of the asp,
and the weaned child shall put his hand on the adder's den.
They shall not hurt or destroy
in all my holy mountain;
for the earth shall be full of the knowledge of the Lord
as the waters cover the sea.
[The nations] shall beat their swords into plowshares,
and their spears into pruning hooks;
nation shall not lift up sword against nation,
neither shall they learn war any more. (Isaiah 11:6–9, 2:4)

Later on, the early Christians were a type of cosmopolitan, seeing themselves without a specific state, but united with all other Christians in a universal brotherhood: "In Christ there is neither Jew nor Greek, neither slave, nor free, neither male nor female, but you are all one in Christ" (Gal. 3:28). Every believer is a Christian cosmopolitan, for there is but one king in heaven, God, and no state but the kingdom of God. Race, gender, ethnicity, and class have been annihilated.

In the nineteenth century, the Russian count and writer Leo Tolstoy (1828–1910) was the foremost cosmopolitan, characterizing patriotism as a kind of corporate insanity. In a little-known essay, written in the 1890s, Tolstoy condemns the idea of patriotism as a superstitious and dangerous emotion, tending to produce war and xenophobic behavior. It falsely supposes that one's own nation is superior to all others, so that it is always justified in settling grievances violently by use of force.[11] But moral people, especially Christians who follow Christ in his glorification of peace, should eschew such folly, which promises only division, death, and destruction. Instead, they should commit themselves to universal peace and brotherhood. Tolstoy recounts two contemporary celebrations of the Franco-Russian Alliance, one in Kronstadt, Russia, and the other in Toulon, France, both aimed at cementing the alliance and at conducting hostile maneuvers against Germany. He comments that such mass hysteria and misplaced loyalty are promoted by the leaders of nations with the assistance of the media and the educational system to ensure that cannon fodder, (i.e., the common people) is available for their future self-aggrandizing adventures. Patriotism, which is nationalism brought to consciousness, is nourished by senseless jingoism in the garden of xenophobia, for it depends on finding an outsider to hate sufficiently so as to enable the people in the in-group to live in peace and cooperate with one another, so long as their hate is directed outward. But a moral conscience must condemn such evil and work for a cosmopolitan outlook, wherein all human life is viewed as sacred.

In the twentieth century, the French philosopher Jacques Maritain (1888–1973), the Indian Nobel laureate Rabindranath Tagore (1861–1941), and Mortimer Adler (1903–2001) promoted the ideal of world government and citizenship. Maritain argued for the death of the dysfunctional nation–state and the inauguration of world government, in which peace and justice will be guaranteed. Given the possibility of nations destroying each other through atomic weapons, an international authority is necessary to ensure peace; the traditional nation–state no longer serves a viable purpose and will have to give up its sovereignty in favor of an international government. Maritain defends his proposal via the idea of a universal natural law, which he believes to be inherent in all human beings and which can be recognized by all rational beings.[12]

The attraction of cosmopolitanism is that it seems to embody the heart of the moral point of view, impartially applying moral principles to all humans. If there is a universal morality applying to all people everywhere and that can be realized in each human life, one joining us all in a common moral brotherhood, then why get sidetracked by the fetish of particular bureaucratic states? Marx and Engels perceived just this point when they prophesied that in the communist utopia, the state would "wither away" and humans would live in an anarchistic utopia, much like that described by the prophet Isaiah. The promise is of universal peace; an end to war, militarism, and state violence; the end of the bipolar us against them. Instead, we would live in a world where each contributed according to his or her ability and received according to his or her need, a world of peace, prosperity, and global justice.

Stoics, Marxists, and secular cosmopolitans seek to implement the universal moral order in a nonreligious manner, creating a secular equivalent to the kingdom of heaven on earth. Isn't it true that if we all lived deeply moral lives, as brothers and sisters, we would not need the state, nor its army, nor its police force, nor its lawyers? It seems so simple. It is what we learned in kindergarten, that utopian community of peace and plenty. So why aren't we all cosmopolitans? Why do nationalism and particularism with their conflict-creating us against them mentality reign instead? Why don't the Israelis and Palestinians embrace the peaceable kingdom of Isaiah and stop the bloodshed on the West Bank? Why don't the Serbs and Kosovo Albanians accept it? Why don't Hindus and Muslims embrace it in Kashmir? Why don't Protestants and Catholics accept it in Northern Ireland?

Why don't we all become world citizens instead of Americans, Russians, Mexicans, Canadians, British, French, or Chinese? What is the answer?

THE PROMISE OF NATIONALISM

Cosmopolitanism may look appealing in the abstract, but nationalism is an even more powerful force in the world and has much to be said for (and against) it. As we noted in the introduction to this book, modern nationalism is the quest for self-determinism, for sovereignty, wherein each nation or complex of nations becomes an autonomous political body. David Carment has estimated that there are over 500 ethnic minorities in the world, many of them seeking self-determination.[13] Let us examine the arguments for and against nationalism.

The first argument is the *self-determination argument.* This argument holds that people should be in charge of their own destinies, and that groups of people should govern themselves both locally and corporately as much as possible. Since 1648, with the Peace of Westphalia, which ended the Thirty Years War between Protestants and Catholics, the nation–state has been recognized in Western society as the sole agency of coercion within a territory. Since that time, borders have been regarded as sacrosanct, not to be infringed except in a just war of defense. The American Founding Fathers, in the Declaration of Independence, justified the war of independence from Britain on the grounds of self-determination: "When in the Course of human events, it becomes necessary for one people to dissolve the political bands which have connected them with another" and assert "separate and equal" status, that is the "Right of the People." The value or right of self-determination is surely important. It is an extension of our individual autonomy. Just as you and I want to be free to direct our own lives, we want our government to be free from external coercion. This is the quest of the Kurds in Iraq, the Palestinians in Israel, the Chechnyans in Russia, the Uighurs in Central Asia and China, the Quebecquois in Canada, and even the native Hawaiians in Hawaii. Perhaps the internecine bloodshed in Bosnia, Kosovo, Israel, Rwanda, and Chechnya could have been avoided if the revolting groups had been given independence. Although self-determination as an extension of autonomy may be a valid goal, that point itself does not establish a justification for an independent nation–state. A further premise is needed to support the idea of a sovereign nation–state. All this argument supports is autonomy, not absolute self-determination. When it violates the human rights of some of its subjects, a nation–state may forfeit its right to self-governance, as Serbia did in its recent policies of ethnic cleansing. A sovereign world government could contain semiautonomous nation–states, just as the sovereign United States of America contains 50 semiautonomous states (or semiautonomous jurisdictions). This model could be the basis for national enclaves with local self-governance, including restrictions on commerce, trade, and immigration. But this sub-jurisdiction would be held accountable for protecting human rights and supporting the superstate. It would not have complete discretion regarding interstate relationships.

Ideally, a world government could accommodate the legitimate claims of ethnic groups for self-governance, and the ultimate trajectory of morality may reside in this course. But in a world where the ghosts of past evils still haunt the present, it is probably a reasonable concession to human nature to support some nationalist claims for a separate state. But secession from the larger body should be allowed only as a last resort, like a divorce, when all attempts at reconciliation have failed, and a separate identity is the lesser of evils.[14] Untangling groups within a territory is often a herculean task.

As we found in India after independence in 1947, when Muslims were forced to migrate to Pakistan and Hindus from present Pakistan to modern India, and, more recently, in Bosnia, where Bosnian Muslims, Croats and Serbs often lived in the same neighborhoods and apartment complexes, great suffering may be caused by uprooting and transferring people from one location to another.

The second argument for nationalism is the *personal identity argument*. Identifying with a national group seems to give us something that we deeply need, a larger ego, an extended self, a deeper and more concrete identity. Just as we all value our family, its intimate and passionate relations defining who we are, similarly we need the sense of belonging that comes via association with larger groups—our community, our school or club, our church, and, especially, our nation. Just as the deep relationships of family—being a child of A and B, having children C and D, being the brother or sister of E and F—give profound meaning to our lives, so the nation gives meaning on another, more abstract, but still particular level. These intimate persons are not replaceable the way a doctor or bus driver or car salesperson is. My relationship to my wife consists in a shared history, memories of our first date in Greenwich Village, our honeymoon in the Pocono Mountains, our hikes together in the Alps and the Grand Canyon, the birth of our children, those beautiful moments in exotic places, our struggles and adventures and special joys and sorrows. She is not replaceable, even if cloning should be possible. She is unique. As such, she constitutes a vital part of my identity. In an analogous manner, our relationship to our community and nation is also irreplaceable, unique, and precious, constituting a vital part of our identity.

Some philosophers, such as Alasdair MacIntyre, Michael Sandel, and David Miller, go even further with this feature of our moral repertoire and argue that it is precisely these particular relations, not the abstract universal principles, that generate our ethics. These philosophers actually reject classic universalist ethics, the idea that ethics consists in universal moral principles, applicable to all people at all times. Instead, they argue that universalism is too abstract to justify our special obligations to family, community, and nation. Morality flourishes in concrete relationships that give meaning and purpose to our lives; we misconstrue the subject when we transform it into the abstract, bloodless universal principles of the core morality.[15]

What are we to make of their argument? Should particularism replace universalism? The particularist may be conflating the context of *discovery* with the context of *justification*. It is no doubt true that we discover what morality is about through the intimacy of family and communal interaction, but I don't see how this undermines universalism. The universalist agrees that we have special obligations to family, friends, and community, but this obligation is particular not just to us, but to all people in all communities everywhere. For example, rule-utilitarianians argue that we will maximize utility if we concentrate on helping those close to us, our family and community, rather than trying to give equal attention to people in other countries, for we understand our close relations better than we do strangers and foreigners and are more likely to maximize welfare if we concentrate on their needs. Of course, we have obligations to people in other countries, but they seldom override our obligations to our fellow compatriots.

We may compare a nation to a team. Take a football team. The members cooperate with one another for a common purpose—to play well and win the game. They are concerned with helping their own team members in a way they are not concerned with the good of members of rival teams. They may respect and admire rival team members and refrain from fouls and unnecessary harm, but they aim to win the game, to be the best team in the league, and this requires giving special attention to the needs of fellow teammates consistent with the good of the whole. If a fellow teammate forgets a play or runs a wrong pattern, other members have a duty to correct him; they don't have a duty to correct an opposing player's mistake. Indeed, they hope members of the opposing team will forget more plays and run more wrong patterns. Likewise, members of other teams have special obligations to their teammates that they don't have to rival team members.

Similarly, although we have general duties to people of other nations, we have special duties to our compatriots that we don't have to those others. But this does not prove particularism—it is consistent with universalism. Since all people have special duties to people in their own countries, we don't need particularism to justify our special duties to our own nation; they rest on universal principles.[16]

Let us return to the thesis that nationhood makes a valuable contribution to personal identity. Traditionally, most nations have been made up of people with a common ethnicity and culture, a single language and history. The genius of the United States of America is that it has been forged out of many cultures and ethnicities into one nation. Immigrants left their countries of origin for the promise of a better life. They left England, Ireland, Scandinavia, Russia, Poland, Italy, China, Cuba, and Mexico and adopted a new heritage: *pluribus unum*, "Out of many, one." While most nations are formed naturally by people living in a common territory sharing common problems and religion and language, America is, for the most part, a "voluntary nation."[17] The new citizen identifies with a new culture, not his or her native one. He or she learns a new language, adopts new customs, learns to appreciate new literature, identifies with a new history, celebrates new holidays—the Fourth of July, Memorial Day, President's Day, Martin Luther King Jr's birthday—all significant holidays of the adopted land. New music such as the National Anthem and sprightly folk songs, become part of one's repertoire. The new citizen comes to feel the glory of Washington crossing the Delaware to defeat the British, and to agonize over the 600,000 soldiers killed fighting the Civil War, but also to be grateful that the war rid the nation of its great evil, chattel slavery. The new citizen will take pride in the country's role in the two World Wars of the past century and perhaps regret the debacle of the War in Vietnam. From the Flag to the Fourth of July, from the Statue of Liberty to Silicon Valley, from Wall Street to the White House, new symbols and places will embed themselves in his or her psyche. This is our history. The future of this land is our and our children's future, and so we care for the land, try to preserve its resources and pass them on, as an inestimable patrimony, to new generations. In this, nationalists of all nations have a similar psychological commitment.

The apex and climax of the nation is the nation–state, the full formalization of the association of people committed to a common purpose. The state imposes institutions onto the people—a governing body, an army to protect them from external harm, a police force and judicial system to protect them from internal harm and to help them resolve conflicts of interest equitably. It claims sovereignty, the sole agent with the right to use coercion within the territory. If the nation represents the substance of the people, their culture, language, rituals and practices, the state represents the form that gives the substance shape and structure, molding our experience in discrete ways.

Without denying the dark side of nationalism, which often involves hatred of the other and violence and gratuitous suffering, the advocates of nationalism argue that we cannot live without its deep psychological benefits. Cosmopolitanism may look good in the abstract, but it cannot give humans that particular sense of belonging that the nation affords. It is simply impossible to identify with 6 billion other human beings who live on this planet and with their cultures. We need particular symbols, places, and people with which to identify, and nationalism amply provides for this.

A third argument enlisted in the defense of nationalism is the *argument from self-defense*. We need to preserve and protect our culture and our people from harm and destruction. The Israeli writer Amos Os puts the point most forcefully:

> I think that the nation-state is a tool, an instrument . . . but I am not enamored of this instrument . . . I would be more than happy to live in a world composed of dozens of civilizations, each developing . . . without any one emerging as a nation-state: no flag, no emblem, no passport, no anthem. No nothing. Only spiritual civilizations tied somehow to their lands, without the tools of statehood and without the instruments of war.
>
> But the Jewish people has already staged a long-running one-man show of that sort. The international audience sometimes applauded, sometimes threw stones, and occasionally slaughtered the actor. No one joined us; no one copied the model the Jews were forced to sustain for two thousand years . . . For me this drama ended with the murder of Europe's Jews by Hitler. And I am forced to take it upon myself to play the "game of nations" with all the tools of statehood . . . To play the game with an emblem, and a flag, and a passport and an army, and even war, provided that such war is an absolute existential necessity. I accept those rules of the game because existence without the tools of statehood is a matter of mortal danger, but I accept them only up to a point. To take pride in these tools of statehood? To worship these toys? To crow about them? Not I . . . Nationalism itself is, in my eyes, the curse of mankind.[18]

The nation–state may be a necessary evil, as it does provide for the protection of our culture and the people associated with it. Of course, as Os makes eminently clear, this argument is contingent on a world of hostility to one's culture, an anti-Semitic world in this case. On a smaller scale, the hostility could be localized to an individual state, causing a national group like the Palestinians in Israel, the Kurds in Iraq, or the Chechnyans in Russia to make a claim to secession and an independent state of their own. But one could also imagine a cosmopolitan system wherein prejudice and unjust discrimination were driven underground, if not destroyed altogether.

Fourth is the *multicultural argument for nationalism*: The world is a better or more interesting place if it contains diverse cultures. Even if some cultures are correctly judged superior to others, a diverse world is better than a homogeneous one. This may be true, but it does little to support the idea of a nation–state. Many cultures could exist side by side in the world, just as they do in the United States. We could have Italian cosmopolitans, Irish cosmopolitans, African cosmopolitans, Chinese cosmopolitans, and so on. So the multicultural argument doesn't necessarily support strong nationalism. However, it might support a weaker form of nationalism. We might need autonomous societies to protect cultures.

AN ASSESSMENT OF THE DEBATE BETWEEN NATIONALISM AND COSMOPOLITANISM

There is truth in the claims of nationalism; self-determination is a valid moral ideal. And we do need to identify with groups such as the family and community and other associations to find meaning in life. But it seems to be a long stretch from a sense of identification with our family to an identification with our nation. The nationalist rejects the cosmopolitan prescription of being a world citizen because the world is simply too large a body to identify with. Judith Lichtenberg points out that if I can't identify with 6 billion people, I can't identify with 260 million (U.S. population) either.[19] Even thought we recognize the problem that the nation is an artificial invention, a myth, it may nevertheless afford us a set of common symbols and cultural artifacts, such as a common language, literature, and history, that do promote human flourishing. So the meaning-identity analogy is plausible, after all. The team analogy may be a valid way of seeing the useful function of the nation in giving our lives meaning and purpose. Lichtenberg's criticism, though literally valid, may miss the point: Nationalism has to do with symbols and meaning, not natural facts. But if a form of nationalism is morally justified, it may best be a moderate, restricted, form, one combined with cosmopolitanism.

Two related problems remain for the justification of nationalism: those of territory and of resources or property. Cosmopolitans criticize nationalists for their strong theory of property rights. Why should America or Saudi Arabia get a monopoly on its resources, which are just part of the natural lottery? The United Sates and Saudi Arabia didn't do anything to deserve their superior natural resources. They were just more fortunate than poorer countries. Thus, wouldn't it be fairer for the resources of these and all other countries to be distributed more equitably? In Chapter 5, we criticized Rawls's argument on the natural lottery regarding our talents, saying that just because we don't deserve our natural abilities doesn't mean that we don't deserve how we develop these abilities. Could the same argument be used to justify our rights to our natural resources? It seems not, for resources are not analogous to talents. As Charles Beitz notes, "Resources do not stand in the same relation to personal identity as talents. It would be inappropriate to take the sort of pride in the diamond deposits in one's backyard that one takes in the ability to play *Appassionata*."[20] Of course, being good stewards of our resources, including sharing them with the needy, may justify some ownership.

In a world government, nations might be made stewards of their land and resources, but not permitted complete sovereignty over their uses. Richer nations would have a duty to redistribute some of their wealth to poorer nations in which not even people's basic needs were met. Peter Singer argues from a utilitarian perspective that "if it is in our power to prevent something bad from happening, without thereby sacrificing something of comparable moral importance, we ought to do it."[21] What changes might we need to make in our lifestyles if we attempted to live according to Singer's challenge? However, until such a cosmopolitan regime is established, it's hard to see either nations or individuals giving up sovereignty to their territory and resources. Even though Beitz's point about resources versus talents is cogent, nations do behave as though their resources are analogous to talents and convincing them otherwise will be a difficult job.

Cosmopolitanism appears to be a worthy ideal, embodying, as it does, the moral point of view in respecting individuals, rather than nations, races, religious or ethnic groups, as the centers of meaning, but the ideal is fraught with seemingly insuperable problems. First, what kind of institution would be required to draw up and enforce the global scheme of taxation required for the kinds of wealth redistribution schemes that might be warranted? Would its coercive powers be an unacceptable violation of individual and national liberties? Second, even if we could ensure a just world government to carry out a taxation scheme, how could it be certain that the funds distributed actually went to the poor and were not siphoned off by a corrupt elite and deposited into their Swiss bank accounts (as happens all too frequently with foreign aid to developing countries)? Third, how do we guarantee that after the funds get to the poor, long-term good would result from the redistribution scheme? Fourth, it would also seem that population control should be a necessary condition for aid, for otherwise the ratchet effect would occur (that is, monetary input in an apparent emergency situation staves off immediate starvation and disaster, enabling people to propagate further, resulting in a larger crisis in 10 or 20 years). A British advocate of world hunger relief, Onora

O'Neill, has conceded that if noncoercive methods fail to control population growth, coercive ones might be warranted:

> If [noncoercive] policies fail, and just productive and redistributive measures too cannot meet needs, direct coercion of procreative decisions would not be unjust. Such emergencies would arise only when recklessly fertile people persist in having children whose needs could not be met, by their parents or by others, either by increasing or by reallocating resources. Such procreators act on a maxim that cannot be widely shared without exacerbating needs and so increasing injustice. Preventing such reckless procreation would coerce less than would failing to prevent it.[22]

For example, the Rwandan population has been growing at a rate of as high as 8 percent per annum, resulting in a doubling of the population every 8½ years or so. The Chinese policy of limiting families to one or two children appears harsh to many of us, but it may be seen as an emergency measure (to counteract the fanatical pronatalist policies of Mao Tse-Tung), and it is having a beneficial effect in slowing population growth (compared with India, where rapid growth continues).

Last, how can one compare what constitutes a good life in different kinds of societies? The per capita GDP of many Western countries is around $25,000, whereas in the third world it may be around $250, or 100 times less. Someone from a third world country, say an Amazonian Indian in Brazil, may not value college education as much as Westerners and may live in a tribe that has a pattern of caring for the elderly, obviating the need for expensive retirement policies. In fact, the Amazonian Indian, upon being exposed to Western culture, may prefer to remain living in the rain forest.

These problems may not be insuperable, but they should give us pause. Until we understand the full implications of what we are doing, a move toward institutionalizing cosmopolitanism should proceed cautiously. Nonetheless, the principle of humanity, embodied in the moral point of view, which focuses on the rights and duties of individuals, not groups, races, or nations, does point to a robust cosmopolitanism, which, it would seem, should be institutionalized into a democratic world government.

Another problem related to international relations concerns intervention in the internal affairs of a nation–state, such as that occurring in Somalia, Afghanistan, Rwanda, Malawi, Serbia, and Kosovo, when human rights violations, such as the oppression of women and ethnic cleansing, become extreme. Even if we accept the principle of national sovereignty, intervention by other nations may be justified. The widespread ethnic cleansing that took place in the former Yugoslavia in the 1990s is a prime example of a case when the intervention of other nations might be warranted. Working out the criteria for when to intervene and when not to intervene, is one of the most urgent problems facing us. We want to be constructive, rather than add to the destruction in these war-torn lands, but it is notoriously difficult to determine the likelihood of success. Such interventions are risky and should be embarked upon only when all attempts at peaceful solutions have been exhausted, when there is widespread international support, when there is willingness for a long-term occupancy, and when there is a reasonable chance of success.

Cosmopolitan institutions threaten the very existence of the traditional nation–state, so much a part of our world since the eighteenth century. If our ultimate allegiance is to a superglobal state, then what is the role of the nation? Does it have moral legitimacy?

Many philosophers would say no; the nation lacks any ultimate moral justification. It is, at best, a temporary and necessary evil, organizing people in restricted manners until the principle of universal humanity can take hold on our collective consciousness. Einstein, as the epigraph at the beginning of this chapter notes, characterized nationalism as an infantile disease, "the measles of mankind," from which we must recover if we are to survive. But, as our analysis suggests, this may be a hard reaction. Certainly, there is a hard version of nationalism, epitomized in the slogan "My country, right or wrong, my country!" which is not justified, because it makes nationalism into an absolute, something that cannot be justified. Such extreme nationalism is no more justified than giving special privilege to one's race or gender or ethnic group. We have an obligation to oppose our country when it violates human rights, even as some Germans, such as the martyrs Dietrich Bonhoffer and Adam von Trapp, opposed Hitler's Nazism. We must transcend this kind of extreme, immoral nationalism, with its atavistic rituals, its narrow patriotism, and replace it with a universal loyalty. There is a prima facie duty to become moral cosmopolitans, committed to the well-being and rights of every person, regardless of country of origin. There are practical obstacles to overcome, as well as moral ones, so we cannot immediately move into such an international allegiance, but this should be our goal. Moral cosmopolitanism, treating each person as a moral equal, is not equivalent to institutional cosmopolitanism, but it inclines in that direction. The benefits of world government are greater prospects of peace, enforcement of treaties and contracts, fluid trade and economic relations, and the allocation of resources according to need and desert, rather than according to purely the luck of being born in a resource-rich country or family.

But cosmopolitanism is not without problems. It has a checkered past. Marxist-Leninism purported to be the ultimate cosmopolitan philosophy, which gave rise to the Union of Soviet Socialist Republics, the completely "internationalist" society, and Stalin's atrocities. It is estimated that Stalin is responsible for the deaths of more than 50 million people. And Stalin shows that one doesn't have to be religious to be an evil fanatic. You can be an atheist and a socialist and perpetrate evil on a national or global scale. Cosmopolitanism can be a veneer for tyranny. Most of us have been immunized against the idea of world government through the inoculating effects of reading Huxley's *Brave New World* and Orwell's *1984*. Cosmopolitans can propagate questionable moral advice on a more micro scale. The 19th century cosmopolitan William Godwin held that "if two persons are drowning and one is a relative of yours, this should make no difference in your decision as to whom to try to rescue first." Dickens satirizes this "telescopic philanthropy" in the person of Mrs. Jelleby, who could only recognize objects of benevolence at a very great distance.[23] It was said of President Woodrow Wilson that "He loved mankind but loathed individual men." Common sense morality, as we noted above, informs us that such disregard of particular commitments and relationships undermines the very substance of morality, for those special relationships make life worth living. It is our basic communitarian values of family, friends, and community that constitute the bases of moral sentiments. To this extent, the particularists are correct. Our love and moral commitments must begin and always remain tied to particular people, not humanity in the abstract. Furthermore, soft nationalists point out, we may take legitimate pride in our democratic institutions, our practices of equality before the law and moral traditions. These aspects of our culture are worth preserving and defending. From a moral point of view all cultures are not equal. Some instantiate the ideals better than others.

At this point, we might compromise and recognize the validity of both cosmopolitanism and nationalism. Nationalists may be divided into two groups: soft nationalists and hard nationalists. *Hard nationalists* hold that the nation is altogether justified as the ultimate locus of political obligation; internationalism is simply confused or immoral. Even as we have a natural duty to prefer our family to other people and strangers, we have a duty to prefer our nation, to be patriotic. Nationalistic concerns override all other loyalties or obligations. On the other hand, *soft nationalists* maintain that while we do have some obligations to people everywhere and we do need some adjudicating overseer to enforce treaties and prevent war, this doesn't completely override the need for nation–states. Although they agree with hard nationalists that we do have special obligations to our own country, soft nationalists feel that the needs or rights of others may sometimes override our familial obligations, and that our nationalistic obligations may be overridden at times by obligations to humankind at large or to people not citizens of our nation.

Soft nationalists are open to the possibility of world government, recognizing the ideals thereby attained, but they also are troubled by the problems of ensuring local autonomy and preventing unwieldy bureaucracy and tyranny. They also fear the dilution of their morally precious cultural ideals by the forces of multiculturalism.[24] However, suppose we could attain an efficient world government, a sort of United Nations with sovereignty, that is, with authority and power? Then, the soft nationalists maintain, nations would still have local jurisdiction, much like the individual states do within the United States, only with greater autonomy (or semi-sovereignty). We would still have special obligations to people in our own states, relating to them in special moral ways, while at the same time, sharing our resources with people throughout the world.[25]

Conclusion

Because it offers us a special form of personal relationship so vital for personal identity, some form of nationalism may always be part of the human psyche, though it may be a less all-encompassing variety than what we now experience. It will be balanced by a soft form of cosmopolitanism, either informally worked out between nations or by a formal world government, which would still encourage and promote individual nation–state autonomy within its domain. One way or another, increased peace and international cooperation will be necessary as we become better-educated people who live in a global village, where actions in Bosnia, South Africa, or the Island of Timor affect people in Siberia, Buenos Aires, and Los Angeles. However it happens and whatever the exact result in terms of formal structure or lack thereof, the process should encapsulate Darwin's cosmopolitan vision of an expanding moral circle:

> As man advances in civilization, and small tribes are united into larger communities, the simplest reason would tell each individual that he ought to extend his social instincts and sympathies to all the members of the same nation, though personally unknown to him. This point being once reached, there is only an artificial barrier to prevent his sympathies extending to the men of all nations and races. If, indeed, such men are separated from him by greater differences in appearance or habits, experience unfortunately shows us how long it is, before we look at them as our fellow-creatures. Sympathy beyond the confines of man, that is, humanity to the lower animals, seems to be one of the latest acquisitions. It is apparently unfelt by savages, except towards their pets. How little the old Romans knew of it is shown by their abhorrent gladiatorial exhibitions. The very idea of humanity, as far as I could observe, was new to most of the Gauchos of the Pampas. This virtue,

one of the noblest with which man is endowed, seems to arise incidentally from our sympathies becoming more tender and more widely diffused, until they are extended to all sentient beings. As soon as the virtue is honored and practiced by some few men, it spreads through instruction and example to the young, and eventually becomes incorporated in public opinion.[26]

If human beings are to survive and flourish on this planet, we will have to combine the sense of personal meaning epitomized in soft nationalism with the global commitments embodied in cosmopolitanism. How to get the balance right will be the challenge of the next decades.

For Further Reflection

1.   Evaluate the claims of globalism. To what degree is the world getting more interconnected? What are the likely outcomes of this process?

2.   Write a short essay on the best arguments for nationalism. Then write one on the evils of nationalism.

3.   What are the strengths and weaknesses of cosmopolitanism?

4.   Does cosmopolitanism lead to world government? Explain your answer.

5.   Are we moving inexorably toward a world government, and is this good or bad?

6.   Do the rich nations have an obligation to help poorer nations? Should any conditions be attached to such aid? Do recipient nations have an obligation to control population growth?

7.   Should nations intervene in the internal affairs of other nations when human rights are being egregiously violated?

8.   Examine Singer's statement: "If it is in our power to prevent something bad from happening, without thereby sacrificing something of comparable moral importance, we ought to do it." Do you agree with him? What kinds of changes would it require in our lives? Is it too demanding?

Endnotes

1.   Alexis de Tocqueville, *Democracy in America,* quoted in David Miller, *On Nationality* (Oxford University Press, 1995). Miller's book is the best defense of moderate nationalism in the literature. I have profited greatly from it in writing this chapter.

2.   Cited in H. Dukas and B. Hoffman, *Albert Einstein: The Human Side* (Princeton, NJ: Princeton University Press, 1979).

3.   Thucydides, *History of the Peloponnesian War* (fifth century B.C.E.).

4. *Portable Machiavelli,* (Penguin, 1979), p. 127. He continues: "How praiseworthy it is for a prince to keep his word and to live by integrity and not by deceit everyone knows; nevertheless, one sees from the experience of our times that the princes who have accomplished great deeds are those who have cared little for keeping their promises and who have known how to manipulate the minds of men by shrewdness; and in the end they have surpassed those who laid their foundations upon honesty" (p. 133).

5. Hans J. Morganthau, *Politics among the Nations* (NY: Knopf, 1973), p. 10.

6. Quoted in *Ethics and Politics,* Amy Gutmann and Dennis Thompson, eds. (Nelson Hall, 1997). Perhaps the most cynical example of amorality in recent American politics was the Watergate affair, especially the cover-up that led to the impeachment process of President Richard Nixon. The Gutmann and Thompson anthology is a good source for the relationship of morality to politics.

7. George F. Kennan, *Realities of American Foreign Policy* (Princeton, NJ: Princeton University Press, 1954), p. 49. It might be more accurate to say that the realist holds only one moral principle in international relations— that the goals of the state's survival and prospering justify any means of accomplishing those goals.

8. *UN Human Development Report* 1997, p. 12, and CorpWatch: www.corpwatch.org/trac/glob101/background/2001/factsheet.html

9. Thomas Friedman, *The Lexus and the Olive Tree* (Farrar, Straus, & Giroux, 1999), p. 7. The backlash was in evidence in the Seattle riots against the World Trade Organization (WTO) in 2000 and the Toronto protests in 2001.

10. Friedman, op. cit., pp. 26–27. But what happens when those fighting over the olive tree suddenly discover that the true enemy of their traditional ways of life is not their historic opponent, but a vast, impersonal, multinational complex? This is what the antitechnoloy movement is all about. See also Michael Hardt and Antonio Negri, *Empire* (Harvard University Press, 2000).

11. From *Leo Tolstoy's Writings on Civil Disobedience and Nonviolence,* trans. Aylmer Maude (London: Owens, 1899). A selection appears in *Political Philosophy,* L. Pojman, ed. (New York: McGraw-Hill, 2002). For a good discussion of this essay, see Stephen Nathanson, *Patriotism, Morality, and Peace* (Rowman & Littlefield, 1993), chaps. 1 and 2.

12. Jacques Maritain, *Man and the State* (Catholic University Press, 1950).

13. David Carment, "The Ethnic Dimension in World Politics" *Third World Quarterly* (1994).

14. See Alan Buchanan, "Secession," in *A Companion to Contemporary Political Philosophy,* Robert Goodin and Philip Pettit, eds. (Blackwell, 1995), pp. 586–96.

15. Miller, op. cit.; Michael Sandel, *Liberalism and the Limits of Justice* (Cambridge University Press, 1982); Alasdair MacIntyre, "Is Patriotism a Virtue?" in *Political Philosophy,* L. Pojman, ed. (New York: McGraw-Hill, 2002). MacIntyre argues that the idea of patriotism has meaning within a communal

understanding of morality, which it lacks in contemporary liberalism. He points out that while the morality of patriotism may endanger the objectivity of ethics, liberal morality has the problem of dislocating morality from those features of life that are necessary for the full flourishing of the moral individual and the moral life. At this point you might want to review the section on universal moral objectivism in the Introduction to this book.

16. It should also be noted that the particularist, in claiming that morality is embedded in a specific culture, seems to be wedded to moral relativism, a position inherently flawed, as we argued in the Introduction.

17. The ignoble exception to this is chattel slavery, in which black Africans were brought to this country in chains.

18. Amos Os, *In the Land of Israel* (Vintage Books, 1983), p. 130 f, quoted in Stephen Nathanson, "Nationalism and the Limits of Global Humanism," in *The Morality of Nationalism,* Robert McKim and Jeff McMahan, eds. (Oxford University Press, 1997).

19. Judith Lichtenberg, "Nationalism: For and (Mainly) Against," in McKim and McMahan, op. cit.

20. Charles Beitz, *Political Theory and International Relations.* (Princeton, NJ: Princeton University Press, 1999), p. 139.

21. Peter Singer, "Famine, Affluence and Morality," *Philosophy and Public Affairs,* 1:3 (1972).

22. Onora O'Neill, *Faces of Hunger* (Allen & Unwin, 1986), p. 158. Even Singer, in a postscript to his article (see endnote 14) says that our obligation to aid is lessened if the people in danger do nothing to reduce their population growth rate. O'Neill isn't claiming that the individual couples are irrational for wanting more children, only that doing so on a large scale results in the tragedy of the commons (discussed at the end of Chapter 2), where individual freedom practiced by too many leads to tragedy.

23. Charles Dickens, *Bleak House* (Bradbury & Evans, 1853): "Mrs. Jelleby's eyes had the curious habit of looking a long way off. As if they could see nothing nearer than Africa" (p. 26).

24. For a good discussion of the threat of multiculturalism on liberal Western culture, see Arthur M. Schlesinger, *The Disuniting of America: Reflection on a Multicultural Society* (NY:W. Norton, 1992) and Samuel P. Huntington, *The Clash of Civilizations: Remaking of World Order* (Simon & Schuster, 1996). Both argue that we must defend and promote the principle of the "American creed": liberty, democracy, individualism, equality before the law, constitutionalism, private property, and separation of church and state.

25. For a good discussion of extreme versus moderate nationalism, see Nathanson, op. cit.

26. Charles Darwin, *The Descent of Man* (1873).

10

INTERNATIONAL TERRORISM AND THE MORAL RESPONSE

When the sacred month has passed, kill those who join other gods with Allah wherever ye shall find them; and seize them, and lay wait for them with every kind of ambush . . . Strive against (jihad) the infidels and the hypocrites! Be harsh with them. Their ultimate destiny is hell.

—THE KORAN 9:3

INTRODUCTION: THE DAY OF IGNOMINY

ON SEPTEMBER 11 THE WORST terrorist attack on civilians in the history of the United States occurred. Four planes were hijacked by Arab Muslim terrorists, becoming in their hands massive murderous missiles. Two of them crashed into New York's World Trade Center, one into the Pentagon in Arlington, Virginia; and a fourth, headed perhaps for the White House or the Capitol building in Washington, D.C., crashed into a Pennsylvania field. An estimated 3,330 unsuspecting, innocent people were killed, along with the 19 terrorists. This diabolical carousel of contempt and fury was not just an attack on the U.S.A., but on Western culture with its liberal values. Thus with this cataclysmic event a new era in the history of warfare has been inaugurated, one which portends a deeper dimension of evil and a different type of war. The history of the U.S. will hence forth be divided into Before September 11 and After September 11.

Terrorism is not new, of course. In the 1980s 5,431 international terrorist incidents occurred in which 4,684 people died, and in the 1990s, 3,824 incidents occurred with 2,468 deaths. From 1970 to 1995, 64,319 terrorist incidents were recorded, half of them attributed to religious extremists.[1]

If one includes state-sponsored terrorism, the twentieth century will be hard to equal in terms of terrorist atrocities. It is estimated that governments killed 169 million people between 1900 and 1987. Joseph Stalin, the all-time megamurderer, accounted for about 43 million deaths; Mao Tse Tung, 38 million; and Adolf Hitler, 21 million.[2] Northern Ireland and Eng-

216

land have had to endure the terrorist threats of the Irish Republican Army for decades, and Israel has lived with suicide bombings for over 30 years. Indeed, Israel, though the target of some of the worst terrorist attacks in history, shares the responsibility for the onset of modern terror. Seeking to drive the British from Palestine, Zionist paramilitary groups, such as the Irgun, Stern Gang, and Etzel, were early perpetrators of terrorist violence in the Middle East. On July 22, 1946, the Polish Jew Menachem Begin, later to become prime minister of Israel, led a group of saboteurs (the Etzel) into the kitchen of the King David Hotel in Jerusalem, which served as the headquarters of British governmental offices. The group deposited milk cans packed with gelignite in the hotel's lower floor, set the fuses, and then fled. When the explosion occurred 25 minutes later, 91 British, Arabs, and Jews were killed and 45 injured. On April 9, 1948, the Stern Gang and Etzel invaded and captured the village of Deir Yassim, raping women and killing more than 230 Arab men, women, and children, mutilating their bodies.[3] Israel was itself founded on terror. Locked in a desparate battle with Palestinian Nationalists and terrorist groups, like Hamas and the Popular Front for the Liberation of Palestine who do not hesitate to massacre innocent Israelis, the Israeli government, through its policies of violent retaliation, bulldozing of refugee camps, assassination, torture as well as its establishment of settlements in Palestinian territory, must bear some of the responsibility for the ongoing Middle East tragedy.

But Israel and the Palestinian Nationalists may simply have been following a well-established practice of the Middle East: Hama rules.

HAMA RULES: THE BACKGROUND METAPHOR FOR THE TERRORISM OF SEPTEMBER 11, 2001

In his book *From Beirut to Jerusalem,* Thomas Friedman describes atrocities that took place in Hama, Syria, in early February 1982. After an assassination attempt on the Syrian President Hafez Assad was traced to the Muslim Brotherhood, a group of Sunni Muslim militants in the town of Hama, Assad's forces, led by his brother Rifaat, launched an attack on the Brotherhood in Hama. A fierce civil war broke out between the Muslim guerillas and the Syrian military. Prisoners were tortured and buildings, even mosques, were destroyed. In a few weeks much of Hama was in rubble. Assad brought in bulldozers to flatten the rubble, as though he were constructing a parking lot. Between 7,000 and 38,000 people were killed. "Normally, a politician would play down such a ghastly incident and dismiss the high casualty numbers as the enemy's propaganda, but Assad's forces claimed them as a badge of honor."

Friedman argues that the incident illustrates the rules of Arab warfare, Hama rules which come straight out of a Hobbesian state of nature, where life is "solitary, poor, nasty, brutish and short." Destroy or be destroyed. Warring tribes confront each other with no impartial arbiter to enforce mutually agreed upon rules; the only relevant concern is survival, which entails that the enemy must be destroyed by whatever means necessary. Friedman describes the Middle Eastern states as brutal autocracies where leaders (despots) like Assad and Iraq's president Saddam Hussein have survived by using oppressive tactics, including framing their enemies, and by torturing and executing political rivals. "Restraint and magnanimity are luxuries of the self-confident, and the rulers of these countries are anything but secure on their thrones," writes Friedman.[4]

Friedman illustrates his theory with a Bedouin legend about an old man and his turkey. One day an elderly Bedouin discovered that by eating turkey, he could restore his virility. So he bought a small turkey and kept it around his tent, feeding it, so that it would provide a source of renewed strength. One day the turkey was stolen. So the Bedouin called his sons together and said, "Boys, my turkey has been stolen. We are in danger now." His sons laughed, replying, "Father, it's no big deal. What do you need a turkey for?" "Never mind," the father replied, "we must get the turkey back." But his sons didn't take this seriously and soon forgot about the turkey. A few weeks later the Bedouin's sons came to him and said, "Father, our camel has been stolen. What should we do?" "Find my turkey," the Bedouin replied. A few weeks later the sons came to him again, saying that the old man's horse was stolen. "Find my turkey," he responded. Finally, a few weeks after that, someone raped his daughter. The Bedouin gazed at his sons and said, "It's all because of the turkey. When they saw that they could take away my turkey, we lost everything."[5]

To let your enemy take an inch is to give him a mile; it is to lose your wealth, your status, your reputation, your integrity. In such a state the rule is not "an eye for an eye, a tooth for a tooth, a life for life," but "a life for an eye, two lives for a tooth, and the lives of your entire tribe for the life of my turkey." Friedman thinks that Hama rules govern the Middle East conflict. They are the rules by which Israel has learned to play. Friedman notes that Ariel Sharon, the present prime minister of Israel, is the one man Assad has feared and respected because Sharon plays by those rules too. His support of the Lebanese Falangists in the mass killings at Sabra and Chatila and the recent Israeli reprisals against the Palestinian community are evidence of this.

If Friedman's thesis is correct, we in the West are dealing with warriors who are playing by a set of rules different from ours. Our notions of proportionate response and the distinction between combatants and noncombatants don't apply to Osama bin Laden; his deputy, Iman al Zawahiri; and the Al Qaeda. As bin Laden has announced, every American is an enemy and should be destroyed, whether he or she is a soldier or a civilian. In a video made on November 9, 2001, bin Laden gloated over the wonderful success, surpassing the most "optimistic estimates," of killing over 3,000 people in the World Trade Center attacks. The attitude behind these boastings and these attacks bespeaks a different way of evaluating actions. Bin Laden pits Hama rules against Western rules:

> The ruling to kill the Americans and their allies—civilians and military—is an individual duty for every Muslim who can do it in any country in which it is possible to do it, in order to liberate the Al Aksa Mosque and the holy mosque from their grip, and in order for their armies to move out of all the lands of Islam, defeated and unable to threaten any Muslim.[6]

During the terrible cold war, at least we knew that our enemy loved life as much as we and would be motivated by secular self-interest, so a policy of mutual assured destruction (MAD) was feasible. But now we are confronted by enemies who would just as soon cause a nuclear holocaust that would wipe us and them from the face of the earth, liberating them for heavenly bliss. They play by Hama rules with a theocratic touch.

CLASH OF CULTURES

A second characteristic of the recent terrorist attacks is their religious underpinning. Unlike nationalistic terrorist attacks by the IRA, Tamil Tigers, or PLO, the attacks of September 11 were not done in the name of a nation. They were cultural, namely religious, and represent what Samuel Huntington refers to as a clash of civilizations.[7] The terrorist attacks carried out by the Islamic Jihad against the Egyptian government and the Al Qaeda-sponsored attacks against the U.S. embassies in East Africa and the World Trade Center in New York were religious in nature. Osama bin Laden, Iman al Zawahiri and their cohorts have announced that this is a *jihad*, a holy war against the *kafir*, the infidel, the evil empire of the West, and especially, the United States and Israel. The Al Qaeda network sees itself as the vanguard of an Islamic movement, expunging the virulent "Westoxification" from the Muslim world, overthrowing American and Western hegemony in the world by removing American military bases and Western culture from countries such as Saudi Arabia, Egypt, and Kuwait. The attack on America was intended to provoke a violent American reaction, which in turn would ignite a worldwide Islamic uprising against the West.

The clash of civilizations, the culture of Islamic fundamentalism against Western culture, composed of modernity, secularity, and democracy, has become the new battleground for humankind. With the cold war over, ideological differences between cultures reemerge as the source of conflict. Religion, not nationalism, may become the dominant threat to world peace and stability. Although the majority of Muslims may eschew the terrorists' tactics, there is something in Islam that predisposes its followers to violence, the idea of jihad, the holy war against the infidel. Saddam Hussein invoked the jihad, appealing to all Muslims to support Iraq against America in the Gulf War, and Iran's Ayatollah Khomeini has called for a holy war against the West, "the struggle against American aggression, greed, plans and policies will be counted as a jihad and anybody who is killed on that path is a martyr."[8] Muslim schools, *madrasses*, throughout the Muslim world teach children that the West is evil and that they have a duty to perpetuate the jihad against it. Although many Muslims reject Islamic fundamentalism, emphasizing peace, the idea of jihad is an essential part of Islamic teachings, and Islam is embattled in war wherever it consists of a critical mass that confronts a different culture. In Israel, it battles Jews; in Kashmir and India, Hindus; in Nigeria, Protestants; in Lebanon, Maronite Christians; in the Philippines, Catholics; in the Balkans, Orthodox Christians; in the Horn of Africa, Coptic Christians; in Europe and America, Christians and secularists. Tolerance toward the "People of the Book" (Jews and Christians) may be officially advocated by the Koran, but fundamentalists, such as the Wahabi sect in Saudi Arabia and Pakistan, seize upon the notion of the jihad against the kafir to override any tendency toward tolerance.

Religion is a powerful motivating force. Invoking the authority of God and offering the rewards of eternal bliss, it can be an incentive to extreme acts of both virtue and vice. It is hard to reason with religious fundamentalists, for they generally hold their faith or religious assumptions to trump reason. Reason, for them, to reverse Kant's dictum, always functions as a strategy within the "bounds of religion alone."

When Hama rules are married to religious fundamentalism and clash with a different religious or secular culture, we have the potential for violence, for terrorism. Let us now define *terrorism* before turning to the causes of and the moral response to that form of violence.

DEFINITION OF TERRORISM

Terrorism is a type of political violence that intentionally targets civilians (noncombatants) in a ruthlessly destructive, often unpredictable manner.

Terrorism hardly constitutes mindless violence. Instead, it reflects a detailed strategy that uses horrific violence to make people feel weak and vulnerable, often disproportionate to either the terrorist act or to the terrorist's long-term power. This undermining fear is then used to promote concrete political objectives. Although some of these objectives may be morally commendable, their moral quality tends to be annulled by the murderous means employed; thus terrorism must be discouraged by civilized governments. Essentially, terrorism employs *horrific violence against unsuspecting civilians, as well as combatants, to inspire fear and create panic, which in turn will advance the terrorists' political or religious agenda.* Although this definition can be qualified and refined, it will serve my purposes in this chapter.

CAUSES OF TERRORISM

Although cultural attitudes, such as religious ideology, may be a significant cause of terrorism, despair, a sense of hopelessness rooted in oppression, ignorance, poverty, and perceived injustice, may be the contributing cause, the soil in which fundamentalism can grow and flourish. Often it is those who have been frustrated by the powers that be who strike out against what they perceive as their enemy.[9] Perceived oppression evokes sympathy in the hearts of many, even to the point of excusing or romanticizing violent responses against the "oppressor." Hence, the French existentialist philosopher Jean-Paul Sartre, writing in defense of the National Liberation Front in Algeria, stated, "To shoot down a European is to kill two birds with one stone, to destroy an oppressor and the man he oppressed at the same time: there remains a dead man and a free man." Unfortunately for Sartre's analysis, most of the victims of terrorism are unsuspecting, innocent civilians, no more engaged in oppression than a Bedouin sheep herder, a firefighter trying to rescue people from a burning building, a passenger on United Airlines Flight 93, or a woman trying to run a business from the 100th floor of a World Trade Center building. But according to the logic of terror, there is no difference between those people and the commander at Auschwitz who led innocent people to the gas ovens. The attractiveness of terrorism is exacerbated by cultures that encourage violence as a response to perceived harms and wrongs. When a religious or political ideology is present, the tendency to resort to terror may be exponentially increased, so that otherwise normal people may resort to extreme measures in the name of religion, believing that by killing people they are serving God and thereby ensuring themselves eternal bliss.[10] The Islamic Wahabi sect adds jihad to the five traditional pillars of Islam.

Abd al-Salam Faraj's *Faridah al-Gha'ibah* (The Neglected Duty), published in the early 1980s, set forth the religious justification for terrorist violence against the enemies of Islam. Islamic warriors are enjoined to use every means available to achieve their just goal. The reward is an assured place in paradise. Hama rules are joined in holy matrimony with Islamic fundamentalism in Faraj's work. In 1982 Faraj was tried and executed for his part in the assassination of President Anwar Sadat of Egypt.

Peer pressure, religious sanctions, and a quasi-military scheme of hierarchical command-obedience structure, which causes the terrorist to focus on the importance of the action rather than his or her own self-interest, enable the terrorist to act in ways we would normally consider irrational in the extreme. We are revulsed by terrorism, not because the terrorists are cowards, but because their misguided courage is directed at violating the rights of and even murdering unsuspecting innocents. In September 2001 shortly after the Day of Ignominy, CBS's "60 Minutes" produced a documentary, directed by Bob Simon, on the life of suicide bombers. Young Palestinian men were selected by radical Islamic leaders to be martyrs in the jihad against Israelis. The youths, believing this call to jihad was a sacred honor, were indoctrinated to the point of believing that through the act of kamikaze missions, they would become holy martyrs and ascend straight to heaven. A video was made of their lives, recording their commitment to die for their cause. The video was sent to their families, who were led to believe that their sons were dying a holy martyr's death. After such profound commitment, it would be hard for the youth to back out, return home, ring their doorbells, and announce, "Surprise, Mom, I decided that suicide bombing was not in my best interest." The comprehensive cultural reinforcement of the terrorist suicide bomber sets this kind of fundamentalism off from our normal sense of prudent and moral behavior. Poverty and oppression are not sufficient (or even necessary) for terrorism, though they are contributing causes. What is the overriding impetus is a culture that endorses and reinforces violent responses against certain types of persons and property.

Terrorism has existed from time immemorial,[11] but with the onset of modern technology, including rapid transport, the bomb, the airplane, and chemical, biological, radiological, and nuclear warfare, the threat to society has been increased exponentially. Furthermore, television and mass communication in general give terrorism widespread publicity. *Publicity is the oxygen of terrorism.* Terrorist acts displayed on worldwide networks such as CNN compel our attention, and this point has not been lost on the terrorist leaders. It took just a couple of terrorists bombing the Marine barracks in Beirut in 1986, killing 241 servicemen, to cause the withdrawal of American and French forces from Lebanon.

A WAR ON TERRORISM

Although terrorism has an ancient history, there was something horrific about the suddenness and sheer magnitude of the events of September 11. In one fell swoop the terrorists swept away America's *illusion of invulnerability*. In a matter of minutes the twin pillars of capitalism were leveled and thousands of lives destroyed. No one is immune from surprise violence. Our airlines are especially vulnerable and our skyscrapers prime targets. While we were still reeling under this terrible tragedy, five people, beginning with a man in Florida, died of anthrax exposure, and several more people, including NBC's Tom Brokaw, Senate Majority Leader Tom Daschle, and Senator Pat Leahy received envelopes containing anthrax spores.

A war on terrorism has been declared by President George W. Bush, and troops have been deployed to areas of the Middle East and Central Asia, where terrorist camps under the auspices of Osama bin Laden and Al Qaeda prosper.[12] But it will be extremely difficult to defeat sophisticated modern terrorism, for these terrorists have neither a state nor identifiable public buildings or institutions. They operate in small semi-autonomous cells, so they are hard to infiltrate. And if one terrorist base is attacked, the terrorists move into the Afghanistan mountains or establish a new base in Iraq, Pakistan, Turkmenistan, Syria, Somalia, Sudan, or, possibly, Saudi Arabia.

Perhaps the answer is to root out the underlying causes of terrorism, such as poverty, ignorance, oppression, and injustice.[13] While, no doubt, this goal should be part of an enlightened strategy, it is extremely difficult to accomplish, since, in this case, the ignorance and oppression are associated with religion, namely, Muslim (Wahabi) fanaticism, which opposes Western liberal values, including women's rights, tolerance of different lifestyles, and abortion. The same ideology that opposes secular liberal values gives deep meaning to the lives of the adherents of the terrorist groups. The religion of Allah gives purpose, hope, and a practical guide to action to millions of Muslims, who may live more virtuous or at least more disciplined lives than their secular counterparts. It is noteworthy that some of the terrorist leaders say the same thing about contemporary American decadence as do American Christian fundamentalist leaders such as Jerry Falwell, who asserted that God permitted this horror of the Day of Ignominy because of our drift into secularism and permissive liberalism. At bottom, this is a struggle of moral secularity against intolerant religious theocracy, of liberal open society versus the Hama rules of the tribal closed society. As such, it represents a supreme challenge to civilization, not equaled since the rise of Hitler and Stalin.

TERRORISM AND JUST WAR THEORY

What strikes us as especially heinous about the Day of Ignominy was the callous disregard for innocent life, for the incredible imperviousness to destroying the lives of people who were not warriors. Osama bin Laden's announcement that there is no distinction between a soldier and an ordinary American civilian ("Whoever is a taxpayer in America is a legitimate target")[14] strikes us as the epitome of immoral use of force, and its originator, a moral cretin. The terrorist fails to grasp the fundamental distinction between combatant and noncombatant, so a strong moral presumption opposes his or her actions. But, even though normally unjustified, could there be extreme cases where terrorism is morally permitted? Here is where just war theory enters the picture.

St. Augustine (354–430), Thomas Aquinas (1225–1274), and Francisco Suarez (1548–1617), a Roman Catholic Jesuit in the Middle Ages, believed that war, although an evil, could be justified if certain conditions were met. As deontologists, they rejected simple cost-benefit calculations and the whole notion of total war—that all is fair in love and war. They distinguished between moral grounds for going into war (*jus ad bellum*) and right conduct while engaged in war (*jus in bello*).

Jus ad bellum, the right to go to war, could be justified by the following circumstances. The war must be:

1. *Declared by a legitimate authority.* This would rule out revolutionary wars and rebel uprisings.
2. *Declared for a just cause.* The Allies' World War II declaration of war on the Japanese and Germans, who were seen as bent on destroying Western democracy, is often cited as the paradigmatic case of such a just declaration of war. The Gulf War against Iraq was allegedly about the integrity of Kuwait as well as the perceived danger to Saudi Arabia, Syria, and, especially, Israel. It was also about the control of oil in the Middle East.
3. *Declared as a last resort.* Belligerence may commence only after a reasonable determination has been made that war is the only way to accomplish good ends. In the Gulf War against Iraq, some argue that serious efforts at negotiation had failed and sanctions were not working, so war was the only alternative.
4. *Declared with the intention of bringing peace and holding respect (and even love) for the enemy.* The opposition must be respected as human beings even as we attack them.

Regarding carrying on the war (*jus in bello*), two further conditions are given:

5. *Proportionality*. The war must be carried out in moderation, exacting no more casualties than necessary for accomplishing the good end. No more force than necessary to achieve the just goal may be exercised. Pillage, rape, and torture are forbidden. There is no justification for cruel treatment of innocents, prisoners, and the wounded. Nuclear war seems to violate the principle of proportionality.

6. *Discrimination*. Contrary to act-utilitarian theories, just war theory makes a distinction between combatants and noncombatants— those deemed innocent in the fray. It is impermissible to attack nonmilitary targets and noncombatants. Civilian bombing, such as took place in London, Coventry, Hamburg, Hiroshima, and Dresden during World War II, is now outlawed by international law. The massacre of civilians at My Lai is viewed as the nadir of despicable behavior by American forces in the Vietnam War.

Criticism of just war theory centers on its idealized constraints. Critics contend that it is a holdover from the confined medieval battlefield, with knights on horses voluntarily engaging the enemy in the name of the king, with spectators looking on from the safety of a promontory. It has little to do with the modern world, where political legitimacy is often open to question, where conscription may force young men and women to do a dictator's bidding, where the whole infrastructure of a nation may be relevant to the outcome, and where the enemy does not abide by the rules of proportionality and discrimination.

The first condition seems somewhat dubious. What is a legitimate authority? One set up by a democratic election? One widely recognized by its subjects? If so, all revolutions, including the American Revolution, are immoral. This seems counterintuitive. The notion of political legitimacy, discussed in Chapter 1, is a deep and difficult issue about which we can disagree. In the United States, only Congress has the authority to declare war, yet in the past 50 years the United States has been involved in full-scale wars in Korea, Vietnam, and the Middle East, not to mention military actions in Grenada, Lebanon, Libya, and Panama, without a declaration of war by Congress.

Conditions 2, 3, and 4 seem plausible. To justify military violence, one's cause must be just, and we ought to do everything in our power to resolve the dispute before resorting to violence. The aim should be the restoration of peace and mutual respect. The trouble is that people on opposing sides usually think they are right and the enemy wrong. An ample dose of self-serving rationalization typically stands proxy for honest inquiry into the relevant facts, which are often complicated and shrouded in a murky past. Nevertheless, these conditions can be approximated.

Condition 5, proportionality, seems self-evident. If we are to do evil, it must be a lesser evil, and that lesser evil must be the minimum evil necessary to accomplish the morally good goal. Condition 6, discrimination between combatants and noncombatants, has been challenged by some utilitarians. They argue that, since utility is the goal, sometimes the distinction between combatants and noncombatants should be overridden. If by bombing a city in which 10,000 civilian lives would be lost, we could save 15,000 soldiers, we should bomb the city, thereby maximizing utility. Whatever does the least total evil (or promotes the greater good) ought to be done, regardless of the status of the victims, be they civilians or combatants.

Where utilitarians waver is when practices such as torture are considered. If we could save 10 of our soldiers by torturing 1 enemy soldier, should we do it? Is torture one of those unspeakable evils that should transcend (or nearly transcend) the utilitarian calculus? Perhaps utilitarianism is plausible when comparing lives but not when heinous acts such as torture are involved. But then is torture really any worse than mass killing, leaving children orphans, or using nuclear weapons to accomplish purposes of the state? Note that it has recently been revealed that Israel tortured Arab prisoners to gain vital information. Suppose a terrorist has planted a bomb to go off in two hours. If we think that his wife knows where the bomb is, are we justified in torturing her to ascertain the location of the bomb? Deontologists would reject this kind of treatment, but utilitarians would entertain the possibility of implementing it.

The moral distinction between innocents (more correctly, noncombatants) and combatants is especially problematic. Sometimes civilians are wholehearted supporters of a war effort and soldiers are poor youths who have been conscripted against their desire. Soldiers, by the very nature of their profession, take on special risks of life and limb. Soldiers are fair game for enemy fire—until they surrender or are put out of action through being wounded.

Some just war theorists, such as Paul Christopher, hold that soldiers have an exceedingly strong duty not to jeopardize civilians, even at the cost of putting their own lives in danger. For example, during the Korean War, North Korean units put civilian hostages in front of them as they attacked U.S. forces. The U.S. forces had the option of retreating, thus losing vital ground, or killing civilians. What should they have done? Christopher, in accord with his interpretation of just war theory, says that the U.S. soldiers should have attacked the Koreans with bayonets to discriminate between civilians and soldiers. "Once we accept that it is part of the ethos of the soldier to behave courageously and to protect innocents, even at the risk of one's own life, then it becomes clear that it is the civilians' lives that must be safeguarded, not the lives of the soldiers. In this case, for example, the men could assault the enemy/civilian formation and use bayonets to engage the combatants."[15]

This seems extreme. Surely soldiers had a right to defend themselves against the North Koreans and advance their position. The Koreans, not the Americans, risked the lives of the hostages. Utilitarians have no difficulty justifying shooting at the soldiers, even though they foresee that some civilians will die. They foresee, but do not intend, the deaths of the civilians.

Rule-utilitarians tend to take the discrimination condition more seriously than classical act-utilitarians. They hold that ordinarily we ought to distinguish combatants from noncombatants in the way just war theory requires, for in the long run, this rule will produce the most good. War itself is a great evil—at best, a necessary lesser evil. The discrimination between civilians and combatants limits war to a specific zone of minimal evil activity, where it may be contained. Rule-utilitarians adhere to deontological just war theory for most purposes, granting these principles strong prima facie status. But they would allow an act-utilitarian override in extreme emergency. For example, these ethicists would justify President Truman's decision to drop the atomic bomb on Hiroshima in 1945 to end the Second World War and thereby save an estimated million lives. The debate between deontological just war theory and a utilitarian theory of moral military action is deep and far-ranging, going beyond the confines of this book. But if one accepts either the deontological or rule-utilitarian position, which the majority of philosophers do, one can justify violations of the combatant-noncombatant distinction only in extreme cases, such as the bombing of Hiroshima. Osama bin Laden's announcement that there is no distinction between a soldier and an ordinary American civilian ("Whoever is a taxpayer in America is a legitimate target") strikes us as a callous, unjustified disregard of that distinction. The terrorist attacks of September 11 didn't cause civilian casualties as simply unintended consequences of aiming at military targets. The terrorists aimed directly at civilians, hoping to kill as many of them as possible. The terrorists adhered to jihadic Hama rules rather than the restraining conditions of just war theory. They also failed to meet the just war condition 3 ("declared only as a last resort"), for neither discussion of their complaints against us nor attempts at negotiations were ever entered into.

No doubt the Al Qaeda and the terrorists of September 11, following Faraj's Wahabi ideology, believed their terrorist actions were justified, and that their violence was a response to Western evil, whether that evil consisted in our support of Israel or the Gulf War or Western troops in Saudi Arabia. Morality would require that we sit down and reason things out, compromising if necessary, to reach the best accommodation. This is what needs to happen in Israel between the Israelis and the Palestinians, where both sides have committed atrocities. But where one side refuses to negotiate and, instead, commits unprovoked terrorist acts, the attacked partly is justified in using measured violence to protect its interests. But, as we argued above, the violence must be not only a last resort and aimed at restoring peace, but also proportionate to the morally endorsed goals, doing no more damage than necessary to accomplish our purposes. It must be delivered in careful ways so as to distinguish between legitimate targets—combatants and their instruments of destruction—and illegitimate targets—noncombatants and civilians not directly involved in the war effort. While just war theory may have to be qualified by utilitarian considerations in some situations of extreme emergency, it provides the best guide for dealing with organized violence, including terrorism. It certainly informs us that the kind of horrific violence perpetrated by terrorists against innocent passengers in airplanes and in the World Trade Center and in the Pentagon is beyond the pale of morally considerable action. What, then, is the appropriate moral response to terrorism?

THE MORAL RESPONSE

In responding to the Day of Ignominy, we have a number of converging goals. One salient goal is to honor the 3,400 victims of the kamikaze attacks. We can do this by working to create a world where terrorism is reduced to a minimum, which, in turn, entails attacking the causes of terrorism, eradicating the moral swamp that breeds fanaticism, hatred, and indiscriminate violence. We can also honor the fallen more immediately by punishing those who perpetrated this deed, the terrorist leaders who trained, financed, and motivated the terrorists to destroy innocent life and property on September 11. These two goals are conjoined. In the long term, we must create a more just world, one conducive to peace, prosperity, and democracy. But in the short term, we must end those regimes and organizations that sponsor and promote terrorism, such as the Taliban, Al Qaeda, and the Islamic Jihad. A measured, carefully executed military operation in Afghanistan, while not a substitute for a long-range and more comprehensive political strategy, can support, supplement, and augment the goal of global justice. Let me then outline some short-term and long-term goals in assessing the ethical response to the Day of Ignominy.

Short-Term Strategies

I have already mentioned the fact that just war theory would endorse a measured response to the terrorist attacks of September 11, aiming to punish and deter terrorists and reduce their threat to our society. That we are building a broad coalition with other European, Asian, and Middle Eastern nations, and even with Russia in this pursuit is one of the good things resulting from wise handling of the disaster of September 11. Every civilized country has a stake in the battle against terrorism. We should also note, but cannot develop at length in this text, the need for strategies for self-protection to include a homeland counterterrorist policy. Our present policy includes the following four principles:

1. Make no concessions to terrorists and strike no deals.
2. Bring terrorists to justice.
3. Isolate and apply pressure on states that sponsor terrorism, forcing them to change their behavior.
4. Bolster the counterterrorist capabilities of those countries that work with the United States and require assistance.

All this seems responsible and worthy of our national support. In addition, counterterrorism must include cutting off the financial resources of terrorists. Terrorists need a support network, including financial support. By undermining a group's economic ability to wage war, as the United States has recently begun to do, we make terrorist attacks more difficult.[16]

An additional response, which seems entailed by these principles, is a more scrutinizing immigration-control policy. Several of the hijackers of September 11 were here legally, though background checks would have caused officials concern. Investigators reported that Mohammed Atta, a known Egyptian terrorist who is thought to be the mastermind behind the terrorist suicide bombings of September 11, originally entered the United States on a legal visa and when it expired, still used it to gain entry to the United States just before the events of September 11. No background check was ever done on him. The Immigration and Naturalization Act of 1990 (led by Senator Ted Kennedy of Massachusetts) forbids denying a visa to foreigners simply because they are members of terrorist organizations. Even though 15 of the 19 suicide hijackers were in the United States on legal visas, some of them on student visas, the immigration policy remains unchanged. In January 1999, the U.S. Commission on National Security, co-chaired by Senator Gary Hart of Colorado, stated that our immigration system was lax and warned of coming problems: "America will become increasingly vulnerable to hostile attack on our homeland,

and our military superiority will not entirely protect us. Americans will likely die on American soil, possibly in large numbers."[17] "The entire system for monitoring and managing foreign visitors is broken. And why is it we grant visas to students from countries that sponsor terror? After all, we know that terrorists have entered the country on student visas," wrote Mark Krikorian, director of the Center for Immigration Studies in Washington.[18]

A striking case that occurred in Canada is that of the Algerian terrorist Ahmed Rassem, who was apprehended in an attempt to blow up the Los Angeles airport in late 1999. Although Rassem had a forged French passport and a terrorist record, the Canadian immigration authorities allowed him into their country, where he soon obtained welfare benefits. This kind of immigration laxity violates the state's obligation to protect its citizens from attack by securing its borders from external threats. Granted, this issue is not without complications, because we do not want to exclude visitors or immigrants altogether. Millions of foreigners enter our country each year, many of whom outstay their visas; but better monitoring of these people is necessary if we are to safeguard our freedom.

National ID cards may have to be issued in the years to come if this proves the best way to protect our liberty. Authorities would use such IDs to detect illegal aliens, those who have overstayed their visa permissions, and criminals. Such identification, which has been public policy in some European nations, need not curtail our freedom, though it may invade a certain privacy—a price that it may be worth paying to preserve our security and liberty.

Long-Term Strategies

NATIONAL CONSCRIPTION   Some good has already come out of the tragedy of September 11. Our country is united in an almost unprecedented way. Democrats and Republicans are bonding and cooperating to build a more vibrant and secure nation. Young people wanting to serve their country have been enlisting in the FBI, the CIA, and the military services. We should take this opportunity to develop new opportunities for national and world service. A new model of national conscription seems a plausible option. Each able-bodied youth should be required to serve our nation or the world in some beneficial capacity, such as the military, AmeriCorps, Domestic Youth Corps, or Peace Corps. In a recent *New York Times* essay, "A New Start for National Service," Senators John McCain and Evan Bayh call for the government to institute new service programs to involve youth in civil defense, community service, and international service. In return, the government would fund the college or vocational education of these young people.[19] Such programs have the virtues of helping young people internalize a moral patriotism and, at the same time, of promoting worthy goals, such as educating the poor, ministering to the sick and elderly, and serving one's nation and the world. If such programs are appropriately organized and administered, they will not hinder personal autonomy, but provide a channel for service. Serving one's country provides a mechanism for expressing one's gratitude for all the benefits membership provides us; creates a mechanism for identifying with the moral goals of the nation, thus internalizing a sense of citizenship; and enables us to help make this a better nation. Though the immediate sphere of service should be one's own country, eventually, the circle should be expanded to include the entire world. This leads to the next point, the recognition of a universal morality with universal human rights.

SPREADING THE MESSAGE OF A UNIVERSAL MORALITY WITH UNIVERSAL HUMAN RIGHTS   The moral point of view, as we noted in the Introduction of this book, is universalistic, based on rationally approved, impartial principles, recognizing a universal humanity, rather than particular groups or persons, as the bearer of moral consideration. When seeking to rescue a drowning man, we do not ask him, "Are you an American or an Arab?" before seeking to save him. We rescue him because he is a human being. We must come to see all humanity as tied together in a common moral network. If all do not hang together, each will hang alone. Since morality is universalistic, its primary focus must be on the individual, not the nation, race, gender or religious group. We are all human beings, and only accidentally, citizens of the United States, Afghanistan, Germany, Japan, Brazil, or Nigeria. Many of us are grateful to be Americans, but we didn't earn this property and should recognize that our common humanity overrides specific racial, nationalistic identity. A global perspective must replace nationalism and tribalism as the leitmotif of ethical living. A nonreligious ethic, based on rational reflection and yielding universal human values, must become the underpinning of a renewed cosmopolitanism. The threats to morality today come from religious particularism, naive egoism, ethical relativism, and deconstructionism—a euphemism for moral nihilism. A defensible moral objectivism, the core of which is accepted by a consensus of moral philosophers, must permeate our society as well as every other society under the sun. At present, most people derive their moral principles unreflectively either from religion or from narrow tribal ideology. An educational process inculcating universal norms in people everywhere is a crucial task for the leaders of the 21st century. Principles such as forbidding murder (the unjust killing of innocents), dishonesty, and exploitation, and promoting reciprocal cooperation, freedom, and universal justice must be seen as the necessary conditions for the good life, civilization, and peace. This leads to the ultimate long-range goal, world government (the cosmopolitan moral imperative).

THE COSMOPOLITAN MORAL IMPERATIVE. THE POSSIBILITY OF WORLD GOVERNMENT: Peace, justice, and the struggle against terrorism and violence may be attainable only by institutional cosmopolitanism—world government. There are two arguments for world government. The first one is the *moral point of view argument,* which we have just adumbrated (above) and which I will elaborate below. The second argument is from the *trend toward globalism,* which I have discussed in Chapter 9. To review: Because of the growth of trade, commercialism, rapid communication, and the Internet, and the spread of English as the lingua franca of commercial and diplomatic communication, and because of the need for global environmental regulation and international law to solve interstate conflict, we need an impartial arbiter to adjudicate conflicts of interest fairly. Some kind of international agency is needed. The United Nations and the international court in The Hague are already beginning to play this role, but something more formal and autonomous is likely to be needed. To these reasons for a world court or governing body, we may now add the need to combat terrorism through an institution with broad powers, including crossing national boundaries and pursuing terrorists wherever they may be hiding. Fighting the brushfires of terrorist wars and working to keep world peace may be best accomplished by each nation–state relinquishing sovereignty, while maintaining significant autonomy, much like the 50 states do within the government of the United States. So long as individual states maintain basic human rights and work together to contribute to justice and peace, they are free to differ on cultural and legal matters. If state A desires a law against abortion or the death penalty, whereas other states permit these institutions, state A would be permitted to pass such legislation. While the overall government would contribute to the welfare of the whole, especially to the worst-off people and states, states would have primary obligations to their own people, just as families have primary obligations to help their own members, while not neglecting their duties to others.

Conclusion

September 11, the Day of Ignominy, has changed America and the world. We have been shocked out of our complacency, disabused of our illusion of invulnerability, and forced to face global terrorism. I have argued that the Day of Ignominy may become the Day of Opportunity, if we use it to take countermeasures to terrorism and the causes of terrorism and to begin to ameliorate the oppression and injustice in our nation and the world. I have outlined some short-term and long-term strategies. The main strategy is a renewed commitment to the moral point of view, to a moral code that substitutes rationally justified principles and policies, such as those contained in the core universal morality and just war theory, for Hama rules of tribal vengeance. The most ambitious and controversial implication of this commitment to a core morality is a version of institutional cosmopolitanism, world government, based on rational morality. To offset the tendency to irrational Hamatic rules, we need an impartial arbiter to enforce objective principles and universal law, which would be part of an international governing system. World government also seems a fitting response to the growing pressures of globalism. In Chapter 9, I have also argued for preserving nationalism because of its ability to develop the opportunities for close personal relationships and loyalties, so vital for personal identity. Some form of nationalism will always be part of the human psyche, though, one hopes, it will be a less bombastic, narrow, and exclusivist variety than the hard nationalism that we now experience. It will be balanced by a soft form of cosmopolitanism, either informally worked out between nations or by a formal world government that would still encourage and promote individual nation–state autonomy within its domain. The model is one of expanding concentric circles, beginning with the close circle of one's family and friends and expanding to one's community, then to one's nation, and finally, to the entire world. One way or another, increased peace and international cooperation will be necessary as we become better-educated people who live in a global village, where human beings flourish, and where we more closely approximate a world in which each child will have an equal opportunity to find fulfillment with justice. This, it seems to me, is the long-term goal of political philosophy.

For Further Reflection

1. Assess the discussion on the responses to terrorism. Do you agree with the short and long term responses? Explain your answer.
2. What are the principles of Just War Theory? Which principles do you think strongest and which weakest? Discuss your answer.
3. Could someone we call a terrorist justify his or her acts through Just War Theory?
4. Discuss the causes of terrorism and what should be done about it.
5. Should we promote world government? Why or why not?

Endnotes

1. Quoted in Magnus Ranstorp, "Terrorism in the Name of Religion" *Journal of International Affairs* (1996).

2. R. J. Rummel, *Death by Government* (Transaction, 1994). Long before Lord Acton, in the eighteenth century, Edmund Burke wrote, "Power gradually extirpates from the mind every humane and gentle virtue."

3. Howard Sachar, *A History of Israel: From the Rise of Zionism to Our Time* (Knopf, 1996), pp. 267, 333. I do not mean to pick out Israel as worse than the Arab nations or Palestine leaders. On the contrary, Israel, at least, approximates a democracy, whereas few of its Arab neighbors, including Saudi Arabia and Egypt, make the slightest pretensions thereof. While the Irgun, Etzel, and Stern Gang were carrying out terrorist acts on Palestinians, Palestinian groups led by such men as Fawzi el Kutub and Abdul Khader Husseini were blowing up Israelis. Note that many incidents of America's treatment of the Native Americans would be considered terrorist acts.

4. Thomas Friedman, *From Beirut to Jerusalem* (Farrar, Straaus & Giroux; 1989), p. 95.

5. Op. cit., p. 89.

6. Osama bin Laden, quoted in Jeffrey Goldberg, "The Education of a Holy Warrior" *New York Times Magazine,* June 25, 2000.

7. See Samuel Huntington's "The Clash of Civilizations?" *Foreign Affairs* (Summer 1993) for an analysis of this phenomenon. Other religious terrorist groups besides Sunni Wahabi Islam and Islamic Jihad have perpetrated terrorist acts. They include the Shiite Hezbollah (Party of God), the Japanese Aum Shinrikyo (The Supreme Truth), and Christian survivalist movements.

8. Op. cit., p. 35. In this regard, Bernard Lewis wrote in 1990, "We are facing a movement far exceeding the level of issues and policies and governments that pursue them. This is no less than a clash of civilizations—perhaps irrational but surely historic reaction of an ancient rival against our Judeo-Christian heritage, our secular present, and the world-wide expansion of both" (quoted in Huntington, op. cit., p.32).

9. Some on the political left have blamed globalization for the recent spate of terrorist attacks. David Held of the London School of Economics writes: "In our global age shaped by the flickering images of television and new information systems, the gross inequalities of life chances found in many of the world's regions feed a frenzy of anger, hostility, and resentment . . . [W]ithout an attempt to anchor globalization in meaningful principles of social justice, there can be no durable solution to the kind of crimes we have just seen" (*OpenDemocracy,* an online magazine). Rooting globalism in principles of social justice surely is called for, but the fact is that the Islamic societies (Afghanistan, Algeria, Iran, Iraq, Libya, Saudi Arabia, Sudan, Syria, and Yemen) that spawn the kind of virulent terrorism we have just seen are among those that eschew globalism. None belongs to the World Trade

Organization, the pivotal globalist organization. Islamic nations tend to be collectivist and closed societies. Globalism is a disruptive process, but it fails to explain Islamic extremism because it hasn't touched most of that world. But perhaps it is the fear of modernity that contributes to the violent Islamic attacks on the West. See Brink Lindsey, "Why Globalization Didn't Create 9/11," *New Republic* (November 12, 2001).

10. See Salman Rushdie, "Yes, This Is about Islam," *New York Times* November 2, 2001.

11. The idea of jihad, or a holy war of terrorism, occurs in the Jewish/Christian Bible. See, for example, the Old Testament book of Exodus (23:23) where God commands Israel to blot out all its neighbors, "the Amonites, and the Hivites, and the Hittites, and the Perizites, and the Canaanaites, the Jebusites," and the book of Joshua, Chapter 8, where in the battle for Ai, God commands Joshua to kill all the people in the city.

12. A particular problem is that of finding and instituting a more progressive government in Afghanistan to replace the Taliban. As I write, a *loya jirga*, a Grand Council of Afghan leaders, has been convened by the former king, the 87-year-old King Zahir Shah, who has been living in Italy for several years. However, the ethnic, tribal, and political divisions in Afghanistan are so intense that providing a transition to enlightened democratic government will probably demand sustained U.S. and U.N. military, economic, and political support for a long time. Afghanistan's literacy rate of 32 percent and life expectancy of 46 years underscore these long-term concerns.

13. Alan Kreuger, in his review of recent research on the relationship between poverty and ignorance to crime and terrorism, argues that there is at best only a weak and indirect correlation between economic and educational conditions and hate crimes, such as terrorism. See Alan B. Krueger, "The Economic Scene," *New York Times*, December 13, 2001.

14. In 1998 he endosed the fatwa calling for the killing of every American: "The ruling to kill the Americans and their allies — civilians and military — is an individual duty for every Muslim who can do it in any country in which it is possible to do it, in order to liberate the Al Aksa Mosque and the holy mosque from their grip, and in order for their armies to move out of all the lands of Islam, defeated and unable to threaten any Muslim," quoted in Goldberg, op cit.

15. Paul Christopher, *The Ethics of War and Peace* (Englewood Cliffs, NJ: Prentice-Hall, 1994), pp. 174–75.

16. For a cogent analysis of this thesis, see James Adams, *The Financing of Terror* (Simon & Schuster, 1986).

17. Quoted in "Immigration and Terror," *Middle American News* (November 2001).

18. Ibid.

19. John McCain and Evan Bayh, "A New Start for National Service," *New York Times*, November 6, 2001. The two senators plan to introduce legislation in the Senate to effect such a program.

BIBLIOGRAPHY

Introduction

Barker, Ernest. *Principles of Social and Political Theory*. Oxford, England: Oxford University Press, 1951.

Jacobs, Lesley A. *An Introduction to Modern Political Philosophy*. Upper Saddle River, NJ: Prentice-Hall, 1997.

Miller, David. *On Nationality*. Oxford, England: Oxford University Press, 1995.

Narveson, Jan F., ed. *For and Against the State*. Lanham, MD: Rowman & Littlefield, 1996.

Plamenatz, J. P. *Consent, Freedom and Political Obligation*. Oxford, England: Oxford University Press, 1968.

Pojman, Louis P. *Ethics: Discovering Right and Wrong*. Wadsworth, 2001. Belmont, CA:

————, ed. *Political Philosophy: Modern and Contemporary Readings*. New York: McGraw-Hill, 2002.

Quinton, Anthony, ed. *Political Philosophy*. Oxford, England: Oxford University Press, 1967.

Raphael, D. D. *Problems of Political Philosophy*. New York: Macmillan, 1970.

Raz, Joseph. *The Morality of Freedom*. Oxford, England: Oxford University Press, 1986.

Sidgwick, Henry. *The Elements of Politics*. New York: Macmillan, 1891.

Simmons, A. John. *Moral Principles and Political Obligation*. Princeton, NJ: Princeton University Press, 1979.

————. *On the Edge of Anarchy*. Princeton, NJ: Princeton University Press, 1993.

Strauss, L. *The City and Man*. Chicago: Rand McNally, 1964.

Thomas, Geoffrey. *Introduction to Political Philosophy*. London: Duckworth, 2000.

Chapter 1

Barker, Ernest. *Principles of Social and Political Theory*. Oxford, England: Oxford University Press, 1951.

Jacobs, Lesey A. *An Introduction to Modern Political Philosophy*. Prentice-Hall, 1997.

Kropotkin, Peter. *Mutual Aid*. Heinmann, 1902.

Narveson, Jan F., ed. *For and Against the State*. Lanham, MD: Rowman & Littlefield, 1996.

Plamenatz, J. P. *Consent, Freedom and Political Obligation*. Oxford, England: Oxford University Press, 1968.

Pojman, Louis P., ed. *Political Philosophy: Modern and Contemporary Readings*. New York: McGraw-Hill, 2002.

Quinton, Anthony, ed. *Political Philosophy*. Oxford, England: Oxford University Press, 1967.

Raphael, D. D. *Problems of Political Philosophy*. New York: Macmillan, 1970.

Raz, Joseph. *The Morality of Freedom*. Oxford, England: Oxford University Press, 1986.

Sidgwick, Henry. *The Elements of Politics*. New York: Macmillan, 1891.

Simmons, A. John. *Moral Principles and Political Obligation*. Princeton, NJ: Princeton University Press, 1979.
———. *On the Edge of Anarchy*. Princeton, NJ: Princeton University Press, 1993.

Strauss, L. *The City and Man*. Chicago: Rand McNally, 1964.

Thomas, Geoffrey. *Introduction to Political Philosophy*. London: Duckworth, 2000.

Wolff, Robert Paul. *In Defense of Anarchism*. New York: Harper & Row, 1976.

Chapter 2

Berlin, Isaiah. *Four Essays on Liberty*. Oxford, England: Oxford University Press, 1969.

Dworkin, Gerald. "Paternalism," *The Monist* 56, (1972). Reprinted in Louis Pojman, ed. *Political Philosophy: Modern and Contemporary Readings*. New York: McGraw-Hill, 2001.

Feinberg, Joel. *Offenses to Others*. Oxford, England: Oxford University Press, 1985.

Fish, Stanley. *There's No Such Thing as Free Speech and It's a Good Thing Too*. Oxford, England: Oxford University Press, 1994.

Gray, J. *Mill on Liberty: A Defense*. London: Routledge, 1996.

Kleinig, John. *Paternalism*. Rowman & Allenheld, 1983.

Mill, John Stuart. *On Liberty*. Hackett, 1978.

Nozick, Robert. *Anarchy, State and Utopia*. New York: Basic Books, 1974.

Pojman, Louis, ed. *Political Philosophy: Modern and Contemporary Readings*. New York: McGraw-Hill, 2002.

Rees, J. C. *John Stuart Mill on Liberty*. Oxford, England: Oxford University Press, 1985.

Sartorius, Rolf, ed. *Paternalism*. University of Minnesota Press, 1983.

Stephen, James Fitzjames. *Liberty, Equality, Fraternity*. Chicago: University of Chicago Press, 1991.

Wolff, Jonathan. *An Introduction to Political Philosophy*. Oxford, England: Oxford University Press, 1996.

Chapters 3 and 4

Abernethy, G. L., ed. *The Idea of Equality: An Anthology*. Richmond, VA, 1959.

Ackerman, Bruce. *Social Justice in the Liberal State*. New Haven, CT: Yale University Press, 1980.

Alexander, Larry, and Maimon Schwarzchild. "Liberalism, Neutrality, and Equality of Welfare vs. Equality of Resource." *Philosophy and Public Affairs* 16:1 (Winter 1987), pp. 85–110.

Arneson, Ricahrd J. "Against Complex Equality." *Public Affairs Quarterly* 4:2 (April 1990).
———. "Equality." In *A Companion to Contemporary Political Philosophy*, eds. Robert Goodin and Philip Pettit, Basil Blackwell, 1993.
———. Equality and Equal Opportunity for Welfare." *Philosophical Studies* (1989), pp. 77–93.
———. "Liberalism, Distributive Subjectivism, and Equal Opportunity for Welfare."

Philosophy and Public Affairs 19:2 (Spring 1992), pp. 158–94.

Bedau, Hugo Adam. "Egalitarianism and the Idea of Equality." In *Nomos IX: Equality*, eds. J. Roland Pennock and John W. Chapman, New York: Atherton Press, 1967, pp. 3–27.

Benn, Stanley I. "Egalitarianism and the Equal Consideration of Interests." In *Nomos IX: Equality*, eds. J. Roland Pennock and John W. Chapman, New York: Atherton Press, 1967, pp. 38–60.

———. "Equality, Moral and Social." In *Encyclopedia of Philosophy*. New York: Macmillan and Free Press, 1967, Vol. 3, pp. 38–41.

Berlin, Isaiah. "Equality as an Ideal." In *Justice and Social Policy*, ed. Frederick A. Olafson. Englewood Cliffs, NJ: Prentice-Hall, 1961, pp. 128–50.

Bowie, Norman, ed. *Equality Opportunity*. Boulder, CO: Westview, 1988.

Carritt, E. F. "Liberty and Equality." *Law Quarterly Review* 56 (1940), pp. 61–74. Reprinted in Anthony Quinton, ed. *Political Philosophy*. Oxford, England: Oxford University Press, 1967.

Charvet, John. "The Idea of Equality as a Substantive Principle in Society" *Political Studies* 17 (March 1969), pp. 1–13.

Cohen, G. A. "Self-Ownership, World-Ownership, and Equality." In *Justice and Equality Here and Now*, ed. F. Lucash. Ithaca, NY: Cornell University Press, 1986.

———. "On the Currency of Egalitarian Justice" *Ethics* 99 (1989), pp. 906–44.

Dworkin, Ronald. *A Matter of Principle*. Cambridge, MA: Harvard University Press, 1985.

———. "What Is Equality?" "Part 1, Equality of Welfare." "Part 2, Equality of Resources." *Philosophy and Public Affairs* 10: 3 and 4 (Summer and Fall, 1981), pp. 185–246, 283–345.

———. "Why Liberals Should Care about Equality." *New York Review of Books*, February 3, 1983. Reprinted in Ronald Dworkin, *A Matter of Principle*. Cambridge, MA: Harvard University Press, 1983.

Flew, Antony. *The Politics of Procrustes: Contradictions of Enforced Equality*. Buffalo, NY: Prometheus Books, 1981.

Frankfurt, Harry. "Equality as a Moral Ideal." *Ethics* 98 (1987), pp. 21–43.

Gellner, Ernest. "The Social Roots of Egalitarianism." In *Culture, Identity and Politics*. Cambridge University Press, 1987.

Green, S. J. D. "Competitive Equality of Opportunity: A Defense." *Ethics* 100 (1989), pp. 5–32.

Gutmann, Amy. *Liberal Equality*. Cambridge University Press, 1980.

Hare, R. M. "Justice and Equality." In *Justice and Economic Distribution*, eds. John Arthur and William H. Shaw. Englewood Cliffs, NJ: Prentice-Hall, 1978.

Jencks, Christopher, et al. *Inequality: A Reassessment of the Effect of Family and Schooling in America*. New York: Basic Books, 1972.

Kristol, Irving. "About Equality." *Commentary* 54 (November 1972), pp. 41–47.

Kymlicka, Will. *Liberalism, Community and Culture*. Oxford, England: Oxford University Press, 1989.

———. *Contemporary Political Philosophy*. Oxford, England: Oxford University Press, 1990.

Lakoff, Sanford. *Equality in Political Philosophy*. Boston: Beacon Press, 1964.

Landesman, Bruce. "Egalitarianism." *Canadian Journal of Philosophy* 13:1 (March 1983).

Letwin, William, ed. *Against Equality*. London: Macmillan, 1983.

Levin, Michael E. "Equality of Opportunity." *Philosophical Quarterly* 31:123 (April 1981), pp. 110–25.

Lucas, J. R. "Against Equality." *Philosophy* 40 (1965), pp. 296–307.

———. "Against Equality Again." In *Against Equality*, ed. William Letwin. London: Macmillan, 1983.

McKerlie, Dennis. "Equality and Time." *Ethics* 99 (1989), pp. 475–91.

Nagel, Thomas. *Mortal Questions*. Cambridge University Press, 1979.

———. *Equality and Partiality*. Oxford, England: Oxford University Press, 1991.

Narveson, Jan. "On Dworkinian Equality." *Social Philosophy and Policy* 1 (1983), pp. 1–23.

Nielsen, Kai. *Equality and Liberty: A Defense of Radical Egalitarianism*. Totowa, NJ: Rowman and Allenheld, 1985.

Norman, Richard. *Free and Equal: A Philosophical Examination of Political Values*. Oxford, England: Clarendon Press, 1987.

———. "Equality Is Compatible with Liberty." In *Contemporary Political Philosophy*, ed. Keith Graham. Cambridge University Press, 1982.

Oppenheim, Felix E. "Egalitarianism as a Descriptive Concept." *American Philosophical Quarterly* 7 (1970), pp. 143–52.

Phelps Brown, Henry. *Egalitarianism and the Generation of Inequality*. Oxford, England: Oxford University Press, 1988.

Pojman, Louis. "Are Equal Rights Founded on Equal Human Worth?" *Philosophy and Phenomenological Research* (October 1992).

———. "Equality: A Plethora of Concepts." *Philosophy and Behavior* .

Pojman, Louis, and Robert Westmoreland, eds. *Equality*.

Oxford, England: Oxford University Press, 1997.

Pole, J. R. *The Pursuit of Equality in American History*. Cambridge University Press, 1978.

Rae, Douglas. *Equalities*. Cambridge: MA: Harvard University Press, 1981.

Rakowski, Eric. *Equal Justice*. Oxford, England: Oxford University Press, 1992.

Rawls, John. *A Theory of Justice*. Cambridge, MA: Harvard University Press, 1971.

———. "A Kantian Conception of Equality." *Cambridge Review* 96:2225 (February 1975).

Raz, Joseph. "Principles of Equality." *Mind* 87 (1978), pp. 321–42.

Rees, John. *Equality*. New York: Praeger, 1971.

Rousseau, Jean-Jacques. *Discourse on the Origin of Inequality among Men*. 1755.

Schaar, John. "Equality of Opportunity and Beyond." *Nomos IX: Equality*, eds. R. Pennock and J. Chapman. New York: Atherton Press, 1967, pp. 228–49.

Sen, Amartya. "Equality of What?" *The Tanner Lectures on Human Values*, Vol. 1. Salt Lake City: The University of Utah Press, 1980.

———. *Inequality Reexamined*. Oxford, England: Clarendon Press, 1992.

Sikora, R. I. "Six Viewpoints for Assessing Egalitarian Distribution Schemes." *Ethics* 99 (1989), pp. 492–502.

Spiegelberg, Herbert. "A Defence of Human Equality." *Philosophical Review*, 53:2 (1944), pp. 101–24.

Temkin, Larry S. "Inequality." *Philosophy and Public Affairs* 15 (1986), pp. 99–121.

———. *Inequality*. Oxford, England: Oxford University Press, 1993.

Thomas, D. A. Lloyd. "Competitive Equality of Opportunity." *Mind* 86:343 (July 1977), pp. 388–404.

————. "Equality within the Limits of Reason Alone." *Mind* 88:352 (October 1979), pp. 538–53.

Thomson, David. *The Babeuf Plot.* London: Kegan Paul, 1947.

————. *Equality.* Cambridge, England: Cambridge University Press, 1949.

Tocqueville, Alexis de. *Democracy in America,* trans. T. Lawrence, ed. J. P. Mayer. New York: HarperCollins, 1988.

Vlastos, Gregory. "Justice and Equality." In *Social Justice,* ed. Richard B. Brandt. Englewood Cliffs, NJ: Prentice-Hall, 1962, pp. 31–72.

Walzer, Michael. *Spheres of Justice: A Defense of Pluralism and Equality.* New York: Basic Books, 1983.

Westen, Peter. *Speaking of Equality.* Princeton, NJ: Princeton University Press, 1990.

————. "The Concept of Equal Opportunity." *Ethics* 95 (July 1985).

Chapter 5

Arthur, John, and William Shaw, eds. *Justice and Economic Distribution.* Englewood Cliffs, NJ: Prentice-Hall, 1978.

Barry, Brian. *The Liberal Theory of Justice.* Oxford, England: Oxford University Press, 1973.

Buchanan, Allen. *Ethics, Efficiency and the Market.* Rowman & Allenheld, 1985.

Campbell, Tom. *Justice.* New York: Macmillan, 1988.

Feinberg, Joel. *Social Philosophy.* Englewood Cliffs, NJ: Prentice-Hall, 1973.

Gutmann, Amy. *Liberal Equality.* Cambridge University Press, 1980.

Hare, R. M. "Justice and Equality." In *Justice and Economic Distribution,* eds. John Arthur and William H. Shaw. Englewood Cliffs, NJ: Prentice-Hall, 1978.

Miller, David. *Social Justice.* Oxford, England: Oxford University Press, 1973.

Murray, Charles. *Losing Ground.* New York: Basic Books, 1984.

Nathanson, Stephen. *Economic Justice.* Englewood Cliffs, NJ: Prentice-Hall, 1998.

Nozick, Robert. *Anarchy, State and Utopia.* New York: Basic Books, 1973.

Pojman, Louis P., ed. *Modern and Contemporary Political Philosophy.* New York: McGraw-Hill, 2002.

Pojman, Louis P., and Owen McLeod, eds. *Desert.* Oxford, England: Oxford University Press, 1998.

Rawls, John. *A Theory of Justice.* Cambridge, MA: Harvard University Press, 1971.

Sandel, Michael. *Liberalism and the Limits of Justice.* Cambridge University Press, 1982.

Solomon, Robert, and Mark Murphy, eds. *What Is Justice?* New York: Oxford University Press, 1990.

Sterba, James. *How to Make People Just.* Rowman & Littlefield, 1988.

Sterbe, James. *Justice for Here and Now.* New York: Cambridge University Press, 1998.

Wolgast, Elizabeth. *The Grammar of Justice.* Ithaca, NY: Cornell University Press, 1987

Chapter 6

Ackerman, Bruce. *Social Justice in the Liberal State.* New Haven, CT: Yale University Press, 1980.

Aristotle. *The Politics of Aristotle* (several editions, including Oxford, England: Oxford University Press, 1946).

Bellamy, R. and Martin Hollis, eds. *Pluralism and Liberal Neutrality.* London: Cass Press, 1999.

Devlin, Patrick. *The Enforcement of Morals.* Oxford, England: Oxford University Press, 1965.

Dworkin, Ronald. *Taking Rights Seriously.* Cambridge, MA: Harvard University Press, 1978.

———. *Law's Empire.* Cambridge, MA: Harvard University Press, 1986.

Fuller, Lon. *The Morality of the Law.* New Haven, CT: Yale University Press, 1964.

George, Robert. *Making Men Moral.* Clarendon Press, 1993.

Haksar, Vinet. *Equality, Liberty, and Perfectionism.* Oxford, England: Oxford University Press, 1977.

Hart, H. L. A. *Law, Liberty and Morality.* Oxford, England: Oxford University Press, 1963.

Hurka, T. "Perfectionism." In *The Encyclopedia of Ethics,* ed. Lawrence Becker. New York: Garland Press, 1992.

Larmore, Charles. *Patterns of Moral Complexity.* Cambridge University Press, 1987.

Popper, Karl. *The Open Society and Its Enemies.* Routledge & Kegan Paul, 1944.

Rawls, John. *A Theory of Justice.* Cambridge, MA: Harvard University Press, 1971.

Sher, George. *Beyond Neutrality.* Cambridge University Press, 1997.

Waldron, Jeremy. *Liberal Rights, Collected Papers 1981–1991.* Cambridge University Press, 1998.

Chapter 7

Baier, Kurt. *The Moral Point of View.* Ithaca, NY: Cornell University Press, 1958.

Brandt, Richard. *Morality, Utilitarianism and Rights.* New York: Cambridge University Press, 1992.

Dworkin, Ronald. *Taking Rights Seriously.* Cambridge, MA: Harvard University Press, 1977.

Feinberg, Joel, "The Nature and Value of Rights." *Journal of Value Inquiry* 4, 1970.

Gerwirth, Alan. *Human Rights.* Chicago: University of Chicago Press, 1982.

Hohfeld, Wesley Newcomb. *Fundamental Legal Conceptions.* New Haven, CT: Yale University Press, 1919, especially pp. 35–64.

Lomasky, Loren. *Persons, Rights, and Moral Community.* Oxford, England: Oxford University Press, 1987.

Lyons, David, ed. *Rights.* Wadsworth, 1979. Contains a good collection of articles.

Nickel, James. *Making Sense of Human Rights.* University of California Press, 1987.

Paul, Ellen; Fred Miller; and Jeffery Paul, eds. *Human Rights.* Blackwell, 1984. Contains a good collection of articles.

Pennock, J. R., and J. W. Chapman, eds. *Human Rights.* New York: New York University Press, 1981.

Shue, Henry. *Basic Rights: Subsistence, Affluence and U.S. Foreign Policy.* Princeton, NJ: Princeton University Press, 1980.

Smith, Tara. *Moral Rights and Political Freedom.* Rowman and Littlefield, 1995.

Sumner, L. W. *The Moral Foundation of Rights.* Oxford, England: Oxford: Clarendon Press, 1987.

Waldron, Jeremy. *The Right to Private Property.* Oxford, England: Clarendon Press, 1988.

———. *Theories of Rights.* Oxford University Press, 1984.

Wellman, Carl. *A Theory of Rights.* Rowman and Allanheld, 1985.

———. *The Proliferation of Rights.* Westview Press, 1999.

Wolgast, Elizabeth. *The Grammar of Justice.* Ithaca, NY: Cornell University Press, 1987

Chapter 8

Bedau, Hugo Adam, ed. *The Death Penalty in America,* 3rd ed. New York: Oxford, 1982.

Berns, Walter. *For Capital Punishment: The Inevitability of Caprice and Mistake.* New York: Norton, 1974.

Gerber, Rudolph, and Patrick McAnany, eds. *Contemporary Punishment.* Notre Dame, IN: University of Notre Dame Press, 1972.

Menninger, Karl. *The Crime of Punishment.* New York: Viking Press, 1968.

Murphy, Jeffrie, ed. *Punishment and Rehabilitation,* 2nd ed. Belmont, CA: Wadsworth, 1985.

Nathanson, Stephen. *An Eye For an Eye.* Lanham, MD: Rowman & Littlefield, 1987.

Pojman, Louis P., and Jeffrey Reiman. *The Death Penalty: For and Against.* Lanham, MD: Rowman and Littlefield, 1998.

Sorell, Tom. *Moral Theory and Capital Punishment.* Oxford, England: Blackwell, 1987.

Szumski, Bonnie, Lynn Hall, and Susan Bursell, eds. *The Death Penalty: Opposing Viewpoints.* St. Paul, MN: Greenhaven Press, 1986.

Chapter 9

Beitz, Charles. *Political Theory and International Relations.* Princeton, NJ: Princeton University Press, 1999.

Brown, Chris. *International Relations Theory.* Harvester-Wheatshelf, 1992.

Calhoun, Craig. *Nationalism.* Open University Press, 1997.

Friedman, Thomas. *The Lexus and the Olive Tree.* Farrar, Straus & Giroux, 1999.

Hardt, Michael, and Antonio Negri. *Empire.* Cambridge, MA: Harvard University Press, 2000.

Keohane, Robert and Joseph Nye. "Complex Interdependence and the Role of Force." In *International Politics,* 4th ed., eds. Robert Art and Robert Jervis. New York: HarperCollins, 1996.

Lichtenberg, Judith "Nationalism: For and (Mainly) Against." In *The Morality of Nationalism,* eds. Robert McKim and Jeff McMahan, Oxford, England: Oxford University Press, 1997.

Mapel, David, and Terry Nardin, eds. *International Society.* Princeton, NJ: Princeton University Press, 1998.

Maritain, Jacques. *Man and the State.* Catholic University Press, 1950.

McKim, Robert, and Jeff McMahan, eds. *The Morality of Nationalism.* Oxford, England: Oxford University Press, 1997.

Miller, David. *On Nationality.* Oxford, England: Oxford University Press, 1996.

Morganthau, Hans J. *Politics among Nations,* 6th ed. New York: Knopf, 1985.

Nussbaum, Martha C., et. al. *For Love of Country: Debating the Limits of Patriotism.* Beacon Press, 1996.

Pogge, Thomas. "Cosmopolitanism and Sovereignty." *Ethics* 103, 1992.

Pojman, Louis, ed. *Political Philosophy: Modern and Contemporary Readings.* New York: McGraw-Hill, 2002.

Shapiro, Ian, and Lea Brilmayer, eds. *Global Justice.* New York: New York University Press, 1999.

Singer, Peter. *The Expanding Circle.* Oxford, England: Oxford University Press, 1981.

Walzer, Michael. *Spheres of Justice.* New York: Basic Books, 1983.

Waltz, Kenneth. "The Anarchic Structure of World Politics." In

International Politics, 4th ed., eds. Robert Art and Robert Jervis. New York: HarperCollins, 1996.

Chapter 10

Chasdi, Richard. *Serenade of Suffering: A Portrait of Middle East Terrorism.* Lanham, MD: Lexington Books, 1999.

Chomsky, Noam. *9–11.* New York: Seven Stories Press, 2001.

Egendorf, Laura, ed. *Terrorism.* Greenhaven Press, 2000.

Huntington, Samuel. "The Clash of Civilizations?" *Foreign Affairs* (Summer 1993).

Laquer, Walter. *The Age of Terrorism.* Boston: Little, Brown, 1987.

Pillar, Paul R. *Terrorism and U.S. Foreign Policy.* Brookings Institute Press, 2001.

Ranstorp, Magnus. "Terrorism in the Name of Religion." *Journal of International Affairs*, 1996.

Rummel, R. J. *Death by Government.* Transaction, 1994.

White, Jonathan. *Terrorism: An Introduction.* Wadsworth, 2002.

INDEX